MASTERWORKS OF THE BRITISH CINEMA

# MASTERWORKS
# OF THE
# BRITISH CINEMA

The Lady Vanishes
Brief Encounter
Henry V

*faber and faber*
LONDON · BOSTON

This collection first published in 1990
by Faber and Faber Limited
3 Queen Square London WC1N 3AU

Printed in England by Clays Ltd, St Ives plc

This collection © Faber and Faber Limited, 1990

*The Lady Vanishes* first published in 1984 by Lorrimer
Publishing Limited. Original screenplay and film © 1938
Gainsborough Pictures, G.B., now copyright the Rank
Organization PLC

*Brief Encounter* first published in 1974 by Lorrimer
Publishing Limited, revised edition 1984. The screenplay
*Brief Encounter* © 1945 by Noël Coward Estate

*Henry V* first published in 1984 by Lorrimer Publishing
Limited. Original screenplay, dialogue transcript and
photographs of the motion pictures based thereon, © 1945
by the Rank Organization PLC

A CIP record for this book is available from the British Library
ISBN 0-571-14384-9

# CONTENTS

# THE LADY VANISHES

# ACKNOWLEDGEMENTS

Our thanks are due to Cyril Howard of Pinewood Studios for making the publication of this screenplay possible, to the British Film Institute for its research facilities and photographic stills, and especially to Elaine Crowther for preparing this continuity from the release script and the film itself.

# INTRODUCTION
## Andrew Sinclair

*The Lady Vanishes* was made in 1938 at a time of suspended disbelief and uneasy diplomacy in Europe. The British Prime Minister, Neville Chamberlain, had arranged 'a peace in our time' with Hitler at Munich, a peace that few expected to last for long. Parts of Czechoslovakia had been sacrificed to German expansion. Poland was threatened in the same way. A Second World War seemed imminent because of plots and claims and subterfuges in Central Europe. Alfred Hitchcock chose to film a novel, *The Wheel Spins*, by Ethel Lina White: it was set on a train making its way through that troubled region, menaced by conflict, bubbling with intrigue.

Although *The Lady Vanishes* chose wit and suspense rather than a political message, its relevance as well as the brilliance of its making led to instant acclaim, particularly in America, where it won the New York Critics Award. Both Orson Welles and James Thurber saw it a dozen times, while the acute Howard Barnes compared Hitchcock's craftsmanship with a Cezanne canvas or a Stravinsky score. Along with *The Thirty-Nine Steps*, this film remains the most popular of the Hitchcock films made in Britain, both for its mastery of technique and lightness of touch.

It was filmed on a small budget on a ninety-foot stage in Islington. There was no exterior shooting: Hitchcock did marvels with miniatures, rear projection and glass shots. It was Michael Redgrave's first film role: Margaret Lockwood had never worked with Hitchcock before. 'He never really mixed with the actors,' she recalled. 'He knew exactly what he wanted, where the camera had to be set up. So you did what he wanted, that was it! I could speak for hours with Carol Reed, but Hitch . . .'

7

At Hitchcock's direction, the two screenwriters, Frank Launder and Sidney Gilliat, made significant changes from the novel. The hero Gilbert was metamorphosed from a dam engineer to a collector of folk music. A banker became a magician in order to introduce the sequence of the trick cabinet and the poster of the Vanishing Lady. Miss Froy was transposed from a gullible governess into a British secret agent, while Hitchcock made his purpose clear in the lines explaining her name, Froy, not Freud. 'It rhymes with joy.' Hitchcock intended to make a thriller of joyous action, not of psychological motivation. The lady vanishes, she does not withdraw into herself.

Various themes thread the script, the theme of families – true and false – against traitors and nations: the theme of unwilling commitment because of necessity: the theme of misunderstanding through language: and the theme of identity, whether a person exists or does not.

The whole of an identity, at one moment, appears an illusion, a vanishing trick. Appearances are not realities. But Hitchcock does not labour over philosophy or significance. He conjures with the art of film.

After a witty introduction in the snow-bound resort hotel, Hitchcock builds suspense on suspense, deception on revelation, like a maestro playing the fifty-two card trick. With the heroine, we cannot believe the evidence of her eyes. Miss Froy's handwriting on the window, the only surety of her existence, disappears like the Uncertainty Principle on the moment of its discovery. The bandaged patient may contain the vanished lady, or a corpse, or anyone. As for the nun in high heels, she is the stuff of dream as well as deception. And the illusion of the moving train itself, although filmed in a small studio, hustles us towards an excitement, a denouement, and explosions of laughter to relieve the suspense. *The Lady Vanishes* is Hitchcock at his most worldly and assured. Yet beneath the entertainment, there is the menace of a Europe about to plunge into the horror of war.

## CAST

| | |
|---|---|
| Margaret Lockwood | Iris Henderson |
| Michael Redgrave | Gilbert Redman |
| Paul Lukas | Dr. Hartz |
| Dame May Whitty | Miss Froy |
| Cecil Parker | Eric Todhunter |
| Linden Travers | Margaret |
| Mary Clare | Baroness |
| Naunton Wayne | Caldicott |
| Basil Radford | Charters |
| Emile Boreo | Manager |
| Googie Withers | Blanche |
| Philip Leaver | Doppo |
| Catherine Lacey | Nun |
| Charles Oliver | Officer |
| Sally Stewart | Julie |
| Zelma Vas Dias | Signora Doppo |
| Josephine Wilson | Madame Kummer |
| Kathleen Tremaine | Anna |

## CREDITS

| | |
|---|---|
| Producer | Edward Black |
| Director | Alfred Hitchcock |
| from the novel "The Wheel Spins" by | Ethel Lina White |
| Screenplay | Frank Launder, Sidney Gilliat |
| Continuity | Alma Reville |
| Photography | Jack Cock |
| Assistant cameraman | Leo Harris |
| Location photography | Jack Parry, Maurice Oakley |
| Music by | Cecil Milner |
| Musical Director | Louis Levy |
| Editors | Alfred Roome |
| | R.E. Dearing |
| Art Director | Alec Vetchinsky |
| Assisted by | Maurice Carter, Albert Jullion |
| Sound recordist | Sidney Wiles |

NOTE: The Bandrieken spoken throughout the film is a fictitious language. The English translations are put down to convey the meaning of the sequence.

# THE LADY VANISHES

*The film opens with an exterior shot of snow-capped mountains over which the titles are superimposed.*
*Camera tracks and pans down from the peaks into the village and on to an hotel.*
*The hotel foyer is packed with travellers.* MISS FROY *passes through, depositing her key with* BORIS, *the hotel manager, who is standing behind the reception desk.* CALDICOTT *and* CHARTERS *impatiently wait in the foyer, not knowing what is going on. Everyone is talking rapidly and loudly; it is late afternoon.*
BORIS *is talking into the telephone.*

BORIS: 'Allo. Prosto. Prosto. (Hallo. Quickly. Quickly).
Signorina. Signore.
Se la moledicate le trena bianga de meno parpicheri, commi radiostroni del maruma ha! ha! Mesdames, Messier, le train va arrive seulment de matin (Hallo . . . hallo . . . quickly . . . quickly. The train is held up until tomorrow. What a rush for rooms there's going to be . . . Ladies and gentlemen, the train will not leave until tomorrow morning.)

CALDICOTT: What's all this fuss about, Charters?

CHARTERS: Hanged if I know.

BORIS: Mein Darmen unt Herron. Bitterscheoun reaistronen . . . (My dear ladies and gentlemen . . . will you please register now).

*The reception desk becomes crowded with travellers.* CHARTERS *and* CALDICOTT *look on bemused.*

BORIS: Dankerschern (Thank you very much). Dankerschern. Ladies and gentlemen, I'm very sorry the train is a little bit uphold, and if you wish to stay in my hotel

. . . you will have to register immediately.

CHARTERS: Why the deuce didn't he say so in the first place?

*They make for the reception desk.* BORIS *leaves.*
*Outside the hotel* BORIS *meets* IRIS, BLANCHE, *and* JULIE *about to enter. They are dressed in hill-walking clothing and are tired. He stops them on the hotel steps.*

BORIS: How do you do, Miss Henderson. How do you do, ladies. It is a great honour to have you with us again.

IRIS: It's nice to see you too, Boris. You haven't changed a bit since last Friday.

BLANCHE: Mm . . . I see you haven't shaved either.

JULIE: Is everything ready?

BORIS: Everything is ready. I didn't change anything.

IRIS: Not even the sheets, we know. Lead on, Boris.

BORIS: You see, I didn't expect you to come so quickly.

IRIS: Well, our legs gave out on us. We had to do the last lap in a farm cart.

BORIS: Oh!

BLANCHE: I see we've got company. Don't tell me Cooks are running cheap tours here.

IRIS: What is it, Boris?

BORIS: The havelunch!

JULIE: Have a lunch?

IRIS: Avalanche, Boris. Avalanche.

BORIS: You see, in the spring, we've got many avalanches. You know, the snow go like that. Boom! And everything disappears. Even trains disappear under the avalanche.

IRIS: But I'm going home tomorrow. How long before they dig it out?

BORIS: By morning. It's lucky for you you can leave by this train, instead of your own. How did you said it? It's a bad wind that blow nowhere no good.

BLANCHE: And talking of wind, we haven't eaten since dawn.

IRIS: Serve us some supper, Boris, in our room.

JULIE: I could eat a horse.

IRIS: Don't put ideas into his head. Er . . . some chicken, Boris, and a magnum of champagne.

*They all enter the hotel and we see* CALDICOTT, CHARTERS *and the travellers still crowded in to the foyer.*

IRIS *off:* And make it snappy.

BLANCHE *off:* Bandrika may have a Dictator . . .

IRIS, BLANCHE, JULIE *and* BORIS *come back into shot.*

BLANCHE: . . . but tonight we're painting it red.

*The action cuts to the foyer. We see a medium-length camera shot of* CALDICOTT *and* CHARTERS *surrounded by travellers.*

CHARTERS: Meanwhile, we have to stand here cooling our heels, I suppose, eh? Confounded impudence.

CALDICOTT: Third rate country. What do you expect?

CHARTERS: Wonder who all those women were?

CALDICOTT: Probably Americans, I should think. You know, almighty dollar, old man.

CHARTERS: Oh, well, I suppose we'll have to wait here. If only we hadn't missed that train at Budapest.

CALDICOTT: I don't want to rub it in, but if you hadn't insisted on standing up until they'd finished their National Anthem . . .

CHARTERS: Yes, but you must show respect, Caldicott. If I'd known it was going to last twenty minutes . . .

13

CALDICOTT: Well, it's always been my contention that the Hungarian Rhapsody is not their National Anthem. In any case, we were the only two standing.

CHARTERS: That's true.

CALDICOTT: Well, I suppose we shall be in time after all.

CHARTERS: I doubt it. That last report was pretty ghastly, do you remember? England on the brink.

CALDICOTT: Yes, but that's newspaper sensationalism. The old country's been in some tight corners before.

CHARTERS: Looks pretty black. I mean, even if we get away first thing tomorrow morning, there's still the connection at Basle. We'll probably be hours.

CALDICOTT: Mm . . . that's true.

CHARTERS: Somebody surely can help us. Oh, sir! Do you happen to know what time the train leaves Basle for England?

*Pan to include* BENNING.

BENNING: Ich sprekker kein Englisch (I don't speak English).

CHARTERS: Oh, really! The fellow doesn't speak English.

*The camera has moved to a long shot of* BORIS *on the telephone.*

BORIS *into phone*: 'Allo . . . Alex . . . Na Kruska natra trappa par kartiska, yah denecatisca champagne Miss Henderson. Griska, Griska, oi veys mille (Hallo, Alex . . . Put everything else aside and take some chicken and a magnum of champagne to Miss Henderson).

BORIS *comes off the telephone and turns to face the travellers, all of whom wish to have some accommodation. A* WOMAN *breaks into a torrent of rapid French saying she wants a double room with a bath. Camera pans onto* CALDICOTT *and* CHARTERS, *who are reading a railway timetable beside the reception desk.*

CHARTERS: Here's one leaves Basle, twenty-one twenty.

CALDICOTT: Twenty-one twenty?

CHARTERS: Yes.

CALDICOTT: Twenty, twenty. Twelve from twenty.

*Cut back to the hotel reception desk where* BORIS *is being harrassed by visitors.*

BORIS: I regret, sir, there is only left two single rooms in front, or a little double room at the back.

TODHUNTER: We'll, er . . . take the two singles.

BORIS: Very well, sir. Here is . . . Thank you.

TODHUNTER *snatches the key and he and* "MRS." TODHUNTER *move away from the reception desk.*

"MRS." TODHUNTER: At least you might have asked me which I preferred.

TODHUNTER: My dear, a small double room at the back in a place like this . . .

"MRS." TODHUNTER: You weren't so particular in Paris last autumn.

TODHUNTER: It was quite different then. The Exhibition was at its height.

"MRS." TODHUNTER: I realise that now. There's no need to rub it in.

CALDICOTT *and* CHARTERS *finally reach the front of the queue in front of the reception desk.*

CALDICOTT: We want a private suite with a bath.

CHARTERS: Facing the mountains.

CALDICOTT: And with a shower, of course.

CHARTERS: Hot and cold.

CALDICOTT: And a private thingummy, if you've got one.

BORIS: Well, I'm sorry, gentlemen, the only thing I've got is the maid's room.

CALDICOTT: Maid's room!

CHARTERS: What's that?

BORIS: Well, I'm sorry. The whole hotel is packed. Jammed to the sky.

CALDICOTT: But that's impossible. We haven't fixed up yet.

CHARTERS: Hang it all, you can't expect to put the two of us up in the maid's room.

BORIS: Well, don't get excited, I'll remove the maid out.

CHARTERS: I should think so. What? What are you talking about?

CALDICOTT: Look here, I think I'd sooner sleep on the train.

BORIS: There is no 'eating in the train.

CALDICOTT: No eating on the train?

BORIS: Yes, I mean heating. Brrr.

CALDICOTT: Oh, there's no heating on the train.

CHARTERS: That's awkward. All right, we'll take it.

BORIS: Just a minute, on one condition. You have to have the maid come to your room, er . . . remove her wardrobe.

*As* CHARTERS, CALDICOTT *and* BORIS *stand looking at one another,* ANNA *comes into the shot.*

BORIS: Anna! She's a good girl, and I don't want to lose her. La cracka des tequa le freita del la castilla aratita la couta heh (Will it be all right for those two gentlemen to have your room)?

ANNA *smiles. The camera cuts rapidly between* ANNA *and* CHARTERS *and* CALDICOTT *and back again.*

CHARTERS: We'd better go and dress.

CALDICOTT: Rather primitive humour, I thought.

CHARTERS: Grown-up children, you know. That was rather an awkward situation, over that girl.

CALDICOTT: Pity he couldn't have given us one each.

CHARTERS: Eh?

CALDICOTT: I mean a room apiece.

CHARTERS: Oh!

> CHARTERS *and* CALDICOTT *ascend the stairs. We cut to the interior of* IRIS'S *bedroom. There is a long shot of* JULIE *and* BLANCHE. IRIS *is standing on a table; she is in her lingerie.*

IRIS: I, Iris Matilda Henderson. A spinster of no particular parish, do hereby solemnly renounce my maidenly past . . .

> *The camera cuts from* IRIS *to* RUDOLPH, *the waiter, entering with a tray. His face registers surprise at* IRIS *on the table. We focus on* RUDOLPH *as he tries to place the contents of the tray on the table that* IRIS *is on, and his reactions to* IRIS'S *legs. The camera cuts between his face and* IRIS'S *legs and the faces of* BLANCHE *and* JULIE.

IRIS *off:* . . . and do declare that on Thursday next, the twenty-sixth inst., being in my right mind, I shall take the veil . . . and the orange blossom . . . and change my name to Lady Charles . . .

> RUDOLPH *stares at* IRIS'S *legs in front of him.*

IRIS *off:* Fotheringail.

BLANCHE *off:* Can't you get him to change his name instead?

JULIE *off:* The only thing I like about him is his moustache.

> *We cut to a medium camera shot of* IRIS *still on the table.*

17

IRIS: You're a couple of cynics. I'm very fond of him.

*We see* IRIS'S *legs again and* RUDOLPH'S *face.*

BLANCHE *off:* Well, I'm fond of rabbits, but they have to be kept down.

IRIS *off:* Rudolph, give me a hand.

RUDOLPH *helps* IRIS *down from the table.*

BLANCHE: Have you ever read about that little thing called love?

JULIE: It used to be very popular.

IRIS: Child, the carpet is already laid at St. George's, Hanover Square, and Father is simply aching to have a coat of arms on the jam label.

JULIE: To Iris, and the happy days she's leaving behind.

BLANCHE: And the blue-blooded cheque-chaser she's dashing to London to marry.

JULIE: The blue-blooded cheque-chaser.

IRIS: I've no regrets. I've been everywhere and done everything. I've eaten caviare at Cannes, sausage rolls at the dogs. I've played Baccarat at Biarritz, and darts with the rural dean. What is there left for me but marriage?

*We cut to the corridor of the hotel.* RUDOLPH *is closing the girls' bedroom door as* ANNA *ascends the stairs to the landing. She joins him.*

ANNA: Ques embraces sedara enduro on-train stirrana (This is a nice thing having to give up one's own bedroom to passengers on the train).

RUDOLPH: Craman vin cam fin satto (Who is going in to your room)?

ANNA: En fun das l'englistos (Two Englishmen).

RUDOLPH: L'englistos (Englishmen)?

ANNA: Griska (That's right).

*We are in* ANNA'S *bedroom.* CALDICOTT *and* CHARTERS *are dressing for dinner.*

CHARTERS: It's this hanging about that gets me. If only we knew what was happening in England.

CALDICOTT: Mustn't lose grip, Charters.

*A knock is heard at the door.*

CALDICOTT: Come in.

ANNA *enters.*

ANNA: Pereskai (Begging your pardon).

*In a series of reaction shots, we see* ANNA *look at* CALDICOTT *and* CHARTERS. *She joins them.*

ANNA: Pas que roben depouli (Can I change my clothes)?

CALDICOTT: Did you follow that?

CHARTERS: I did. Tell her this has gone far enough.

CALDICOTT: No, er . . . no change . . . er here. Mm, outside.

ANNA: Pereskai (Begging your pardon).

CALDICOTT: She doesn't understand.

CHARTERS: No, come on.

CHARTERS *and* CALDICOTT *leave* ANNA *in her room, and walk out of the camera shot down the hotel landing. We cut to* CHARTERS *and* CALDICOTT *now in the hotel foyer. They walk to a table and pick up some newspapers.*

CHARTERS: Nothing newer than last month.

CALDICOTT: I don't suppose there is such a thing as a wireless set hereabouts.

CHARTERS: Awful being in the dark like this, you know, Caldicott.

CALDICOTT: Our communications cut off in a time of crisis.

*The camera moves from them to* BORIS *who is talking into the telephone receiver on the reception desk.*

BORIS: Hallo, hallo, hallo, London?

*We see* CHARTERS *and* CALDICOTT *look at one another as they overhear* BORIS'S *conversation.*

BORIS: (*into phone*) You want Mr. Seltzer? Yes, hold on. I'm going right to find him . . . where he is.

CALDICOTT *and* CHARTERS *watch* BORIS *leave, look at one another and move to the reception desk.*

CHARTERS: London!

CALDICOTT: Go on, risk it.

CHARTERS: (*into phone*) Hallo . . . hallo. You . . . you in London. What? No, no, no, I'm not Mr. Seltzer. Name's Charters. I don't suppose you know me. What? You needn't worry, they've just gone to fetch him. Tell me, what's happening to England? Blowing a gale? No, you don't follow me, sir. I'm enquiring about the Test Match in Manchester. Cricket, sir, cricket! What, you don't know? You can't be in England and not know the test score. The fellow says he doesn't know.

CALDICOTT: Silly ass.

CHARTERS: (*into phone*) Hallo, can't you find out? Oh, nonsense, it won't take a second. All right, if you won't, you won't.

CHARTERS *replaces the telephone receiver on the hook.*

CHARTERS: Wasting my time. The fellow's an ignoramus.

BORIS *enters in the background with* MR. SELTZER.

BORIS: Mr. Seltzer, at last your call's come through to London.

CHARTERS *and* CALDICOTT *look sheepishly at one another and walk away.*

BORIS *off:* (*into phone*) Hallo, hallo, hallo, karistica

crastica fatistica London? Me di castia London. Oh! saeme dein a-calle porte (What has happened to my call to London? I've been cut off from London . . . Oh! what clumsiness).

*Cut to the interior of the dining room as* CALDICOTT *and* CHARTERS *enter.* MISS FROY *is seen sitting at a table. The room is crowded. The people seated with* MISS FROY *get up to leave and* CALDICOTT, CHARTERS *and other guests are seen trying to obtain these seats.* CALDICOTT *and* CHARTERS *succeed by pushing and forcing themselves in front of the others. A* WAITER *enters.*

WAITER: Pairdum . . . (Excuse me)! Rayni cartodo escht finido . . . (There is no food left).

CHARTERS: Thank you, waiter.

WAITER: Rayni cartodo escht finido . . . (There is no food left).

CHARTERS: Well, what do you say to a grilled steak?

CALDICOTT: A very good idea. Well done for me, please.

CHARTERS: On the red side for me.

WAITER: Rayni cartodo escht finido . . . (There is no food left).

CHARTERS: These people have a passion for repeating themselves.

MISS FROY: I . . . I beg your pardon.

CHARTERS: Mm?

MISS FROY: He's trying to explain to you that owing to the large number of visitors there's no food left.

CHARTERS: No food? What sort of place is this? Do they expect us to share a blasted dog box with a servant girl on an empty stomach? Is that hospitality? Is that organisation?

*The camera cuts from* CHARTERS *to* CALDICOTT *to the*

WAITER *to* MISS FROY. CHARTERS'S *face registers unease as he realises he has forgotten his manners. He turns to* MISS FROY.

CHARTERS: Oh, thank you.

CALDICOTT: I'm hungry, you know.

CHARTERS: What a country! I don't wonder they have revolutions.

MISS FROY: You're very welcome to what's left of the cheese. Of course, it's not like beefsteak but it's awfully rich in vitamins.

CHARTERS: Oh, really . . . thank you very much.

MISS FROY: I'm afraid they're not accustomed to catering for so many people. Bandrika is one of Europe's few undiscovered corners.

CHARTERS: That's probably because there's nothing worth discovering, I should think.

MISS FROY: You may not know it as well as I do. I'm feeling quite miserable at the thought of leaving it.

CALDICOTT: After you with the cheese, please!

CHARTERS: Certainly, old man. Why not? You're going home.

MISS FROY: Tomorrow. My little charges are quite grown up. I'm a governess and . . . and music teacher, you know. In the six years I've lived here, I've grown to love the country. Especially the mountains. I sometimes think they're like very friendly neighbours. You know, the big father and mother mountains with their white snow hats, and their nephews and nieces, not quite so big with smaller hats.

*A* SINGER *can be heard playing a guitar.* CALDICOTT *and* CHARTERS *look at one another, bored with the old lady.*

MISS FROY: Right down to the tiniest hillock without any hat at all. Of course, that's just my fancy.

CHARTERS: Oh, really?

MISS FROY: I like to watch them from my bedroom every night when there's a moon. I'm so glad there's a moon tonight. Do you hear that music? Everyone sings here. The people are just like happy children, with laughter on their lips and music in their hearts.

CHARTERS: It's not reflected in their politics, you know.

MISS FROY: I never think you should judge any country by its politics. After all, we English are quite honest by nature, aren't we? You'll excuse me if I run away? Good night, good night.

MISS FROY *exits*.

CHARTERS: Queer sort of bird.

CALDICOTT: Trifle whimsical, I thought.

CHARTERS: After six years in this hole we'd be whimsical.

CALDICOTT: Oh, I don't think so, old man. She was very decent about that cheese.

CHARTERS: I see she's finished the pickles.

*Cut to the hotel corridor outside* IRIS'S *room. We see* BLANCHE, JULIE *and* IRIS *standing together*.

BLANCHE: Good night, Iris. Listen, someone's serenading.

IRIS: Oh, let him. Nothing will keep me awake tonight. Good night, my children.

IRIS *kisses* BLANCHE *and* JULIE.
*As the women part, we see a long shot of* IRIS *with* MISS FROY *in the foreground unlocking her bedroom door, which is next to* IRIS'S *room. We go with* MISS FROY *into her bedroom. The* SINGER *can still be heard.* MISS FROY *sways with the music. We see a quick shot of the* SINGER *and then come back to* MISS FROY *by her bedroom window, listening to the* SINGER. *Stamping and the sound of a clarinet being played can be heard from upstairs.*

23

MISS FROY *looks annoyed.*
*In the hotel corridor we see* MISS FROY *and* IRIS *coming from their rooms as the clarinet "noise" persists.*

IRIS: What's happening? An earthquake?

MISS FROY: That would hardly account for the music, would it? What a horrible noise. What can they be doing?

IRIS: I don't know, but I'll soon find out.

> *We follow* IRIS *back into her bedroom.* MISS FROY *stands in the doorway.* IRIS *sits on the side of her bed and talks into the telephone.*

IRIS: Hallo.

*We see a shot of the chandelier vibrating.* IRIS *looks at* MISS FROY.

IRIS: Musical country this.

MISS FROY: Yes, I . . . I feel quite sorry for that poor singer outside having to compete with this.

IRIS: *(into phone)* Boris? Miss Henderson speaking. Look, someone upstairs is playing musical chairs with an elephant. Move one of them out, will you? I want to get some sleep. All right. *(putting down the telephone)* That ought to settle it.

MISS FROY: Thank you so much.

> IRIS *walks back into the corridor with* MISS FROY.

MISS FROY: Some people have so little consideration for others, which makes life so much more difficult than it need be, don't you think? Good night and thank you so much. I expect you'll be going back on the train in the morning.

IRIS: Yes.

MISS FROY: Then I hope we shall meet again under . . . under quieter circumstances. Good night.

IRIS: Good night.

MISS FROY: And thank you so much.

MISS FROY *exits and* BORIS *enters.*

BORIS: Sagri morrida . . . pierci ectenda (Miss, please, I'll fix everything).

IRIS: You'd better.

*Back in* IRIS'S *bedroom she sits on her bed and sighs as the chandelier continues to vibrate.*
BORIS *is seen walking along the landing above* IRIS'S *room. He stands outside* GILBERT'S *room and knocks. There is no answer.* BORIS *enters. The camera pans to include three* SERVANTS, *folk dancing to* GILBERT'S *music.* GILBERT *is sprawled across his bed, music sheets in front of him, playing his clarinet.*

GILBERT: Hold it. Splendid, don't move, don't move.

GILBERT *makes notes of the* SERVANTS' *positions on his paper, taking no notice of* BORIS.

BORIS: Er . . . If you please, sir.

GILBERT: Get out! One, two.

GILBERT *goes back to his music and the* SERVANTS *continue to dance.*

BORIS: Please, sir, will you kindly stop? They are all complaining . . . in the whole hotel. You make too much noise.

GILBERT: Too much what?

BORIS: Too much noise.

GILBERT: You dare to call it a noise. The ancient music with which your present ancestors celebrated every wedding for countless generations. The dance they danced when your father married your mother, always supposing you were born in wedlock, which I doubt. Look at them.

*We see a shot of the three* SERVANTS, *now motionless, trying to hold their positions as* GILBERT *is not playing his clarinet.* BORIS *looks incredulous.*

GILBERT: I take it you're the manager of this hotel?

BORIS: Sure I am the manager of the hotel.

GILBERT: Fortunately I am accustomed to squalor. Tell me, who's complaining?

BORIS: The young English lady underneath.

GILBERT: Well, you tell the young English lady underneath that I am putting on record for the benefit of mankind, one of the lost folk dances of Central Europe and furthermore that she does not own this hotel. Get out!

BORIS: But, sir, you don't understand.

BORIS *exits.*

GILBERT: Now, one, two!

GILBERT *continues his studies. Meanwhile,* IRIS'S *chandelier continues to vibrate. We cut to* BORIS *now back in* IRIS'S *room.*

BORIS: And do you know what he said? "Who does she think she is, the Queen of Sheba? She thinks she owns this hotel?"

IRIS: Well, can't you get rid of him?

BORIS: Impossible.

IRIS: Are you sure?

IRIS *takes bank notes from her handbag.*

BORIS: I begin to wonder. It's come back to me. I have got an idea. You see, the German lady she will call him up on the telephone and she say "Young man, it is my room. I did pay for it. Get out quickly." How's that?

IRIS: Good enough.

BORIS: We will inject him with a little . . . he'll never forget as long as he live.

26

*We are in* ANNA'S *room. There is a shot of an open newspaper being held in front of the camera.*

CALDICOTT *off:* Nothing but baseball. You know, we used to call it rounders. Children play it with a rubber ball and a stick. Not a word about cricket. Americans have got no sense of proportion.

*A knock is heard at the door.*

CALDICOTT *calling off:* Come in.

*The newspaper is moved to reveal* CHARTERS *and* CALDICOTT *in bed.* ANNA *enters and looks around. Everybody looks at each other, then she turns around and leaves.* CALDICOTT *and* CHARTERS *say nothing. They are looking at each other.* ANNA *comes in again.*

ANNA: Goodernaght (Good evening).

ANNA *goes out.*

CHARTERS: Can't stand this ridiculous lack of privacy . . . lock the door.

CHARTERS *gets out of bed and we follow him to the door – in his pyjama top only. Just as he gets to the door,* ANNA *pops her head round it.*

CHARTERS: Oh!

ANNA: Goodernaght (Good evening).

*The film cuts to* IRIS *in bed. Without knocking,* GILBERT *enters. He leans on the doorpost in an outdoor coat and hat, with his suitcase and bags. They look at each other, camera cutting rapidly between their expressions.*

IRIS: Who are you? What do you want?

GILBERT *produces his clarinet and plays a few notes.*

GILBERT: Recognise the signature tune?

IRIS: Will you please get out?

GILBERT *enters the room and looks around. He walks towards the bed.*

27

GILBERT: Oh, this is a much better room. In fact, definitely an acceptable room.

*There are more exchanges of glances between* IRIS *and* GILBERT. GILBERT *removes her lingerie that is hanging on the bedhead, and places his hat and coat on them instead.*

IRIS *off:* What exactly do you think you're doing? Keep away!

GILBERT: Would you hold those for a minute?

GILBERT *hands his clarinet to* IRIS *and takes his pyjamas from a suitcase.*

IRIS: Put those back at once.

GILBERT: Now, which side do you like to sleep?

IRIS: Do you want me to throw you out?

GILBERT: Well, in that case, I'll sleep in the middle. Smart of you to bribe the manager.

GILBERT *enters the bathroom and prepares to wash.* IRIS *gets out of bed and follows him to the bathroom door.*

GILBERT: An eye for an eye and a tooth for a toothbrush.

IRIS: I suppose you realise you're behaving like a complete cad?

GILBERT: On the contrary, you're perfectly at liberty to sleep in the corridor if you want to.

IRIS *turns and goes back to the bed. She picks up the telephone and talks into it.*

IRIS: Hallo.

GILBERT: Oh, I shouldn't if I were you. I'd only tell everyone you invited me here.

*There is a medium shot of* IRIS *replacing the telephone receiver.*

GILBERT: And when I say everyone, I mean everyone. I have a powerful voice.

GILBERT *closes the bathroom door.*

IRIS: Come out of there at once!

GILBERT: Not until you bribe the manager to restore me to my attic.

IRIS: Come out of that bathroom.

IRIS (*into phone*): Hallo, Boris? Look, I was thinking, I might change my mind about that room upstairs . . .

*We cut to* GILBERT *coming from the bathroom.*

GILBERT: Oh, by the way, you might have my things taken upstairs, would you?

IRIS: You're the most contemptible person I've ever met in all my life!

GILBERT *goes to the door. He turns around as he opens it and smiles towards* IRIS.

*GILBERT: Confidentially, I think you're a bit of a stinker, too.*

*MISS FROY leans out of her bedroom balcony, listening to the* SINGER *playing the guitar.*
*The* SINGER *is seen performing as two hands come in to the picture and close around his throat.*
*MISS FROY tosses down a coin just as the music ceases, and she moves from the window to prepare for bed.*
*We cut to an exterior shot of Zolney Station with a train at the platform.* CALDICOTT *and* CHARTERS *are seen walking along the platform.*

CALDICOTT: If we get to Basle in time, we should see the last day of the match.

CHARTERS: Hope the weather's like this in Manchester. A perfect wicket for our fellows.

*We cut to a shot of local people on the platform, together with* MR. *and* MRS. TODHUNTER, *walking beside the train looking into the compartments.*

MRS. TODHUNTER: Isn't it somewhere along here?

TODHUNTER: If you don't hurry, Margaret, we shan't get that compartment to ourselves, you know.

MRS. TODHUNTER: Does it matter?

*We cut to another section of the train.* IRIS, JULIE *and* BLANCHE *are standing together on the platform.*

JULIE: Well, there's still time to change your mind, Iris.

BLANCHE: Yes, why not send Charles a greeting telegram and tell him he's all washed up?

IRIS: No, it's too late. This time next week, I shall be a slightly sunburnt offering on an altar in Hanover Square. I shan't mind, really.

MISS FROY *comes into the shot, walking towards the women and looking absentmindedly about her.*

MISS FROY: Ah, good morning. I can't find my bag. It's a brown hold-all, you know. Have you seen it? No, of course not. Thank you.

IRIS, JULIE *and* BLANCHE *look at each other as* MISS FROY *walks off.*

MISS FROY *off:* I gave it to the porter. I can't imagine what I could have done with it.

IRIS: Oh, she's dropped her glasses.

IRIS *bends down and picks them up from the platform and follows after* MISS FROY.
*We see a window box being tipped over a ledge above* MISS FROY, *as* IRIS *walks over to her.*

IRIS: You dropped your glasses.

*The window box falls into the picture and hits* IRIS *on the head.*

MISS FROY: Oh, thank you, my dear. Oh, dear, oh, dear, oh, dear!

> BLANCHE *and* JULIE *enter the scene and hold* IRIS, *who is rubbing her head.*

BLANCHE: Are you hurt?

IRIS: I don't know. What was it?

GUARD: Magrabtund masca nunzo dar treni (Take your place on the train, please).

BLANCHE: Never mind about that. This cockeyed station of yours has practically brained my friend.

MISS FROY: Yes, indeed.

BLANCHE: Well, what are you going to do about it?

GUARD: Tempar mag rabtung . . . (I can't keep the train any longer).

MISS FROY: He says he can't hold the train.

JULIE: Well, I like that!

BLANCHE: Hurry up. It's going.

IRIS: I'll be all right, really.

JULIE: Are you sure?

IRIS: Yes, sure.

MISS FROY: Don't worry, I'll look after her. Such carelessness.

> *Men shovelling snow from the railway track are shown, as the train creaks and begins to pull very slowly away from the station.*
> *We cut to an interior shot of a first class compartment where* IRIS *is seen looking out of the window at* BLANCHE *and* JULIE *on the platform.*

BLANCHE: Are you sure you're all right?

JULIE: Send us a copy of the *Times*.

BLANCHE: Write and tell us all about it. Good luck. Look after yourself.

*As the train picks up speed, we see rapid cuts to the faces of* BLANCHE, JULIE *and* IRIS.
*This sequence dissolves to a montage of train wheels,* BLANCHE *and* JULIE.
*Now dissolve back to* IRIS'S *first class compartment.*

MISS FROY: There, there, you'll be all right in a minute. Just take everything quietly. Put some of this *eau de cologne* on your head.

*As* IRIS *pats her forehead she gazes at the other members of the compartment:* SIGNOR DOPPO, *a* CHILD, *the* BARONESS, SIGNORA DOPPO, *and back to* MISS FROY.

MISS FROY: Do you feel any better?

IRIS: Yes, thank you. I'm all right now.

MISS FROY: What you need is a good strong cup of tea. I'll ring for the attendant.

IRIS: No, no, please, don't bother. I'll go to the dining car myself. I need some air.

MISS FROY: Well, in that case, I'll come with you. If you don't mind, that is?

IRIS: No, of course not.

*They walk into the corridor. As they begin carefully walking along it,* MISS FROY *stumbles and falls into the* TODHUNTERS' *compartment.*

MISS FROY: Oh, I beg your pardon. I'm so sorry.

TODHUNTER *stands and closes the door and pulls down the blind.* MISS FROY *smiles at* IRIS.

MISS FROY: You can always tell a honeymoon couple, you know. They're so shy.

*The scene cuts to the interior of the* TODHUNTERS' *compartment. Only* MR. *and* MRS. TODHUNTER *are there.*

MRS. TODHUNTER: Why did you do that?

TODHUNTER: We don't want people staring at us.

MRS. TODHUNTER: Anyone would think the whole legal profession were dogging you.

TODHUNTER: Well, one would be enough.

MRS. TODHUNTER: You even thought that beggar in Damascus was a barrister in disguise.

TODHUNTER: I merely said his face was distinguished enough for a judge.

MRS. TODHUNTER: You hurried off in the opposite direction I noticed.

TODHUNTER: That's not true. I was looking for the street called 'Straight'.

MRS. TODHUNTER: You weren't so careful the first few days.

TODHUNTER: I know. I know.

MRS. TODHUNTER: And anyway, as for you meeting someone you know, what about me? Robert thinks I'm cruising with Mother.

*We cut to an interior shot of the dining car as* IRIS *and* MISS FROY *enter in the background.*

MISS FROY: If one is feeling a little bit shaky I always think it's best to sit in the middle of the coach . . . preferably facing the engine.

*IRIS and* MISS FROY *sit opposite each other. The* STEWARD *enters.* CHARTERS *and* CALDICOTT *have the table at the side of them, separated by the way through the carriage.*

MISS FROY: A pot of tea for two, please.

STEWARD: Very good, madam.

MISS FROY: Oh, and just a minute, will you please tell

them to make it from this. I don't drink any other. And make absolutely sure that the water is really boiling, do you understand?

*We see* MISS FROY *taking a package from her handbag, handing it to the* STEWARD *who leaves.*

MISS FROY: It's a little fad of mine. My dear father and mother, who I'm thankful to say are still alive and enjoying good health, invariably drink it, and so I follow their footsteps. Do you know, a million Mexicans drink it? At least that's what it says on the packet.

IRIS: It's very kind of you to help me like this. I don't think we've introduced ourselves. My name's Iris Henderson, I'm going home to be married.

MISS FROY: Really? Oh, how very exciting. I do hope you'll be happy.

IRIS: Thank you.

MISS FROY: You'll have children, won't you? They make such a difference. I always think it's being with kiddies so much that's made me, if I may say so, young for my age. I'm a governess, you know. My name's Froy.

*The train has picked up speed and there is a lot of noise.* IRIS *has difficulty in hearing* MISS FROY.

IRIS: Did you say Freud?

MISS FROY: No, O.Y., not E.U.D. . . . Froy.

IRIS: I'm sorry I can't hear.

*We see* MISS FROY *solve their problem by writing her name on the window.*

MISS FROY: Froy, it rhymes with joy.

*The* STEWARD *enters with the tea tray.*

MISS FROY: Thank you. Please reserve two places for lunch, will you?

*The* STEWARD *exits.*

MISS FROY: That is, if you'd care to have it with me.

IRIS: Of course.

*We move to* CHARTERS *and* CALDICOTT *at the adjoining table, in deep conversation.*

CHARTERS: Nothing more about it, it simply wasn't out, that's all. But for the Umpire's blunder he'd probably still be batting.

CALDICOTT: What do you mean? I don't understand.

CHARTERS: I'll show you. Look here. I saw the whole thing.

CHARTERS *tips the sugar lumps onto the table.*

CHARTERS: Now then. There's Hammond, there's the bowler, and there's the Umpire.

*We cut to* MISS FROY *and* IRIS *at their table.*

MISS FROY: Sugar?

IRIS: Two, please.

MISS FROY: Dear me, there is no sugar.

MISS FROY *looks around her and sees* CHARTERS *and* CALDICOTT, *still playing with the sugar lumps.*

CHARTERS: Now watch this very, very carefully, Caldicott. Gimmett was bowling.

MISS FROY: May I trouble you for the sugar, please?

CHARTERS: What?

MISS FROY: The sugar, please.

CHARTERS *and* CALDICOTT *replace the sugar lumps in the bowl in disgust, and hand it over to* MISS FROY.

MISS FROY: Thank you so much.

*We see an exterior low angle shot of the train crossing a bridge, and then cut back to* IRIS *and* MISS FROY *re-entering their compartment from the corridor.*

35

MISS FROY: If I were you I'd try and get a little sleep. It'll make you feel quite well again. There's a most intriguing acrostic in the *Needlewoman*. I'm going to try and unravel it before you wake up.

IRIS *settles down in her seat. She gazes quickly at the same members of her compartment and at* MISS FROY *reading, before falling asleep.*
*A montage of shots helps convey the passing of time and miles. There are shots of the engine, telegraph wires, railway lines repeated rapidly. The camera comes back into* IRIS'S *compartment where everyone is still seated – except that* MISS FROY'S *seat is empty.*

ATTENDANT *off:* Prandoor . . . billet resach (Reservations for lunch, please).

*The* ATTENDANT *enters and goes up to each person individually in the compartment.*

ATTENDANT: Reservations for lunch, please.

SIGNOR DOPPO: Bin may (Three please).

ATTENDANT: Daf (For the first lunch)?

SIGNOR DOPPO: Bin daf (Three places for the first lunch).

ATTENDANT: Madame has booked for lunch?

IRIS: Oh, I think my friend did. She's got the tickets.

IRIS *gets up and looks up and down the corridor, then turns back to the compartment.*

IRIS: Have you seen my friend?

SIGNOR DOPPO: Non (No).

IRIS: My friend. Where is she? La signora Inglese. The English lady, where is she?

BARONESS: There has been no English lady here.

IRIS: What?

BARONESS: There has been no English lady here.

IRIS: But there has. She sat there in the corner.

*They all look at one another.* IRIS *is dumbfounded and talks directly to* SIGNOR DOPPO.

IRIS: You saw her, you spoke to her, she sat next to you. But this is ridiculous. She took me to the dining car and came back here with me.

BARONESS: You went and came back alone.

IRIS: Maybe you don't understand. I mean the lady who looked after me when I was knocked out.

SIGNOR DOPPO: Ah perhaps it make you forget, eh?

IRIS: Well I may be very dense, but if this is some sort of a joke I'm afraid I don't see the point.

IRIS *leaves the compartment. The camera follows her along the corridor and into the dining car. The* STEWARD *enters in the foreground and* IRIS *follows him out to the next corridor.*

IRIS: Oh, Steward. You served me tea just now.

STEWARD: Yes, madame.

IRIS: Have you seen the lady I was with. The English lady.

STEWARD: But madame was alone.

HEAD STEWARD *off:* Caproki Eugene (They heard Eugene).

*The* HEAD STEWARD *enters.*

HEAD STEWARD: Pardon, madame. He make mistake.

IRIS: Well, of course, he must remember the little English lady. She ordered the tea and paid for it.

STEWARD: No, it was you who paid.

HEAD STEWARD: Caproki (She heard).

STEWARD: Nagra additan (Look at the bill).

HEAD STEWARD: He say to look at the bill. I will look, madame.

IRIS: But she gave you a special packet of tea. You can't have forgotten that.

STEWARD: The tea was ours, madame. I received no packet.

IRIS: But you did. I know what happened.

HEAD STEWARD: Pardon, madame. The bill. Tea for one.

IRIS: But that's not right.

HEAD STEWARD: Perhaps madame would care to examine the bills herself.

IRIS: No, I wouldn't. The whole thing's too absurd.

> IRIS *leaves her compartment as the train continues its journey. She walks along the corridor and down the train until she enters a fourth class compartment.* GILBERT *is there, but she does not notice him at first.*

IRIS: Please have you seen a lady pass through . . . Oh!

GILBERT: Well, well. If it isn't Old Stinker. If I thought you were going to be on this train I'd have stayed another week in the hotel. Lady? No, why?

IRIS: It doesn't matter. You probably wouldn't recognise one anyway.

> IRIS *sways as if she is about to faint.* GILBERT *goes across to her past an old man smoking a pipe.*

GILBERT: Hallo! Feeling queer? It's that pipe of yours, George. Why don't you throw your old socks away. Never mind, thanks for the help all the same. Now, come on, sit down and take it easy. What's the trouble?

IRIS: If you must know something fell on my head.

GILBERT: When? Infancy?

IRIS: At the station.

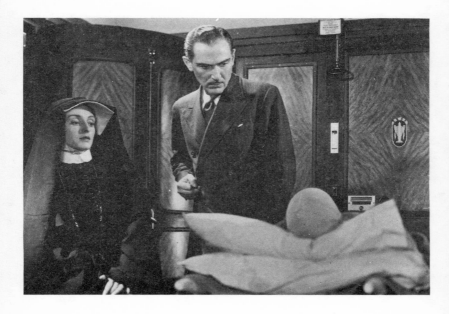

GILBERT: Oh, bad luck! Can I help?

IRIS: No, only by going away.

GILBERT: No, no, no, no, my father always taught me, never desert a lady in trouble. He even carried that as far as marrying mother.

IRIS: I say, did you see a little lady last night in the hotel in tweeds?

GILBERT: I only saw one little lady and she was hardly in tweeds.

IRIS: Yes, but she was in my compartment, and now I can't find her.

GILBERT: Well, she must be still on the train. We haven't stopped since we started.

IRIS: Of course she's still on the train. I know that.

GILBERT: All right, all right. Nobody said she isn't.

IRIS: Yes, but that's just what they are saying.

GILBERT: Who?

IRIS: The rest of the people in the compartment and the Steward. They insist they never saw her.

GILBERT: All of them?

IRIS: All of them.

GILBERT: You were saying you got a knock on the head.

IRIS: What do you mean?

GILBERT: Oh, never mind. Do you talk the lingo?

IRIS: No.

GILBERT: Oh, well, they probably thought you were trying to borrow some money. Come on, let's knock the idea out of their stupid heads. A most unfortunate remark, I beg your pardon.

IRIS *and* GILBERT *walk down the corridor, where* IRIS

*spots* SIGNOR DOPPO *and* DR. HARTZ *talking together.*

IRIS: That's one of them. The little dark man.

GILBERT: I say, excuse me. I think there's been a little misunderstanding. This young lady seems to have lost her friend.

DR. HARTZ: Yes, I have heard. The gentleman has been explaining to me. Most interesting, and I think under the circumstances we shall all introduce ourselves.

SIGNOR DOPPO: I am Italian citizen. My wife and child.

GILBERT: How do you do. Bonny little chap. How old is he?

SIGNOR DOPPO: Nineteen thirty-four class.

GILBERT: Ah!

SIGNOR DOPPO: And the lady in the corner is the Baroness Athena.

GILBERT: Oh, yes. I met her husband, and he presented prizes at the Folk Dances Festival. Minister of Propaganda.

DR. HARTZ: And I am Doctor Egon Hartz of Prague. You may have heard of me.

GILBERT: Not the brain specialist?

DR. HARTZ: The same.

GILBERT: Yes, you flew over to England the other day and operated on one of our cabinet ministers.

DR. HARTZ: Oh, yes.

GILBERT: Tell me, did you find anything?

DR. HARTZ: A slight Cerebral Confusion.

GILBERT: Oh, well, that's better than nothing.

DR. HARTZ: But I am picking up a similar case at the next station, but so much more complicated. I shall operate at the National Hospital tonight. Among other things a cranial fracture with compression. You understand?

GILBERT: Oh yes, a wallop on the bean.

IRIS: I suppose you haven't seen my friend?

DR. HARTZ: Unfortunately no.

GILBERT: I'll just take a word with the Baroness.

GILBERT *enters the first class compartment and goes towards the* BARONESS, *who is seated by the window.*

GILBERT: Bakara vaskin fermera baronak (Excuse me, have you seen an elderly lady in here, Baroness)?

BARONESS: Nagray femora (I have seen no elderly lady).

GILBERT: Excuee avete visto la Signora (Excuse me, have you seen this lady)?

SIGNORA DOPPO: Non no la seen her (No, I haven't seen her).

IRIS: What do they say?

GILBERT: Well, they both say they've never seen her.

IRIS: But that's not true. She was sitting where you are.

DR. HARTZ: Can you describe her?

IRIS: Well, it's a bit difficult. You see she was sort of middle-aged, and ordinary.

GILBERT: What was she wearing?

IRIS: Tweeds, oatmeal flecked with brown, a three-quarter coat with patch pockets, a scarf, felt hat, brown shoes, a tussore shirt and . . . and a small blue handkerchief in her breast pocket. I can't remember any more.

GILBERT: You couldn't have been paying attention. Now listen, you both went along to tea?

IRIS: Yes.

GILBERT: Well, surely you met somebody.

IRIS: I suppose we did, but wait a moment, let me think. Oh yes, there was an Englishman who passed the sugar.

GILBERT: Right you are. Now, let's go along and dig him out.

DR. HARTZ: Pardon. May I come with you? This is most interesting to me.

GILBERT: Well, we don't like people muscling in, but we'll make you a member.

IRIS: Wait a moment, there was somebody else. As we passed this compartment Miss Froy stumbled in, there was a tall gentleman and a lady.

GILBERT: Right, now we're getting somewhere. If we can really find someone who saw her, we'll have the place searched.

TODHUNTER *comes into the picture.*

TODHUNTER: Can I be of any assistance?

IRIS: That's the gentleman.

GILBERT: Well, do you happen to remember seeing this young lady pass the compartment with a little English woman?

TODHUNTER: I'm, er . . . I'm afraid not.

IRIS: But you must have. She almost fell into your compartment. Surely you haven't forgotten. It's very important. Everybody's saying she wasn't on the train, but I know she is and I'm going to find her even if I have to stop the train to do it.

CHARTERS *is in the corridor, knocking on a compartment door.*

CHARTERS: I say, Caldicott. It's Charters. Can I come in?

CALDICOTT *appears.*

CHARTERS: You know that girl we saw in the hotel? She's

back there kicking up a devil of a fuss, says she's lost her friend.

CALDICOTT: Well, she hasn't been in here, old man.

CHARTERS: But the point is, she threatens to stop the train.

CALDICOTT: Oh, Lord!

CHARTERS: If we miss our connection at Basle, we'll never make Manchester in time.

CALDICOTT: This is serious.

CHARTERS: Let's hide in here.

TODHUNTER: (*to* IRIS) I'm sorry, I haven't the faintest recollection. You must be making a mistake.

GILBERT: Well, he obviously doesn't remember. Let's go and look for the other fellow.

*We have an interior shot of the* TODHUNTERS' *compartment.*

MRS. TODHUNTER: Who were you talking to outside?

TODHUNTER: Oh, nobody . . . just some people in the corridor . . . arguing.

*Back in the corridor we see* GILBERT *and* IRIS *walking along as* CHARTERS *comes from the other direction.*

IRIS: There he is . . . that's the man.

GILBERT: Oh, I say, I'm so sorry – I wonder if I can bother you . . . I wonder if you can help us.

CHARTERS: How?

IRIS: Well, I was having tea about an hour ago with an English lady . . . you saw her, didn't you?

CHARTERS: Well, I don't know . . . I mean . . . I was talking to my friend, wasn't I?

CALDICOTT: Indubitably.

IRIS: Yes, but you were sitting at the next table . . . she turned and borrowed the sugar . . . you must remember.

CHARTERS: Oh, yes . . . I recall passing the sugar.

IRIS: Well, then you saw her.

CHARTERS: I repeat – we were deep in conversation – we were discussing cricket.

IRIS: Well, I don't see how a thing like cricket can make you forget seeing people.

CHARTERS: Oh, don't you? Well, if that's your attitude, obviously there's nothing more to be said . . . Come, Caldicott . . . thing like cricket.

  CALDICOTT *and* CHARTERS *exit.*

GILBERT: Wrong tactics . . . we should have told him we were looking for a lost cricket ball.

IRIS: Yes, but he spoke to her . . . there must be some explanation.

  *DR. HARTZ enters.*

DR. HARTZ: There is. Please forgive me, I'm quite possibly wrong but I have known cases where a sudden shock or blow has induced the most vivid impressions.

IRIS: I understand – you don't believe me.

DR. HARTZ: Oh, it's not a question of belief – even a simple concussion may have curious effects upon an imaginative person.

IRIS: Yes, but I can remember every little detail . . . her name . . . Miss Froy . . . everything.

DR. HARTZ: So interesting. You know, if one had time, one could trace the cause of the hallucination.

GILBERT: Hallucination?

DR. HARTZ: Oh, precisely. There is no Miss Froy. There never was a Miss Froy. Merely a vivid subjective image.

IRIS: But I met her last night at the hotel.

DR. HARTZ: You thought you did.

GILBERT: But what about the name?

DR. HARTZ: Oh, some past association. An advertisement or a character in a novel, subconsciously remembered. No, there is no reason to be frightened, if you are quiet and relaxed.

IRIS: Thank you very much.

DR. HARTZ *looks out of a train window*.

DR. HARTZ: Dravaka. If you will excuse me, this is where my patient comes aboard. Excuse me. Most interesting.

DR. HARTZ *exits*.

GILBERT: We're stopping.

IRIS: This is our first stop, isn't it? Well, then, Miss Froy must still be on the train. Look, you look out of this window and see if she gets off this side. I'll take the other.

GILBERT: Most interesting . . .

*We see* IRIS *opening the window as* GILBERT *crosses the compartment to open the window opposite* IRIS.

GILBERT: What was she dressed in? Scotch tweeds, wasn't it?

IRIS: Oatmeal tweeds.

GILBERT: I knew it had something to do with porridge.

*We see an exterior shot of the station. Two* ATTENDANTS *enter in the background, wheeling a* PATIENT *on a stretcher, accompanied by* DR. HARTZ *and a* NUN.

DR. HARTZ: Escht tranquir (Don't let your patient be disturbed).

NUN: Din, Doktor (Very good, Doctor).

DR. HARTZ: Gentil . . . gentil . . . Coren cara (Gently . . .

gently . . . carry her carefully).

*There is a shot of* GILBERT *at his window in the corridor, looking up and down the track outside.* IRIS *is seen doing the same from her compartment window. The railway lines reveal no* MISS FROY.
*We cut to* TODHUNTER *who is looking out of his compartment.* MRS. TODHUNTER *is in the background.*

MRS. TODHUNTER: How long does it take to get a divorce? Eric?

TODHUNTER: I'm sorry, I wasn't listening.

MRS. TODHUNTER: I said, how long does it take to get a divorce?

TODHUNTER: That depends. Why?

MRS. TODHUNTER: I was only wondering whether we could take our honeymoon next spring. I mean the official one.

TODHUNTER: The difficulties are considerable. For one thing the courts are very crowded just now. Although, I suppose we barristers ought not to complain about that. As a matter of fact with the . . . with conditions as they are now, my chances of becoming a judge are very rosy. That is if, er . . . nothing untoward occurs.

MRS. TODHUNTER: Such as you being mixed up in a divorce case yourself?

TODHUNTER: Er . . . yes.

MRS. TODHUNTER: In that first careless rapture of yours, you said you didn't care what happened.

TODHUNTER: You must think of it from my point of view. The law, like Caesar's wife, must be above suspicion.

MRS. TODHUNTER: Even when the law spends six weeks with Caesar's wife?

TODHUNTER: Look here.

MRS. TODHUNTER: Now, I know why you've been running around like a scared rabbit. Why you lied so elaborately a few minutes ago.

TODHUNTER: I lied?

MRS. TODHUNTER: Yes, to those people in the corridor. I heard every word you said.

TODHUNTER: It was merely that I didn't wish to be mixed up in any enquiry.

MRS. TODHUNTER: Enquiry? Just because a little woman can't be found?

TODHUNTER: That girl was making a fuss. If the woman had disappeared and I'd admitted having seen her, we might become vital witnesses. My name might even appear in the papers, coupled with yours. A scandal like that might lead anywhere . . . anywhere . . .

MRS. TODHUNTER: Yes, I suppose it might.

*We cut to an exterior shot of the engine as it starts to move. Back in the carriage we focus on* IRIS *and* GILBERT.

GILBERT: Nobody?

IRIS: Nobody.

GILBERT: The only things that came out my side were two bits of orange peel and a paper bag.

IRIS: I know there's a Miss Froy. She's as real as you are.

GILBERT: That's what you say and you believe it. But there doesn't appear to be anybody else who has seen her.

MRS. TODHUNTER *off:* I saw her . . .

*She approaches* IRIS *and* GILBERT *and joins them.*

MRS. TODHUNTER: . . . I think.

IRIS: You did?

MRS. TODHUNTER: A little woman in tweeds.

IRIS: Yes.

MRS. TODHUNTER: Wearing a three-quarter coat.

IRIS: With a scarf.

MRS. TODHUNTER: That's right. I saw her with you when you passed the compartment.

IRIS: I knew I was right. But your husband said he hadn't seen her.

MRS. TODHUNTER: Oh, he didn't notice, but as soon as he mentioned it I remembered at once.

GILBERT: You win. You know, this calls for action. Are you prepared to make a statement?

MRS. TODHUNTER: Of course, if it helps.

DR. HARTZ *enters.*

DR. HARTZ: Ah, pardon, my patient has just arrived. The most fascinating complication.

IRIS: We have some news for you. This lady actually saw Miss Froy.

DR. HARTZ: So.

GILBERT: We are going to have the train searched.

IRIS: You'll have to think of a fresh theory now, Doctor.

DR. HARTZ: It is not necessary. My theory was a perfectly good one, the facts were misleading. I hope you will find your friend. Excuse me.

MRS. TODHUNTER: I'll be in here if you want me.

GILBERT: Right you are. Come along.

*We cut to an interior shot of the* TODHUNTERS' *compartment as* MRS. TODHUNTER *re-enters.*

MRS. TODHUNTER: Eric, I was only going to mention that I told that girl I'd seen her friend.

TODHUNTER: What's that? Have you taken leave of your senses?

MRS. TODHUNTER: On the contrary, I've come to them.

TODHUNTER: What do you mean?

MRS. TODHUNTER: If there's a scandal, there'll be a divorce. You couldn't let me down, could you? You'd have to do the decent thing as reluctantly as only you know how.

TODHUNTER: You forget one very important thing, Margaret. Your husband would divorce you, I've no doubt, but whatever happens, my wife will never divorce me.

*The camera cuts back to the corridor, where* GILBERT, IRIS, *the* GUARD *and* SIGNOR DOPPO *are talking together.*

GILBERT: Well, it may seem crazy to you, but I tell you you're going to search the train.

SIGNOR DOPPO: Ah, Signorina, down there they look for you. Your friend, she come back.

IRIS: Come back?

SIGNOR DOPPO: Si, si (Yes).

IRIS: But what happened?

SIGNOR DOPPO: Oh, you go see. She tell you. Sousi (Excuse me).

GILBERT: All right, Athleston, relax. The crisis is over. Come on, let's join the lady.

*Camera pans with them into the first class compartment.* GILBERT *goes up to* MADAME KUMMER, IRIS *follows.*

GILBERT: Here we are.

IRIS: Miss Froy? That isn't Miss Froy.

GILBERT: Isn't it?

IRIS: No.

GILBERT: I say, it's a silly thing to say, but are you Miss Froy?

MADAME KUMMER: No, I am Madame Kummer . . . Ga dossen joelator or hockatch bat kever fronche am nond (I helped her into the carriage when she was hit on the head . . . then went to see some friends).

GILBERT: She says she helped you into the carriage after you got the biff on the head and then went to see some friends.

BARONESS: Norsk revalt de denalt rinda anglisch fomana (When she said English lady I didn't think of Madame Kummer).

GILBERT: The Baroness says as you spoke about an English lady she didn't connect her with Madame Kummer.

DR. HARTZ *comes into the picture and listens intently.*

IRIS: But she wasn't the lady I saw. It was Miss Froy.

GILBERT: Oatmeal tweeds, blouse, blue silk handkerchief.

IRIS: Yes, I know everything's the same, but it isn't her.

DR. HARTZ: I beg your pardon, when did you say you first met this Miss Froy?

IRIS: Last night at the hotel.

DR. HARTZ: Was she wearing a costume like this?

IRIS: Yes, I think she was.

DR. HARTZ: Then I must apologise. You did meet her after all.

IRIS: Then . . .

DR. HARTZ: But not on this train. In your subconscious mind you substituted for the face of Madame Kummer that of Miss Froy.

IRIS: But I didn't. I couldn't have. I tell you. I talked to her here.

GILBERT: That's very easily settled, there's an English woman on the train who said she saw her. If this lady wouldn't mind . . . Madame, abner bresen dak master cav selham (Would you mind coming with us)?

MADAME KUMMER *nods.*

MADAME KUMMER: Non . . . trar taska (No . . . not at all).

GILBERT *(in French):* Bon. Après vous, mesdames (Good. After you, ladies). What a gift of languages the fellow's got!

DR. HARTZ, GILBERT, IRIS *and* MADAME KUMMER *leave the compartment and walk along the corridor to the* TODHUNTERS' *compartment.* GILBERT *knocks.*
*We cut to an interior shot of* TODHUNTERS' *compartment.* TODHUNTER *opens to the door to reveal* GILBERT *first, and then* IRIS *and* MADAME KUMMER *in the background.*

GILBERT: I'm so sorry, but would you tell us please, is this the woman you saw?

IRIS: It isn't a bit like her, is it?

MRS. TODHUNTER: Yes, she's the woman.

IRIS: But it isn't, I tell you, it isn't.

GILBERT: Are you sure?

MRS. TODHUNTER: Perfectly.

IRIS: She isn't. She isn't.

MADAME KUMMER: Bragarsan (Is that all)?

GILBERT: Ascar (Yes, thank you). Well, come on, then. I'm so sorry to have troubled you.

TODHUNTER *closes the door of the compartment.*

MRS. TODHUNTER: Well, aren't you going to say anything? You might at least gloat, if nothing else.

TODHUNTER: What am I expected to say? You only did it to save your own skin.

IRIS *and* GILBERT *are seen walking along the corridor from the* TODHUNTERS' *compartment.*

IRIS: She was lying. I saw it in her face. They're all lying, but why, why?

GILBERT: Now, why don't you sit down and take it easy?

IRIS: Do you believe that nonsense about substituting Miss Froy's face for Madame Kummer's?

GILBERT: Well, I think any change would be an improvement.

IRIS: Listen, Miss Froy was on this train. I know she was, and nothing will convince me otherwise. Must you follow me round like a pet dog?

GILBERT: Well, let's say a watch dog. It's got all the better instincts.

IRIS: Goodbye.

IRIS *moves to her compartment.*
*She imagines a picture of* MISS FROY *and then* SIGNORA DOPPO; *then* MISS FROY *superimposed with the* BARONESS; *then* MISS FROY'S *face with that of* SIGNOR DOPPO; *finally she thinks of* MISS FROY *and* MADAME KUMMER.
*We cut back to the corridor where* GILBERT *is standing, as* IRIS *appears from her compartment in the background.*

IRIS: The Doctor was right. You're all right. I never saw Miss Froy on the train. It didn't happen, I know now.

GILBERT: I'm glad you're going to take it like that. What you want to do is to forget all about it. Make your mind a complete blank. You know, watch me, you can't go wrong.

What about a spot of something to eat, eh?

IRIS: Anything.

GILBERT: That's right, come along.

*We follow* IRIS *and* GILBERT *along the corridor into the dining car. They sit at the very table* IRIS *and* MISS FROY *had taken earlier.*

GILBERT: Would you like a little air?

IRIS: Thanks.

GILBERT *opens the window slightly revealing* MISS FROY'S *name still written on the train window.*

GILBERT: Do you think you could eat anything?

IRIS: I could try.

GILBERT: That's the spirit. You'll feel a different girl tomorrow.

IRIS: I hope so. I don't want to meet my fiancé a nervous wreck.

GILBERT: You're what?

IRIS: I'm being married on Thursday.

GILBERT: You're quite sure you're not imagining that?

IRIS: Positive.

GILBERT: I was afraid so. Ah, food.

IRIS: I couldn't face it.

GILBERT: You know best. Do you mind if I talk with my mouth full?

IRIS: If you must.

GILBERT: Well, since you press me. I'll begin with my father. You know, it's remarkable how many great men begin with their fathers. Oh, something to drink?

IRIS: No. Oh, yes I will, a cup of tea, please.

GILBERT: One tea, and no soup for the lady. You know, my father was a very colourful character. Amongst other things, he was strongly addicted to . . . you'll never guess.

IRIS: Harriman's Herbal Tea.

GILBERT: No, double scotches.

IRIS: A million Mexicans drink it.

GILBERT: Maybe they do, but father didn't.

IRIS: Miss Froy gave the waiter a packet of it.

GILBERT: A packet of what?

IRIS: Harriman's Herbal Tea. She said it was the only sort she liked.

GILBERT: Look here, I thought we agreed that you were going to make your mind a complete blank.

IRIS: But it's so real, I'm sure it happened.

GILBERT: Did we, or did we not?

IRIS: We did. Sorry. Go on telling me about your father.

GILBERT: Well, my father was a very remarkable man . . .

IRIS: Did he play the clarinet?

GILBERT: He did. In fact he never put it down unless it became absolutely necessary. Well, naturally I couldn't help inheriting his love of music.

IRIS: Why not?

GILBERT: That was all he left me. You know, you're remarkably attractive. Has anyone ever told you?

IRIS: We were discussing you.

GILBERT: Oh yes, of course. Do you like me?

IRIS: Not much.

GILBERT: Well, after I'd, er . . . paid my father's debts, I started to travel, before they tried to cash the cheques. At the moment, I'm writing a book on folk dancing. Would you like to buy a copy?

IRIS: I'd love to. When does it see the light of day?

GILBERT: In about four years.

IRIS: That's a very long time.

GILBERT: It's a very long book. Do you know why you fascinate me? I'll tell you. You have two great qualities I used to admire in father. You haven't any manners at all, and you're always seeing things. What's the matter?

IRIS: Look!

*We cut to a shot of* MISS FROY'S *name on the window, as the train passes through a tunnel. Then we are back inside the dining car studying* GILBERT *and* IRIS *at their table, and* MISS FROY'S *name on the window. The train comes out of the tunnel.*

IRIS: It's gone!

GILBERT: What's gone?

IRIS: Miss Froy's name on the window. You saw it. You must have seen it. She's on the train.

GILBERT: Steady! Steady!

GILBERT *takes a glass from a* MAN *passing the table, and offers it to* IRIS.

IRIS: No. No. We've got to find her. Something's happening to her.

GILBERT: Take it easy.

IRIS: Stop the train. Listen, everybody. There's a woman on this train. Miss Froy. Some of you must have seen her. They're hiding her somewhere. I appeal to you, all of you, to stop the train.

DR. HARTZ *and* GILBERT *enter the picture.*

IRIS: Please, help me. Please make them stop the train. Do

you hear? Why don't you do something before it's too late?

DR. HARTZ: Please. Please.

IRIS: I know you think I'm crazy, but I'm not. I'm not. For heaven's sake, stop this train. Leave me alone. Leave me alone.

*We follow* IRIS *across the dining car, and see her pulling the communication cord. Then she faints.*
*There is an interior shot of* CHARTERS' *compartment.* CHARTERS *and* CALDICOTT *are sitting opposite each other.*

CHARTERS: Ten minutes late, thanks to that fool of a girl. If she gets up to any more of her tricks, we shall be too late for the last day of the match.

CALDICOTT: I suppose you couldn't put it to her in some way.

CHARTERS: What?

CALDICOTT: Well, people just don't vanish and so forth.

CHARTERS: But she has.

CALDICOTT: What?

CHARTERS: Vanished.

CALDICOTT: Who?

CHARTERS: The old dame.

CALDICOTT: Yes.

CHARTERS: Well?

CALDICOTT: But how could she?

CHARTERS: What?

CALDICOTT: Vanish.

CHARTERS: I don't know.

CALDICOTT: That just explains my point. People don't just disappear into thin air.

CHARTERS: It's done in India.

CALDICOTT: What?

CHARTERS: The rope trick.

CALDICOTT: Oh, that. It never comes out in a photograph.

*The film cuts to an interior shot of the corridor. From the corridor we see* DR. HARTZ *and* IRIS *in the compartment.* GILBERT *is in the corridor.*

DR. HARTZ: Look now. In half an hour we stop at Morsken, just before the border. I will leave there with my patient for the National Hospital. If you will come with me, you could stay overnight in a private ward. You need peace and rest.

IRIS: Sorry. Nothing doing.

GILBERT *off:* Isn't there anything we can do?

IRIS: Yes, find Miss Froy.

DR. HARTZ: I tell you, my friend, if she does not rest I will not answer for her. It will be best if you persuade her. She likes you.

GILBERT: I'm just about as popular as a dose of strychnine.

DR. HARTZ: If you coat it with sugar, she may swallow it.

*While* GILBERT *is still in the corridor, the camera pans to the* CHEF, *as he appears with a bucket of rubbish, which he throws out of the window. A piece of paper sticking to a window is seen by* GILBERT. *He notices it is part of a Harriman's Herbal Tea packet.*
GILBERT *enters the first class compartment. We see a shot of* SIGNOR DOPPO *and the* BARONESS. GILBERT *goes up to* IRIS.

GILBERT: Cosmopolitan train this. People of all nations. I've just seen at least a million Mexicans in the corridor. Well, I thought I'd look in to tell you to think over what Doctor Hartz said. If you feel like changing your mind, I'll be hanging around.

IRIS *follows* GILBERT *out into the corridor.*

IRIS: What's all the mystery?

GILBERT: You're right. Miss Froy is on this train. I've just seen the packet of tea that you are talking about. They chucked it out with the rubbish.

IRIS: You're a trifle late, aren't you? She may be dead by now.

GILBERT: Dead or alive we'll . . .

MADAME KUMMER *comes to join them.*

GILBERT: For sheer variety, give me an English summer. I remember once spending a Bank holiday at Brighton . . .

MADAME KUMMER *exits.*

GILBERT: Come on, we're going to search this train. There's something definitely queer in the air.

*We cut to an exterior long shot of the train as it continues on its way, before we cut to the interior of the fourth class compartment as* GILBERT *and* IRIS *pass through. They enter the luggage van.*

GILBERT: Looks like a supply service for trunk murderers.

IRIS: Don't!

*There is a long shot of a wicker basket which is moving.*

IRIS: What's that?

GILBERT: It's all right, Miss Froy, it's only us.

IRIS: Hurry up. Quickly.

GILBERT *opens the lid of the basket revealing a calf.*

GILBERT: Maybe it's Miss Froy bewitched. You never know. Well, anyway, I refuse to be discouraged. Faint heart never found old lady. By the way, do you know anything about her?

IRIS: No. Only that she was a governess going back home.

66

What is in this thing?

GILBERT: Can't imagine. Wait a minute. There might be something down here.

*There is a shock as they discover a model of* SIGNOR DOPPO. IRIS *and* GILBERT *look at one another.*

IRIS: What on earth!

GILBERT: Our Italian friend. I've got it. Wait a minute. There you are, the great Doppo.

GILBERT *unrolls a poster.*

GILBERT: His visiting card. Look!

IRIS: What's it say?

GILBERT: The Great Doppo. Magician, illusionist, mind reader. Signor Doppo will appear in all the principal towns and cities. See his fascinating act, The Vanishing . . . Lady.

IRIS: The Vanishing Lady?

GILBERT: Perhaps that's the explanation.

IRIS: What?

GILBERT: Maybe he was practising on Miss Froy.

IRIS: Well, perhaps it's a publicity stunt.

GILBERT: No, I don't think so. That wouldn't account for the Baroness or Madame Kummer.

IRIS: Well, what's your theory?

GILBERT: I don't know. My theory? I'll tell you.

GILBERT *accidentally unfastens a basket in the background. Pigeons fly out of it.*

IRIS: Oh, dear . . . I can't get this one.

GILBERT *goes into a trick cabinet.*

IRIS: Where are you?

*We see a medium shot of the trick cabinet.* GILBERT'S

*voice comes from it as* IRIS *stands next to it.*

GILBERT *off:* I'm in here with a strong smell of camphor balls.

IRIS: I can't see you.

GILBERT *off:* I'm about somewhere.

IRIS *enters the trick cabinet as* GILBERT *reappears.*

GILBERT: Here I am. Where are you?

IRIS *off:* I don't know.

GILBERT: That's what comes of not saying Abracadabra.

*We cut to a shot of a rabbit in the trick cabinet.*

IRIS *off:* Oh!

*We cut to* IRIS *and* GILBERT, *now both happily out of the trick cabinet and back in the luggage van together.*

IRIS: Ouch!

GILBERT: Are you hurt?

IRIS: Not much.

GILBERT: Come and sit down over here.

IRIS: What is that thing?

GILBERT: Well, in magic circles, we call it the disappearing cabinet. You get inside and vanish.

IRIS: Mm . . . so I noticed. You were about to tell me your theory.

GILBERT: Oh, my theory. Well . . .

GILBERT *puts on a Sherlock Holmes hat. His hand comes into the picture.*

GILBERT *off:* . . . My theory, my dear Watson . . .

*Resume shot of* GILBERT *and* IRIS.

GILBERT: . . . is that we are in very deep waters indeed.

IRIS *hands a pipe to* GILBERT.

GILBERT: Oh, thank you very much. Let us marshal our facts over a pipeful of Baker Street shag. In the first place, a little old lady disappears. Everyone that saw her promptly insists that she was never there at all. Right?

IRIS: Right.

GILBERT: We know that she was. Therefore, they did see her. Therefore, they are deliberately lying. Why?

IRIS: I don't know. I'm only Watson.

GILBERT: Well, don't bury yourself in the part. I'll tell you why. Because they daren't face an enquiry, because Miss Froy's probably still somewhere on this train.

IRIS: I told you that hours ago.

GILBERT: Oh, yes, so you did. For that, my dear Watson, you shall have a 'trichonoply" cigar.

IRIS: Oh, thank you.

GILBERT: Now, there's only one thing left to do, you know. Search the train in disguise.

IRIS: As what?

GILBERT: Well, er . . . Old English Gentleman.

IRIS: They'd see through you.

GILBERT: Perhaps you're right. Ah, Will Hay. No, boys, boys, which of you has stolen Miss Froy? Own up. Own up.

GILBERT *has perched glasses on his nose.*

IRIS: Those glasses. Give them to me.

GILBERT: Why?

IRIS: They're Miss Froy's.

GILBERT: Are you sure?

IRIS: Yes. They're exactly the same. Gold-rimmed with . . . Where did you find them?

GILBERT: Why, down here on the floor. The glass is broken.

IRIS: Well, probably in a struggle.

GILBERT: Pick up the glass, Do you realise that this is our first piece of really tangible proof?

*We cut to* SIGNOR DOPPO'S *hand taking* MISS FROY'S *spectacles from* IRIS'S *hand. Pan up to show* GILBERT, SIGNOR DOPPO *and* IRIS.

SIGNOR DOPPO: Will you please give me those spectacles? They belong to me. My spectacles, please.

GILBERT: Yours? Are you sure?

SIGNOR DOPPO: Dietemmi questi occhiali (You doubt my word)?

GILBERT: Ah, naughty, naughty. That's a very large nose for a very small pair of spectacles. So that's the game, is it? We'll soon see about that. These are Miss Froy's glasses and you know it. She's been in here and you know that too.

*There is a shot of the calf in the wicker basket, before we cut back to* GILBERT *and* SIGNOR DOPPO *struggling on the floor.*

GILBERT: Well, don't stand hopping about there like a referee, cooperate. Kick him. See if he's got a false bottom. Wait a minute, I'll get him up.

*There is a quick shot of three white rabbits, then the camera focuses on* IRIS *as she kicks* GILBERT.

GILBERT: Ouch! That doesn't help.

*We have another shot of the white rabbits, followed by a shot of* GILBERT *and* SIGNOR DOPPO *still struggling with each other.*

GILBERT: Quick, pull his ears back. Give them a twist.

GILBERT *and* SIGNOR DOPPO *continue to fight. There seems little* IRIS *can do.*

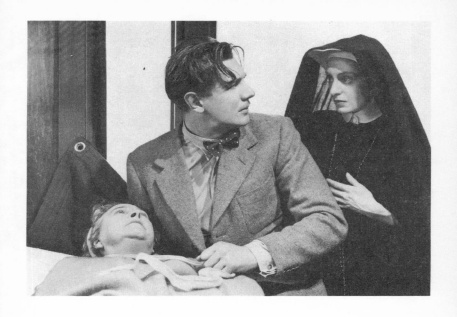

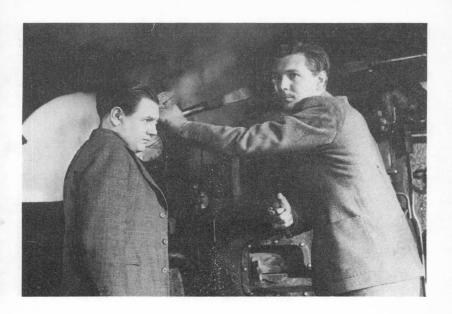

GILBERT: Look out, he's got a knife.

*We cut to a close-up shot of the knife in* SIGNOR DOPPO'S *hand.*

GILBERT: Try and get hold of it before he cuts a slice off me.

IRIS: I can't reach it.

*The camera pans to* IRIS'S *feet and legs standing on a case. As the men's fight comes closer to her, she bends down and bites* SIGNOR DOPPO'S *hand and he drops the knife.* GILBERT *comes into the picture.*

GILBERT: Well done!

*There is another shot of the calf in the wicker basket, before we cut back to* SIGNOR DOPPO *and* GILBERT, *who punches him on the jaw.* DOPPO *staggers back into the trick cabinet.*
*Cut to* DOPPO *coming out of the cabinet, with* IRIS *on the right.*

GILBERT *off:* We know how that thing works. Come out of there.

IRIS *hits* SIGNOR DOPPO *on the head.*

GILBERT: Is he out, do you think? We've got to hide him somewhere. I wonder what's in here?

IRIS: Hurry up! Quick, before he comes to.

GILBERT *lifts the lid of a nearby wooden box.*

GILBERT: It's empty. Bring him along. Oh no, you don't.

GILBERT *places* SIGNOR DOPPO *in the wooden box.*
*Cut to* IRIS *and* GILBERT *sitting on the box.*

GILBERT: Oh!

IRIS: What's the matter?

GILBERT: Garlic. I'll be all right in a minute. Here, hold onto this.

79

IRIS: Oh, yes.

GILBERT: Tie him up. Oh, well, we're getting somewhere at last. We definitely know that Miss Froy was on this train and we know that our friend in here had something to do with it. That ought to keep him quiet until we find her. Ah, hard work, but worth it. Let's have the evidence.

IRIS: Evidence?

GILBERT: Yes, the glasses.

IRIS: You've got them.

GILBERT: No. I haven't got them.

IRIS: Oh!

GILBERT: He's got them.

*We cut to a shot of the inside of the box, which is empty.*

IRIS *off:* He isn't there.

GILBERT *off:* Snookered. It's a false bottom. The twister! He's a contortionist.

*Pan up to* IRIS *and* GILBERT.

IRIS: He's gone all right.

GILBERT: Yes, to find the others and make more trouble. We're in a nasty jam, my dear. We can't fight the whole train. We need allies.

IRIS: Yes, but who can we trust?

GILBERT: That's the snag.

IRIS: There's that Doctor Hartz person.

GILBERT: Yes, you're right. He might help. Come on, let's tell him the symptoms.

IRIS: All right. Oh, wait a minute.

GILBERT *and* IRIS *go back through the train to find* DR. HARTZ. *They stand in the corridor outside the sleeper compartment.*

*Only the* BANDAGED PATIENT *and a* NUN *are inside, so* GILBERT *goes back into the corridor.*

GILBERT: He's not there. I've just had a particularly idiotic idea.

IRIS: Mm, I can quite believe that.

GILBERT: Suppose that patient in there is Miss Froy?

IRIS: Yes. But it didn't come on the train until after Miss Froy had disappeared.

GILBERT: Oh, yes. Yes, that's why it's an idiotic idea. Come on, let's find the doctor.

IRIS: No, no, wait a minute.

GILBERT: What is it?

IRIS: Did you notice anything wrong about that Nun?

GILBERT: No.

IRIS: I don't think she's a Nun at all. They don't wear high heels.

*There is a quick flashback shot to the* NUN'S *feet wearing high-heeled shoes as seen by* GILBERT

GILBERT: Yes, you're right. Listen, did you see Madame Kummer get on the train?

IRIS: No.

GILBERT: Supposing they decoyed Miss Froy into the luggage van and hid her there. At the first stop the patient comes aboard. Head injury, all wrapped up. The patient is Madame Kummer. Madame Kummer becomes Miss Froy and Miss Froy becomes that.

IRIS: Yes. But why should they go to all this trouble to kidnap a harmless little governess?

GILBERT: It isn't a governess at all. Perhaps it's some political thing, you know. Come on, let's investigate.

IRIS *and* GILBERT *enter the sleeping compartment.*

81

GILBERT: Parlez vous Français (Do you speak French)?
Sprechen sie Deutsch (Do you speak German)?
Yarka dar Bandrieken (Do you speak Bandrieken)?
Oh, well, you'll just have to put up with it in English. Can I take a look at your patient, please? Thank you. (*to* IRIS) Keep an eye on the Nun.

> GILBERT *stands over the bandaged patient as* IRIS *and the* NUN *look on.* DR. HARTZ *opens the door.*

DR. HARTZ: What are you doing here? Why are you in here? This is a most serious accident case. You have no business to be here at all, neither of you.

GILBERT: Doctor Harz, we want you to undo those bandages and le us take a look at your patient's face.

DR. HARTZ: Are you out of your senses? There is no face there. Nothing but lumps of raw flesh. Already the case has lost so much blood, nothing but a transfusion can save him. What do you want me to do? Murder my patient?

GILBERT: You're quite sure that this is your patient?

IRIS: We . . . we believe it's Miss Froy.

DR. HARTZ: Miss Froy, You can't be serious. What on earth put such ideas into your heads? I understand she is deaf and dumb.

IRIS: But she may lip read.

DR. HARTZ: Oh, that's impossible. Well, in that case, perhaps you will join me in the dining car? I'll be with you in a moment. I want to be certain my patient hasn't been disturbed.

> GILBERT *and* IRIS *go out of the compartment.*

DR. HARTZ: Cadeskan barogne sar calto drunk (Why did they become suspicious)?

NUN: How the devil do I know how they cottoned on? Somebody must have tipped them off. You never said the old girl was English.

DR. HARTZ: What difference does that make? In a few moments I shall order three drinks in the dining car. Mine will be Chartreuse. Now, one of the stewards is working for us. Now, listen carefully.

*We cut to an interior shot of* IRIS *and* GILBERT *entering the dining car.* CHARTERS *and* CALDICOTT *are also there.*

CHARTERS: There's that girl again.

CALDICOTT: Seems to have recovered. Lucky it blew over.

GILBERT *and* IRIS *are now seated as* DR. HARTZ *enters.*

DR. HARTZ: And now, perhaps, you'll tell me what it's all about?

GILBERT: Now, listen, Doctor, have you ever actually seen your patient?

DR. HARTZ: No, I merely received a message to pick the case up and operate at Morsken.

GILBERT: How do you know that it's not Miss Froy?

IRIS: We believe there's been a substitution, Doctor.

DR. HARTZ: You really mean to say that you think that someone has . . . (*He speaks to a* STEWARD) I want a Green Chartreuse. Won't you join me?

GILBERT: Oh, thanks. I'd like a large brandy, please.

DR. HARTZ: And you?

IRIS: I don't want anything, thanks.

GILBERT: Oh, come, it'll do you good.

IRIS: No, really, I don't want it.

DR. HARTZ: You are very tired. It will pick you up.

IRIS: All right, then. Just a small one.

DR. HARTZ: Two brandies and a Chartreuse.

GILBERT: Tell me, do you know anything about the Nun

who is looking after your patient?

DR. HARTZ: Nun? No. Only that she is from a convent close to where the accident occurred.

GILBERT: Don't you think it's rather peculiar that she's wearing high-heeled shoes?

DR. HARTZ: Oh, is she? Well, that is rather . . . rather curious, isn't it?

IRIS: It's a conspiracy. That's all it can be. All these people on the train say they haven't seen Miss Froy, but they have. We know that, because just now in the luggage van . . .

*Her voice has risen and* CHARTERS *and* CALDICOTT *notice this.*

CHARTERS: She's off again!

CALDICOTT: I hope she doesn't create another scene. Puts the lid on our getting back in time, if she did.

*We cut back to a shot of the table that* GILBERT, IRIS *and* DR. HARTZ *are sitting at.*

IRIS: . . . And then this fellow from the carriage, Doppo's his name, he came along and grabbed the glasses.

GILBERT: And then we went for him and had a bit of a fight.

DR. HARTZ: Oh, a fight?

IRIS *off:* We knocked him out.

DR. HARTZ: Oh!

SIGNOR DOPPO *walks past them between the tables.*

DR. HARTZ: He seems to have made a speedy recovery.

GILBERT: Yes. Oh, that's just bluff.

*The* STEWARD'S *hand comes in to shot with the drinks.*

STEWARD: Gratsia (Thank you).

*There is a quick shot of* SIGNOR DOPPO *sitting nearby,*

*followed by another shot of the drinks on the table as* DR. HARTZ'S *hand comes into the shot.*

DR. HARTZ: Oh, but how could he be involved in a conspiracy? Look at him . . . the poor fellow. He's just a harmless traveller.

GILBERT: He's also a music-hall artist making a tour of Bandrieka.

DR. HARTZ: Well?

GILBERT: And the Baroness's husband is Minister of Propaganda. One word from her and his tour would be cancelled.

DR. HARTZ: Oh, I see.

GILBERT: As for the stewards, if they don't do what they're told, they've got a nice cosy brick wall to lean up against.

*Shots of the drinks on the table intersperse themselves with the conversation.*

DR. HARTZ: But . . . but . . . tell me about the two English travellers over there. They also denied seeing her?

GILBERT: British diplomacy, Doctor. Never climb a fence if you can sit on it. Old Foreign Office proverb.

DR. HARTZ: What I cannot understand is why should anyone want to dispose of the old lady?

GILBERT: Well, that's just what stumps us. All we know is that she was here on this train and now she's . . .

GILBERT *swallows his drink. We see* GILBERT'S *hand replacing his glass on the table.*

GILBERT *off:* . . . gone.

DR. HARTZ: Well, if you're right, it means the whole train is against us.

IRIS: What are we going to do?

DR. HARTZ: Well, in view of what you've just told me, I

shall risk examining the patient. One moment, we mustn't act suspiciously. Behave as if nothing had happened. Drink, that'll steady your nerves. To our health. And may our enemies, if they exist, be unconscious of our purpose. Let's go. We must hurry now.

GILBERT *off:* Come on, drink up.

*We see* IRIS *drinking her brandy before they all go back into the corridor.*

DR. HARTZ: Wait in here.

GILBERT: Right you are.

DR. HARTZ *watches* IRIS *and* GILBERT *enter the compartment before moving on to the sleeper compartment. He enters it.*

NUN: Anything wrong?

DR. HARTZ: Nothing, except they noticed you were wearing high heels. However it makes no difference. We shall reach Morsken in three minutes. Quite an eventful journey.

GILBERT *and* IRIS *are sitting, waiting, in their compartment as* DR. HARTZ *enters.*

IRIS: Well?

DR. HARTZ: Yes, the patient is Miss Froy. She will be taken off the train at Morsken in about three minutes. She will be removed to the hospital there and operated on. Unfortunately the operation will not be successful. Oh, I should perhaps have explained, the operation will be performed by me.

GILBERT *moves towards the door.* DR. HARTZ *holds a gun in his pocket.*

DR. HARTZ: You see, I am in this conspiracy as you term it. You are a very alert young couple, but it's quite useless for you to think, as you are undoubtedly doing, of a way out of your dilemma. The drink you had just now, I regret to say, contained a quantity of Hydrocin. For your benefit, Hydrocin is a very little known drug which has the effect in a small quantity of paralysing the brain and rendering the victim unconscious for a considerable period. In a slightly larger quantity, of course, it induces madness. However you have my word the dose was a normal one.

IRIS *falls over in a faint.*

DR. HARTZ: In a very few moments now you will join your young friend. Need I say how sorry I am having to take such a, how shall I say, melodramatic course. But your persistent meddling made it necessary.

GILBERT *falls back.* DR. HARTZ *leaves the compartment. As he does so,* GILBERT *opens his eyes.*

GILBERT: Are you all right? You must have fainted. Listen, there's a woman next door going to be murdered and we've got to get moving before this stuff takes effect.

IRIS: I did read once that if you keep on the go you can stay awake.

GILBERT: Right, come on, let's get going. It's locked. We can't go that way, we'll be spotted.

GILBERT *starts to open the train window.*

IRIS: You can't do that.

GILBERT: Don't worry, it's only next door, you carry on keeping fit, touch your toes, stand on your head, do anything, only whatever you do, don't fall asleep.

*We have an exterior shot of* GILBERT *climbing out of the window. Another train is approaching. Cut to the interior of the sleeper compartment where the* NUN *and the* PATIENT *are.*
*GILBERT appears in the background and climbs through the window of the sleeper. He and the* NUN *exchange glances.*

NUN: Go on, you needn't be afraid, it is Miss Froy. It's all right, you haven't been drugged. He told me to put

87

something in your drinks, but I didn't do it.

*We see* GILBERT *untying* MISS FROY'S *bandages.*

GILBERT: Who the devil are you? He said you were deaf and dumb.

NUN: Never mind about that now. If you want to save her, you've got to hurry.

*The* NUN *watches as* GILBERT *continues to unwrap the bandages, and* MISS FROY *is indeed revealed.*

NUN: Hartz will be back in a minute. What's going to happen then?

GILBERT: If we can hold them off until we get past Morsken, the frontier's a few miles beyond the station.

MADAME KUMMER *enters in the background.* GILBERT *claps his hand over her mouth.*

NUN: Come on, there's still time.

*We move to the interior of the first class compartment, where* SIGNOR DOPPO, *the* BARONESS *and* DR. HARTZ *are seated.*

DR. HARTZ: Arkda duk jova set . . . finiki (Two thousand, three thousand, four thousand, five thousand, that's the lot).

SIGNOR DOPPO: Cinque cente sememonte dope tutto quelle che koha fatto cos poi de quest' orrechio marsicato de quelle ragazzo. (Only five thousand for all the work that I've done, it's not enough, I want some more).

BARONESS: Margordavsay (Give it to him).

*We cut back to the interior of the sleeper compartment.*

GILBERT: That's Morsken. Have you finished?

GILBERT *opens the door to reveal* IRIS *in the next compartment touching her toes.*

GILBERT: Come on, Miss Froy.

GILBERT *gives* IRIS *a slap.*

GILBERT: Come on, kid, you're not drugged. I'll explain later. Abracadabra.

MISS FROY *enters.*

IRIS: Miss Froy! Oh, I can't believe it.

MISS FROY: Thank you, my dear. Thank you very much.

GILBERT: Careful.

DR. HARTZ *enters the sleeper compartment where the* NUN *is sitting beside* MADAME KUMMER, *who is lying swathed in bandages.*

DR. HARTZ: Ready?

NUN: Yes.

DR. HARTZ *checks the other compartment and sees* GILBERT *and* IRIS *who appear to be unconscious.* MISS FROY *is secretly hidden in the toilet.*

DR. HARTZ: *(to a Guard)* Teraner lena derafo, legas cheto (Keep this door locked).

*Back in the compartment,* GILBERT *and* IRIS *get up. Pan round as* GILBERT *opens the door to the toilet to reveal* MISS FROY.

GILBERT: Are you all right, Miss Froy?

MISS FROY: Yes, thank you. It's rather like the rush hour on the Underground.

*There is a quick, exterior long shot of the train.*

GILBERT: We're slowing down!

*The camera shoots through the compartment window onto a long shot of an ambulance waiting at the station.* DR. HARTZ *leaves the train, and the stretcher bearing* MADAME KUMMER *is taken into a waiting ambulance.* GILBERT *and* IRIS *watch.*
*Cut to the interior of the ambulance.*

DR. HARTZ: Davara . . . davara (Excellent . . . excellent). I'm sorry you've had such an uncomfortable journey, Miss Froy.

DR. HARTZ *unwraps the bandages and discovers his patient is* MADAME KUMMER.

DR. HARTZ: Eranaverek (Damnation).

DR. HARTZ *bursts from the ambulance just as the* NUN *is about to leave the train.*

DR. HARTZ: Get back on the train.

*People on the platform look at* DR. HARTZ. *They are puzzled.*
GILBERT *and* IRIS *are seen waiting anxiously in the compartment.*

IRIS: I hope nothing goes wrong. Aren't we stopping rather a long time?

*There is a long shot of the ambulance moving off as seen from the train.*

GILBERT: The ambulance is going. We'll be off in a jiffy.

*There is an exterior, medium-length shot of a carriage being uncoupled from the rest of the train with* DR. HARTZ *watching. Then we cut back to the interior of the compartment where* GILBERT, IRIS *and* MISS FROY *are.*

GILBERT: Another couple of minutes, we'll be over the border.

*We cut to the interior of the* BARONESS'S *sleeper, where the* NUN, *the* BARONESS *and* DR. HARTZ *are.*

BARONESS: Briden dan karvik jasconey pas hafdon ragenok mantado pondalat (So this is how you repay us, those who treated you so well).

NUN: I know I've been well paid, and I've done plenty of dirty work for it, but this was murder, and she was an Englishwoman.

BARONESS: You are Bandriekan.

NUN: My husband was, but I'm English and you were going to butcher her in cold blood.

DR. HARTZ: Your little diversion made it necessary not only to remove the lady in question, but two others as well.

NUN: You can't do that.

DR. HARTZ: Also, it would be unwise of us to permit the existence of anyone who cannot be trusted.

NUN: You wouldn't dare. I know too much.

BARONESS: Precisely.

*We cut back to the compartment where* GILBERT *and* IRIS *are.*

GILBERT: I think we're over the border now. You can come out, Miss Froy.

MISS FROY *appears.*

MISS FROY: Oh, bless me. What an unpleasant journey.

GILBERT: Never mind, you shall have a corner seat for the rest of the way. There you are. Look here, now that it's over, I think you ought to tell us what's it's all about.

*A scream is heard.*

GILBERT: What was that scream?

IRIS: Surely it was only the train whistle.

GILBERT: It wasn't, it was a woman.

MISS FROY: Be careful.

GILBERT *enters the corridor. He reacts as he finds that the carriage has been disconnected from the rest of the train. Then he goes back into the compartment.*

GILBERT: They've rumbled. We're on a branch line and they've slipped the rear part of the train.

MISS FROY: Oh dear! Oh dear!

GILBERT: Look here! Who are you, and why are these people going to these lengths to get hold of you?

MISS FROY: I really haven't the faintest idea. I'm a children's governess. You know, I can only think they've made some terrible mistake.

GILBERT: Why are you holding out on us? Tell us the truth. You got us involved in this fantastic plot. You might at least trust us.

MISS FROY: I really don't know, I . . .

GILBERT: I wonder if there's anybody else left on the train?

IRIS: There's only the dining car in front, but there won't be anybody there now.

GILBERT: What time do you make it, tea time? All the English will be there. I'm going to have a look. Come on, we'd better stick together.

> GILBERT *is correct. Having made their way along the* corridor, MISS FROY, GILBERT *and* IRIS *enter the dining car. There are* MR. *and* MRS. TODHUNTER, CHARTERS *and* CALDICOTT.

CHARTERS: There's the old girl turned up.

CALDICOTT: Told you it was a lot of fuss about nothing. Bolt must have jammed.

GILBERT: I've got something to say. Will you all please listen? An attempt has been made to abduct this lady by force. And I've got reason to believe that the people who did it are going to try again.

CHARTERS: What the devil's the fellow drivelling about?

GILBERT: Well, if you don't believe me, you can look out of the window. This train has been diverted onto a branch line.

TODHUNTER: What are you talking about?

GILBERT: There's been . . .

TODHUNTER: Abduction . . . diverted trains . . .

IRIS: We're telling you the truth.

TODHUNTER: I'm not in the least interested. You . . . you've annoyed us enough with your ridiculous stories.

CHARTERS: My dear chap, you must have got hold of the wrong end of the stick somewhere.

CALDICOTT: Yes, things like that just don't happen.

MISS FROY: We're not in England now.

CALDICOTT: I don't see what difference that makes.

IRIS: We're stopping.

*We cut to a long shot of two cars parked in a wood, as seen from the train.*

GILBERT: Look, you see those cars, they're here to take Miss Froy away.

CALDICOTT: Nonsense. Look, there go a couple of people.

*We cut to a long shot of* DR. HARTZ *and the* BARONESS *walking towards the cars, still seen from the train.*

CALDICOTT: The cars have obviously come to pick them up.

GILBERT: Well, in that case, why go to the trouble of uncoupling the train and diverting it?

CALDICOTTT: Uncoupling?

GILBERT: There's nothing left of the train beyond the sleeping car.

CALDICOTT: There must be. Our bags are in the first class carriage.

GILBERT: Not any longer. Would you like to come and look?

CALDICOTT: If this is a practical joke, I warn you I shan't think it very funny.

GILBERT *opens the dining car door to reveal the* NUN *who is gagged.*

CALDICOTT: Good Lord!

GILBERT: Let's have some of that brandy.

*They all gather around the* NUN.

CHARTERS: You don't suppose there's something in this fellow's story, Caldicott, do you?

CALDICOTT: Seems a bit queer.

CHARTERS: I mean, after all, people don't go about tying up nuns.

IRIS: Someone's coming.

*We cut to a long shot of an* OFFICER *walking towards the train. Everyone in the dining car looks out of the window and watches the* OFFICER'S *progress.*

TODHUNTER: They can't possibly do anything to us. We're British subjects.

*The* OFFICER *enters the dining car. Track and pan with him to include the group.*

OFFICER: I have come to offer the most sincere apologies. An extremely serious incident has occurred . . . an attempt has been made to interfere with passengers on this train.

*We see the* NUN *whispering to* GILBERT.

OFFICER: Fortunately it was brought to the notice of the authorities. And so if you will be good enough to accompany me to Morsken, I will inform the British Embassy at once. Ladies and gentlemen, the cars are at your disposal.

CALDICOTT: We're very grateful. It's lucky some of you fellows understand English.

OFFICER: Well, I was at Oxford.

CHARTERS: Oh really, so was I.

GILBERT: Hold on, this woman . . . seems to be trying to say something. I don't understand the language, but it may be important. Would you . . .

OFFICER: Certainly.

*The* OFFICER *bends down to the* NUN *. As he does so,* GILBERT *picks up a chair and hits the* OFFICER *on the head with it. The* OFFICER *falls to the floor.*

GILBERT: That's fixed him. That's all right. He's only stunned.

*The* STEWARD *and* CHIEF STEWARD *look on in amazement.* GILBERT *takes the* OFFICER'S *gun.*

CALDICOTT: What the blazes did you do that for?

GILBERT: Well, I was at Cambridge.

CALDICOTT: Well, what's that got to do with it? You heard what he said, didn't you?

GILBERT: I heard what he said. That was a trick to get us off the train.

TODHUNTER: I don't believe it. The man's explanation was quite satisfactory.

CHARTERS: A thing like this might cause a war.

*There is a cut to an exterior shot of the woods, where the* STEWARD *is talking to the* BARONESS *and* DR. HARTZ.

STEWARD: Madra avendra . . . offichara ditata (Terrible things are happening . . . the Officer has been stunned).

*Cut back to the dining car.*

CHARTERS: I'm going outside to tell them what's occurred. It's up to us to apologise and put the matter right.

*In the woods we see the* BARONESS, DR. HARTZ, *and a* SOLDIER.

BARONESS: Brancka (Fire)!

CHARTERS *starts to climb down out of the train, but a* SOLDIER *fires from the wood.* CHARTERS *returns quickly to the dining car, shot in the hand.*

CHARTERS: You were right. Do you mind, old man?

CALDICOTT: Certainly.

CALDICOTT *wraps a handkerchief around* CHARTERS'S *hand. We see* DR. HARTZ, *the* BARONESS *and some* SOLDIERS *by the cars as seen from the train.*
DR. HARTZ *beckons the* CHIEF STEWARD.
MISS FROY, IRIS, CHARTERS, TODHUNTER *and* GILBERT *are still in the dining car.*

CHARTERS: Looks as if they mean business.

GILBERT: I'm afraid so.

TODHUNTER: They can't do anything. It would mean an international situation.

MISS FROY: It's happened before.

*We see a long shot of* DR. HARTZ *and* SOLDIERS *walking towards the train.*

IRIS: They're coming.

NUN: Don't let them in. They'll murder us. They daren't let us go now.

*There is a long shot of* DR. HARTZ *and* SOLDIERS *standing by the train.*

DR. HARTZ: I order you to surrender at once.

GILBERT: Nothing doing. If you come any nearer, I'll fire. I've warned you.

GILBERT *fires and one of the* SOLDIERS *falls.*

GILBERT: Better take cover, they'll start any minute now.

CALDICOTT: Nasty jam, this . . . don't like the look of it.

CHARTERS: Got plenty of ammunition?

GILBERT: Whole pouch full.

CHARTERS: Good.

CALDICOTT: Duck down, you.

TODHUNTER: I'm not going to fight, it's madness.

MRS. TODHUNTER: It will be safer to protest down here.

*We cut to a long shot of the* SOLDIERS *by the cars.*
GILBERT *is looking out of the window.*

GILBERT: Hallo, they're trying to work round to the other
side.

TODHUNTER: You're behaving like a pack of fools . . .
what chance have we got against a lot of armed men?

CALDICOTT: You heard what the Mother Superior said. If
we surrender now, we're in for it.

*The* SOLDIERS *start coming towards the train, as*
GILBERT *fires his gun. The window of the dining car is*
*shattered by a* SOLDIER *firing from nearby the cars. He*
*just misses* GILBERT *who is close to the window. There is*
*a rapid exchange of cuts between the people in the dining*
*car and the* SOLDIERS *outside.*

CALDICOTT: We'll never get to the match now.

MRS. TODHUNTER *off:* Give it to me . . . give it to me.

*We cut to a shot of* MR. *and* MRS. TODHUNTER *struggling.*
CALDICOTT *comes on.*

CALDICOTT: What's going on here?

MRS. TODHUNTER: He's got a gun and he won't use it.

CALDICOTT: What's the idea?

TODHUNTER: I've told you, I won't be a party to this sort
of thing. I don't believe in fighting.

CALDICOTT: Pacifist, eh? Won't work, old boy. Early

Christians tried it and got thrown to the lions. Come on, hand it over.

*Another window in the dining car shatters.*

MRS. TODHUNTER: I'm not afraid to use it.

CALDICOTT *off:* Probably more used to it. I once won a box of cigars.

CHARTERS: He's talking rot . . . he's a damned good shot.

CALDICOTT: Hope the old hand hasn't lost its cunning. You know, I'm half inclined to believe that there's some rational explanation to all this. Oh, rotten shot, only knocked his hat off.

*He fires out of the train window.*

MISS FROY: Would you mind if I talked to you for a minute?

GILBERT: What, now?

MISS FROY: Please forgive me, but it's very important.

GILBERT: Hang on to this for me, will you?

GILBERT *hands his gun to* CHARTERS.

CHARTERS: All right, I'll hold the fort.

MISS FROY: I think it's safer along here. You come too.

GILBERT: Keep your heads down.

*They duck down together.*

MISS FROY: I just wanted to tell you that I must be getting along now.

IRIS: But you can't, you'll never get away. You'll be shot down.

MISS FROY: I must take that risk. Listen carefully. In case I'm unlucky and you get through, I want you to take back a message to a Mr. Callendar at the Foreign Office at Whitehall.

IRIS: Then you are a spy.

MISS FROY: I always think that's such a grim word.

GILBERT: What is the message?

MISS FROY: It's a tune.

GILBERT: Tune?

MISS FROY: It contains, in code, of course, the vital clause of a secret pact between two European countries. I want you to memorise it.

GILBERT: Go ahead.

MISS FROY: The first part of it goes like this.

MISS FROY *starts to hum.*

MISS FROY: Oh, perhaps I'd better write it down. Have you got a piece of paper?

GILBERT: No, don't bother. I was brought up on music. I can memorise anything.

MISS FROY: Very well then.

*She hums the rest of the tune.*

CALDICOTT: Hello, the old girl's gone off her rocker.

TODHUNTER: I don't wonder. Why don't you face it? Those swines out there will go on firing till they kill the lot of us.

*Pan to include* MRS. TODHUNTER *and* CALDICOTT.

MRS. TODHUNTER: For goodness sake, shut up, Eric.

GILBERT *is now humming the tune.*

MISS FROY: That's right. Now we've got two chances instead of one.

GILBERT: You bet.

MISS FROY: You're sure you'll remember it?

GILBERT: Don't worry, I won't stop whistling it.

MISS FROY: I suppose this is my best way out?

GILBERT: Yes, just about.

IRIS: But you may be hit, and even if you do get away they'll stop you at the frontier. We can't let her go like this.

GILBERT: You know, this is a hell of a risk you're taking.

MISS FROY: In this sort of job one must take risks. I'm very grateful to you both for all you've done. I do hope and pray no harm will come to you, and that we shall all meet again . . . one day.

IRIS: I hope so too. Good luck.

GILBERT: Good luck.

MISS FROY: Will you help me out?

GILBERT: Yes, rather.

> GILBERT *helps* MISS FROY *out of a train window.*

GILBERT: Now take the weight . . . on top . . . right you are . . . I've got you.

IRIS: Goodbye.

> IRIS *and* GILBERT *watch as* MISS FROY *runs from the train.* DR. HARTZ *and the* SOLDIERS *see her go too. In the woods,* DR. HARTZ *shouts orders to his men.*

DR. HARTZ: Agrakan (Make sure of her).

> *There is a cut to a long shot of* MISS FROY *disappearing as seen by* GILBERT *and* IRIS.

IRIS: Was she hit?

GILBERT: I'm not sure.

> *As* DR. HARTZ *and the* SOLDIERS *look for* MISS FROY, CALDICOTT *fires the gun out of the window. We see a* SOLDIER *falling backwards.*

CALDICOTT: Well, that's the end of my twelve.

CHARTERS: There's not much left here, either.

GILBERT: We've only got one chance now. We've got to get this train going. Drive it back to the main line and then try and cross the frontier.

CALDICOTT: I say, that's a bit of a tall order, isn't it? Those driver fellows are not likely to do as you tell them, you know.

GILBERT *picks up the gun.*

GILBERT: We'll bluff them with this. Who's coming with me?

CALDICOTT: You can count on me.

CHARTERS: Me too.

GILBERT: We can't all go. You stay here and carry on, and if we have any luck we'll stop the train when we reach the points. And you jump out and switch them over.

CHARTERS *off:* Okay.

TODHUNTER: You idiots, you're just inviting death. I've had enough. Just because I've the sense to try and avoid being murdered, I'm accused of being a pacifist. All right, I'd rather be a rat than die like one. Think for a moment, will you? If we give ourselves up, they daren't murder us in cold blood. They're bound to give us a trial.

MRS. TODHUNTER: Stop jibbering, Eric. Nobody's listening to you.

TODHUNTER: Very well. You.go your way, I'll go mine.

CHARTERS: Hey, where are you off to?

TODHUNTER: I know what I'm about. I'm doing the only sensible thing.

CHARTERS: Oh, let the fellow go if he wants to.

TODHUNTER *comes from the train carrying a white handkerchief. One of the* SOLDIERS *fires.* TODHUNTER *is hit and falls to the ground.*
GILBERT *and* CALDICOTT *climb onto the engine.*

MRS. TODHUNTER: Don't, please. Why aren't we going? Why aren't we going? They said we were going. Why aren't we?

IRIS: If only he can get us away now. He must!

CHARTERS: Only one left. I'll keep that for a sitter.

IRIS: They're moving away from the cars. They're coming towards us.

*We see* DR. HARTZ *and the* SOLDIERS *walking towards the train.*

CHARTERS: Pity we haven't a few more rounds.

MRS. TODHUNTER: It's funny. I told my husband when I left him that I wouldn't see him again.

IRIS: Gilbert! Gilbert!

DR. HARTZ *and the* SOLDIERS *continue walking towards the train.*

CHARTERS: By gad, we're off.

IRIS: This gives us a chance.

DR. HARTZ *and the* SOLDIERS, *seen from the windows, look on, as the train is moving away.*
*Cut to the cab of the engine of the train.* CALDICOTT, GILBERT *and two drivers are there.*

GILBERT: Come on, keep going.

*One of the* SOLDIERS *fires, an engine driver is hit. Now* DR. HARTZ *and his* SOLDIERS *begin following in a car. Another shot is fired. The second engine driver is hit by a bullet and falls from the train.*

CALDICOTT: I say, do you know how to control this thing?

GILBERT: I watched the fellow start it. Anyway, I know something about it. Once drove a miniature engine on the Dymchurch line.

CALDICOTT: Good. I'll look out for the points.

CALDICOTT *spots one of the cars following the train.*
CHARTERS, *in the dining car, spots it too.*

CHARTERS: Blighters are chasing us. Look.

*Everyone looks out of the window as we see a long shot of
one of the pursuing cars.*

IRIS: We can't have far to go.

*There is a cut to the stunned* OFFICER *regaining
consciousness on the floor and seeing the revolver near
him.*
*There is a shot of the revolver as seen by the* OFFICER,
*and then another of the* OFFICER *himself, calculating his
chances.*
*Resume on* CHARTERS, *and* IRIS *and* MRS.
TODHUNTER.

CHARTERS: It's time for my little job changing the points.
Thank heavens we shall be in neutral territory.

*The* OFFICER *rises with the revolver.*

OFFICER: That will not be necessary. I'm sorry, but the
points, as you call them, will not be changed over. Please
be seated.

*Cut back to the cab of the engine, where* CALDICOTT,
*acting as look out, spots the points ahead.*

CALDICOTT: There they are, just ahead of us. Do you
think you can stop it?

GILBERT: Hope so.

*In the dining car, the* OFFICER *brandishes the gun in front
of the others. The* NUN *is behind the* OFFICER.

OFFICER: You'll keep quite still until my friends arrive. If
anyone moves, I'm afraid I shall have to shoot.

IRIS: There's just one thing you don't know, Captain.
There's only one bullet left in that gun, and if you shoot me
. . . you'll give the others a chance. You're in rather a
difficult position, aren't you?

OFFICER: Sit down, please.

*The* OFFICER *is preoccupied with* IRIS *talking.*
CHARTERS *moves in to block the* OFFICER'S *view as the*
NUN *leaves.*

IRIS: All right.

*The train stops close to the points. In the engine,*
CALDICOTT *and* GILBERT *look worried.*

CALDICOTT: Where the devil's Charters?

*The* NUN *jumps from the train and goes to the points*
*junction and moves the points.*
SOLDIERS *in the car commence firing as the* NUN *runs*
*back towards the train.*

CALDICOTT: Go ahead, she's done it.

*The* NUN *runs to the cab of the engine as* GILBERT
*prepares to ease the brake.* GILBERT *and* CALDICOTT
*help her aboard the engine.*

NUN: Ouch! It's all right, it's just my legs.

*On the road, a second car is arriving. The* BARONESS
*alights from it, just in time to watch the train crossing the*
*border. Pan to include* DR. HARTZ.

BARONESS: Barogluts farshadram (They've got away after
all).

DR. HARTZ: Car marniblon. Or as they say in English,
jolly good luck to them.

GILBERT, CALDICOTT *and the* NUN *are delighted.*

CALDICOTT: My word, I'm glad all that's over, aren't you?
Heaven knows what the Government will say about all this.

GILBERT: Nothing at all. They'll hush it up.

CALDICOTT: What?

GILBERT: Hey, take your hand off that thing. I've got to
remember a tune.

CALDICOTT: Remember . . .

*Dissolve to a Channel steamer, then to a train drawing into Victoria Railway Station.*
*Cut to* IRIS *and* GILBERT *in a compartment of the train.*

ATTENDANT: Porter, sir?

GILBERT: No, thanks.

IRIS: Well, we're home, Gilbert. Can't you stop humming that awful tune? You must know it backwards.

GILBERT: Oh, I'm not taking any risks. Will Charles be here to meet you?

IRIS: I expect so.

GILBERT: Well, you'll be pretty busy between now and Thursday.

IRIS: I could meet you for lunch or dinner, if you'd like it.

GILBERT: Sorry, I didn't mean that. Oh, as a matter of fact, I've got to deliver this theme song to Miss Froy, and when I've done that, I'm going to dash up to Yorkshire and finish my book.

IRIS: Oh, I see.

GILBERT: Ready?

IRIS: Yes.

IRIS *and* GILBERT *walk along the platform among other passengers.* CHARTERS *and* CALDICOTT *are just ahead of them.*

CHARTERS: Ample time to catch the six-fifty to Manchester after all.

*They pass a newspaper stand and notice a newsvendor carrying a poster which reads:*
*TEST MATCH*
*ABANDONED:*

*FLOODS*
*LATE EVENING*
*EXTRA NEWS*
CALDICOTT *and* CHARTERS *are speechless.*

GILBERT: Any sign of Charles yet?

IRIS: No, I can't see him.

GILBERT: Well, this is where we say goodbye.

> IRIS *suddenly see* CHARLES *and dives into a taxi.*

GILBERT: What's the matter?

> *From the point of view of* IRIS *and* GILBERT, *we see* CHARLES. *He is too appallingly civilised.*

GILBERT: Charles?

IRIS: Yes, you heartless, callous, selfish, swollen-headed beast, you.

> GILBERT *kisses* IRIS, *who kisses him back.*

TAXI DRIVER: Are you going anywhere?

> GILBERT *and* IRIS *stop kissing each other.*

GILBERT: Foreign Office.

> *Dissolve to the interior lobby of the Foreign Office where* GILBERT *and* IRIS *are waiting together.*

IRIS: Where are we going for our honeymoon?

GILBERT: I don't know. Somewhere quiet. Somewhere where there are no trains.

> *A* MAN *enters in the background.*

MAN: Mr. Callendar will see you now.

GILBERT: Wait a minute. It's gone!

IRIS: What's gone?

GILBERT: The tune. I've forgotten it!

IRIS: No. Oh, no!

GILBERT: Wait a minute, let me concentrate.

GILBERT *starts to hum.*

IRIS: No, no, no, no, that's the Wedding March.

GILBERT: This is awful. I've done nothing else but sing it since the day before yesterday, and . . . and now I've forgotten it completely.

*A piano is heard playing the tune. Track forward with* GILBERT *and* IRIS *into* CALLENDAR'S *room to reveal* MISS FROY *seated at the piano.*

IRIS: Miss Froy!

GILBERT: Well, I'll be hanged.

*Fade out to THE END.*

# BRIEF ENCOUNTER

# INTRODUCTION
## John Russell Taylor

*Brief Encounter* was David Lean's fourth collaboration with Noël Coward, and the one, understandably, where the creative responsibility for the film as a whole is most evenly divided between the two of them. It constitutes almost a declaration of independence on Lean's part from his fruitful but by 1945 no doubt increasingly constricting association with Coward's writing. On his first film, *In Which We Serve*, he had been brought in as co-director with Coward, taking care of the technical end in a sort of one-man-band operation, featuring Coward as author of the original screenplay, director, star and composer of the music. The next two films, *This Happy Breed* and *Blithe Spirit*, were smooth, easy, essentially faithful adaptations of recent Coward stage successes. *Brief Encounter* is something rather different. Though it takes as its starting-point *Still Life*, a one-act play from Coward's 1936 collection, *Tonight at 8.30*, the screenplay elaborates considerably to fill in the background of the two principal characters' 'brief encounter' in a railway station buffet. And it is not just the conventional 'opening-out' process by which snatches of dialogue and whole scenes from the stage play are arbitrarily scattered in a variety of improbable locales in the cause of Cinema. The whole thing is radically rethought in terms of the screen and its possibilities, to such an extent that it becomes more or less an original screenplay on the same theme as the stage play.

The play is a classic essay in British understatement and the good old stiff upper-lip. Two sublimely improbable people, married, settled, middle-aged, find themselves embarrassingly involved in a great romantic passion that they can do nothing about. People like them don't do things like that, and the only possible answer is the decent, dutiful one: they must part for good. The film, by telling us a lot more about them, about their background, about the circumstances of their meetings and their parting, intensifies our understanding of and belief in both their passionate feelings for each other, and the very real problems that they have of squaring these with their normal codes of duty, their natural desire not to hurt people they also love, if not quite with the same intensity.

The film, in fact, becomes a far more emotional, far more romantic statement than the play. Partly this is the effect of a very simple device: that of making Laura the narrator, and telling the whole story from her point of view after the parting, when her despair has reached and just passed its moment of maximum intensity. The narration provides us ready-made with an emotional colouring, an attitude to the story we are being told— and came in for criticism at the time because this was felt to be somehow not playing fair, not doing things the 'cinematic' way. However, the device does work, despite occasional moments of weakening duplication: as a rule what Laura tells us about what is going on inside her, complements the visuals without overwhelming or replacing them.

Much of the effect of the film, though, resides in the way David Lean directs it (something which could not really be said of his three previous films). Throughout his career Lean seems to be rather a cold director, a brilliant technician who steers clear of leaving any personal mark on his subjects and appears, if anything, to be positively embarrassed by any overt displays of emotionalism. *Brief Encounter* might, therefore, depending which way one looks at it, be the ideal subject for him, matching his reticence with its own, or a disaster, encouraging him to cool down to freezing point something which was already pretty chilly and undemonstrative. As it turned out, the first pattern seems to be that which prevailed: the film has, unlike any of Lean's other films, the feeling that intense emotions are there, underneath, made all the more intense by the iron control under which they are held.

Partly this is effected by the moody, chiaroscuro camerawork, which makes the most of rain-washed night streets, clouds of smoke and steam from the steam trains that still rumble or roar through Milford station. Occasionally the camera takes over on its own, as in the once-renowned sequence of Laura's temptation to suicide, in which the angles become more and more extreme until after the express has rushed through (its presence made palpable by the soundtrack and the flashing lights on Laura's anguished face) and our viewpoint is gradually returned to the everyday horizontal, as Laura goes back sensibly to the buffet she just precipitately left.

But most of all the mood of the film, its emotional temperature, is created by one stroke of something like genius: the use of Rachmaninov's Second Piano Concerto on the soundtrack (the practical motivation for this being that the work in question is being played on the radio as Laura starts her reverie). Again, maybe the use of this very highly charged, emotional music is not quite playing fair, at any rate by conventional canons of cinema. But it works, triumphantly by giving at once an extra dimension to the most prosaic, seemingly unemotional exchanges, making us aware that we are in the presence of Harold Pinter's second silence: 'below the words spoken, is the thing known and unspoken. . . . '

At this distance of time *Brief Encounter* assumes another, rather surprising quality—that of a documentary insight into a vanished scene, a vanished way of life.

# Brief Encounter (1945)

From *The Film and The Public* by Roger Manvell (Penguin Books, 1955)

*Brief Encounter* is one of those rare films for which one can never be sure to whom the real credit is due, one of those films one can offer to critics of the artistic integrity of the medium as an example of the unity achieved by the co-operation of many creative minds. That devoted care was given to this picture the result itself is evidence. I do not remember any more moving performance than that given by Celia Johnson. The theme and situation are perfect for so sensitive an actress, and these are the work of Noël Coward. The visual conception, the sympathetic eye that watches Miss Johnson, and relates her work to that of the other people, and to the environment of home, and street, and station which are so much part of her life, is the creative work of the director David Lean.

The theme and situation are universal. They belong to all human beings whether they have individually endured a similar love-tragedy or not. Laura Jesson is a kindly attractive woman with two children. She is married to a kindly, unimaginative husband and lives a contented, unawakened life. She visits the small town of Milford each Thursday, shops, goes to the pictures, and catches her evening train home from Milford Junction. She has a brief encounter in the station refreshment room with a doctor who removes some grit from her eye. He also visits Milford on Thursdays. A chance tea together follows. Then lunch. Then the pictures. Their acquaintance grows into an intense and passionate love. He also is married and has children. But unlike her husband he is a man with a genuine belief in his vocation, and the vital appreciation of life and need for love which go with it, and the sight of him stirs her to her depths and turns each Thursday into a vortex of emotional anticipation. They realize the dangers and difficulties of their situation. They experience the shame of domestic evasion, and lies, and subterfuge. They decide to part.

The film begins with their parting, mercilessly ravaged by an unsuspecting garrulous woman who is one of Laura's acquaintances. We ourselves know little more than this intruder. At home again, stricken with emotional sickness, Laura tells her story in imagination to her husband, who sits trite and dull over his crossword puzzle. The story takes us back and so leads through to their parting again, with our full realization of its pain and tension. It is a brilliant piece of structure and directing. We see the same final touch of his hand on her shoulder with new eyes.

I do not remember a moment when Celia Johnson's performance falters in a part where emotional over-playing or false intonations would have turned the film from a study of life itself into another piece of cinema fiction. It is a uniquely beautiful portrait; our sympathy grows with knowledge, and Laura's beauty grows with our sympathy. The movement of the film and our relation to the character develop with the same tempo of understanding with which we all live and meet and love. It is this quality which makes the film inescapably human, and whilst we watch it we are with this other human being as with a friend.

Celia Johnson has a small pointed face with wide emotional eyes. She looks quite ordinary until it is time for her to look like what she feels. Trevor Howard plays his first considerable part in this film: he does not look ordinary, but he is not required to do so. He has strength, ease, and charm; his performance is quiet and assured. The poetry of this film, its revealing study of a man and a woman almost out of control, reveals a fine balance of their strength and weakness, now one taking the lead, now the other. It would be difficult to find a more profound study of distressed love in the history of the cinema.

Into all this complexity, Milford Junction enters as a poetic image. Its passing express trains have the rush and power of passion, its platforms and subways the loneliness of waiting lovers. Its local trains jerk and shunt with their faithful service of routine domesticity. The imagery of trains has seldom been so finely used as in that last terrifying shot when the express screams by with its windows flashing a staccato rhythm of white lights across Laura's agonized face. It is hysteria visually and aurally personified. It is the image of a moment of intended but uncommitted suicide.

Each detail of background is authentic, the streets, shops, café, and cinema. To touch the film with humour Stanley Holloway and Joyce Carey play out a grotesque love-affair in the station bar, and whilst this happens we can rest from the intense emotions of the main story in the comic casualness of their love-making. All the other characters, too, are exaggerations of reality. But this, strangely enough, does not matter, for they are all seen through the eyes of Laura, and in her suffering are as grotesquely different from herself as the close shots of Dolly Messiter's chattering lips are from Laura's pale face as she sits opposite her in the village train. The film always returns to Laura: it is her story told by herself and addressed without his knowledge to her husband. The main achievement is that of Celia Johnson, but supported throughout by the creative sympathy of her director, David Lean.

CREDITS:

| | |
|---|---|
| In Charge of Production | Anthony Havelock-Allan |
| | Ronald Neame |
| Producer | Noël Coward |
| Director | David Lean |
| Screenplay | Noël Coward |
| Director of Photography | Robert Krasker |
| Art Director | L. P. Williams |
| Editor | Jack Harris |
| Sound Editor | Harry Miller |
| Sound Recordists | Stanley Lambourne |
| | Desmond Dew |
| Production Manager | E. Holding |
| Assistant Director | George Pollock |
| Camera Operator | B. Francke |

CAST:

| | |
|---|---|
| Laura Jesson | Celia Johnson |
| Alec Harvey | Trevor Howard |
| Albert Godby | Stanley Holloway |
| Myrtle Bagot | Joyce Carey |
| Fred Jesson | Cyril Raymond |
| Dolly Messiter | Everley Gregg |
| Beryl Waters | Margaret Barton |
| Stanley | Dennis Harkin |
| Stephen Lynn | Valentine Dyall |
| Mary Norton | Marjorie Mars |
| Mrs Rolandson | Nuna Davey |
| Woman Organist | Irene Handl |
| Bill | Edward Hodge |
| Johnnie | Sydney Bromley |
| Policeman | Wilfrid Babbage |
| Waitress | Avis Scutt |
| Margaret | Henrietta Vincent |
| Bobbie | Richard Thomas |
| Clergyman | George V. Sheldon |

# BRIEF ENCOUNTER

The action of this film takes place during the winter of 1938-39. It is early evening. A local train is pulling into platform Number 1 of Milford Junction Station, as a voice over the loudspeaker announces:

LOUDSPEAKER: *Milford Junction — Milford Junction.*

The train comes closer and closer, and a great cloud of steam is hissed out from the engine. The screen becomes completely white as the main titles appear. With the last title the steam disperses, revealing again the engine, which starts to pull out of the station. ALBERT GODBY is at the ticket barrier. He is somewhere between 30 and 40 years old. His accent is north country. He collects the last few tickets from the passengers of the departing train and moves towards the edge of the platform. An express train is approaching from the distance. ALBERT jumps down from platform Number 1 onto the track, and waits for the express to pass. It roars by, practically blotting out the view. ALBERT watches the train pass, as the lights from the carriage windows flash across his face. From his waistcoat pocket he takes out a watch and chain, and checks the time of the train. The watch reads 5.35. By the look of satisfaction on his face we know that the train is punctual. He puts the watch back and the lights cease flashing on his face. The train has passed, and ALBERT follows it with his eyes as it roars into the tunnel. He crosses the line over which the express has just gone by, jumps onto platform Number 2, and moves towards the refreshment room.

Inside the refreshment room he crosses to the counter, behind which stand MYRTLE BAGOT and her assistant BERYL WATERS. MYRTLE is a buxom and imposing widow. Her hair is piled high, and her expression is reasonably jaunty except on those occasions when a strong sense of refinement gets the better of her. BERYL is pretty but dimmed, not only by MYRTLE's personal effulgence, but by her firm authority.

ALBERT: *Hullo! — Hullo! — Hullo!*

MYRTLE: *Quite a stranger, aren't you?*

ALBERT: *I couldn't get in yesterday.*

MYRTLE bridling: *I wondered what happened to you.*

ALBERT: *I 'ad a bit of a dust-up.*

MYRTLE preparing his tea: *What about?*

ALBERT: *Saw a chap getting out of a first-class compartment, and when he comes to give up 'is ticket it was third-class, and I told 'im he'd have to pay excess, and then he turned a bit nasty and I 'ad to send for Mr Saunders.*

MYRTLE: *Fat lot of good he'd be.*

ALBERT: *He ticked him off proper.*

MYRTLE: *Seein's believing. . . .*

In the far end of the refreshment room, seated at a table, are ALEC HARVEY and LAURA JESSON. He is about 35 and wears a mackintosh and squash hat. She is an attractive woman in her thirties. Her clothes are not smart, but obviously chosen with taste. They are in earnest conversation, but we do not hear what they are saying.

ALBERT off: *I tell you, he ticked 'im off proper — 'You pay the balance at once,' he said, ' or I'll 'and you over to the police.' You should 'ave seen the chap's face at the mention of the word ' police '. Changed his tune then 'e did — paid up quick as lightning.*

MYRTLE off: *That's just what I mean. He hadn't got the courage to handle it himself. He had to call in the police.*

ALBERT off: *Who said he called in the police?*

MYRTLE off: *You did, of course.*

ALBERT off: *I didn't do any such thing. I merely said he mentioned the police, which is quite a different thing from calling them in. He's not a bad lot, Mr Saunders. After all, you can't expect much spirit from a man who's only got one lung and a wife with diabetes.*

MYRTLE off: *I thought something must be wrong when you didn't come.*

Close shot of ALBERT and MYRTLE. BERYL is in the background. Close shots of ALBERT and MYRTLE individually, as they are speaking.

ALBERT: *I'd have popped in to explain, but I had a date, and 'ad to run for it the moment I went off.*

MYRTLE frigidly: *Oh, indeed!*

ALBERT: *A chap I know's getting married.*

MYRTLE: *Very interesting, I'm sure.*

ALBERT: *What's up with you, anyway?*

MYRTLE: *I'm sure I don't know to what you're referring.*

ALBERT: *You're a bit unfriendly all of a sudden.*

MYRTLE ignoring him: *Beryl, hurry up — put some coal in the stove while you're at it.*

BERYL: *Yes, Mrs Bagot.*

MYRTLE: *I'm afraid I really can't stand here wasting my time in idle gossip, Mr Godby.*

ALBERT: *Aren't you going to offer me another cup?*

MYRTLE: *You can 'ave another cup and welcome when you've finished that one. Beryl 'll give it to you — I've got my accounts to do.*

ALBERT: *I'd rather you gave it to me.*

MYRTLE: *Time and tide wait for no man, Mr Godby.*

ALBERT: *I don't know what you're huffy about, but whatever it is I'm very sorry.*

> DOLLY is seen at the counter. Forgetting her tea, she hurries across the room to join LAURA and ALEC.

DOLLY: *Laura! What a lovely surprise!*

LAURA dazed: *Oh, Dolly!*

DOLLY: *My dear, I've shopped until I'm dropping! My feet are nearly falling off, and my throat's parched. I thought of having tea in Spindle's but I was terrified of losing the train. I'm always missing trains, and being late for meals, and Bob gets disagreeable for days at a time — he's been getting those dreadful headaches you know — I've been trying to make him see a doctor, but he won't.* Flopping down at their table: *Oh, dear.*

LAURA: *This is Doctor Harvey.*

ALEC rising: *How do you do!*

DOLLY shaking hands: *How do you do. Would you be a perfect dear and get me my cup of tea? I don't think I could drag my poor old bones back to the counter again. I must get some chocolates for Tony, too, but I can do that afterwards.*

> She offers him money.

ALEC waving it away: *No, please. . . .*

> He goes drearily out of frame towards the counter.

> Close shot of DOLLY and LAURA.

DOLLY: *My dear — what a nice-looking man. Who on earth is he?*

*Really, you're quite a dark horse. I shall telephone Fred in the morning and make mischief — this is a bit of luck. I haven't seen you for ages, and I've been meaning to pop in, but Tony's had measles, you know, and I had all that awful fuss about Phyllis —*

LAURA with an effort: *Oh, how dreadful!*

At the counter, ALEC is standing next to ALBERT, who is finishing his cup of tea. ALBERT leaves and MYRTLE hands ALEC the change for DOLLY's cup of tea.

DOLLY off: *Mind you, I never cared for her much, but still Tony did. Tony adored her, and — but never mind, I'll tell you all about that in the train.*

ALEC picks up DOLLY's tea and moves back to the table. He sits down again.

DOLLY: *Thank you so very much. They've certainly put enough milk in it — but still, it'll be refreshing.* She sips it. *Oh, dear — no sugar.*

ALEC: *It's in the spoon.*

DOLLY: *Oh, of course — what a fool I am — Laura, you look frightfully well. I do wish I'd known you were coming in today, we could have come together and lunched and had a good gossip. I loathe shopping by myself anyway.*

There is the sound of a bell on the platform, and a loudspeaker voice announces the arrival of the Churley train.

LAURA: *There's your train.*

ALEC: *Yes, I know.*

DOLLY: *Aren't you coming with us?*

ALEC: *No, I go in the opposite direction. My practice is in Churley.*

DOLLY: *Oh, I see.*

ALEC: *I'm a general practitioner at the moment.*

LAURA dully: *Doctor Harvey is going out to Africa next week.*

DOLLY: *Oh, how thrilling.*

There is the sound of ALEC's train approaching.

ALEC: *I must go.*

LAURA: *Yes, you must.*

ALEC: *Good-bye.*

DOLLY: *Good-bye.*

ALEC shakes hands with DOLLY, looks at LAURA swiftly once, and gives her shoulder a little squeeze. The train is heard rumbling into the station. He goes over to the door and out onto the platform.

LAURA is gazing at the door through which ALEC has just passed. She seems unaware of the chattering DOLLY at her side, who proceeds to fumble in her handbag for lipstick and a mirror. Close shot of LAURA.

DOLLY: *He'll have to run or he'll miss it — he's got to get right over to the other platform. Talking of missing trains reminds me of that awful bridge at Broadham Junction — you have to go traipsing all up one side, along the top and down the other! Well, last week I'd been over to see Bob's solicitor about renewing the lease of the house — and I arrived at the station with exactly half a minute to spare. . . .*

Close shot of DOLLY, who is applying lipstick to her chattering mouth and watching the operation in her little hand-mirror.

DOLLY: *. . . My dear, I flew — I had Tony with me, and like a fool, I'd brought a new shade for the lamp in the drawing-room — I could just as easily have got it here in Milford.*

Close shot of LAURA.

DOLLY off: *. . . It was the most enormous thing and I could hardly see over it — I've never been in such a frizz in my life — I nearly knocked a woman down.*

The door onto the platform is seen from LAURA's point of view.

DOLLY off: *. . . Of course, by the time I got it home it was battered to bits.*

There is the sound of a bell on the platform as we resume on LAURA and DOLLY.

DOLLY: *Is that a train?*

She addresses MYRTLE.

DOLLY: *Can you tell me, is that the Ketchworth train?*

MYRTLE off: *No, that's the express.*

LAURA: *The boat-train.*

DOLLY: *Oh, yes — that doesn't stop, does it?*

She gets up and crosses to MYRTLE at the counter.

DOLLY: *Express trains are Tony's passion in life — I want some chocolate, please.*

MYRTLE: *Milk or plain?*

DOLLY: *Plain, I think — or no, perhaps milk would be nicer. Have you any with nuts in it?*

The express is heard in the distance.

MYRTLE: *Nestlé's nut-milk — shilling or sixpence?*

DOLLY: *Give me one plain and one nut-milk.*

The noise of the express sounds louder. The express roars through the station as DOLLY finishes buying and paying for her chocolate. She turns to see that LAURA is no longer at the table.

DOLLY: *Oh, where is she?*

MYRTLE looking over the counter: *I never noticed her go.*

There is the sound of a door opening and they both look up. LAURA comes in through the door from Number 2 platform, looking very white and shaky. She shuts the door and leans back against it. DOLLY enters frame.

DOLLY: *My dear, I couldn't think where you'd disappeared to.*

LAURA: *I just wanted to see the express go through.*

DOLLY: *What on earth's the matter? Do you feel ill?*

LAURA: *I feel a little sick.*

LAURA goes slowly over to the table, where DOLLY helps her into a chair. The platform bell goes and the loudspeaker announces the arrival of the Ketchworth train.

LAURA: *That's our train.*

DOLLY goes out of shot towards the counter.

DOLLY off: *Have you any brandy?*

MYRTLE off: *I'm afraid it's out of hours.*

DOLLY off: *Surely — if someone's feeling ill. . . .*

LAURA: *I'm all right really.*

Close shot of DOLLY and MYRTLE.

DOLLY: *Just a sip of brandy will buck you up.* To MYRTLE: *Please. . . .*

MYRTLE: *Very well. . . .*

She pours out some brandy as the train is heard approaching the station.

DOLLY: *How much?*

MYRTLE: *Tenpence, please.*

Resume on LAURA at the table.

DOLLY off: *There!*

The train is heard rumbling into the station. DOLLY moves into frame with the brandy.

DOLLY: *Here you are, dear.* (*Still*)

LAURA taking it: *Thank you.*

She gulps down the brandy as DOLLY proceeds to gather up her parcels. They hurry across the refreshment room and out of the door leading to Number 3 platform.

Outside they cross the platform to the train. A porter opens the door of a third-class compartment. There is the sound of the door slamming, off. Through the carriage window at the far end can be seen platform Number 4. LAURA sits down and DOLLY bustles over to the corner seat opposite her.

DOLLY: *Well, this is a bit of luck, I must say. . . .*

The carriage gives a jolt and the train starts to pull out of the station.

DOLLY: *. . . This train is generally packed.*

DOLLY, having placed her various packages on the seat beside her, leans forward to talk to LAURA.

DOLLY: *I really am worried about you, dear — you look terribly peaky.*

Close shot of LAURA over DOLLY's shoulder.

LAURA: *I'm all right — really I am — I just felt faint for a minute, that's all. It often happens to me you know — I once did it in the middle of Bobbie's school concert! I don't think he's ever forgiven me.*

She gives a little smile. It is obviously an effort, but she succeeds reasonably well.

Close shot of DOLLY over LAURA's shoulder.

DOLLY after a slight pause: *He was certainly very nice-looking.*

LAURA: *Who?*

DOLLY: *Your friend — that Doctor whatever his name was.*

Resume on LAURA, over DOLLY's shoulder.

LAURA: *Yes. He's a nice creature.*

DOLLY: *Have you known him long?*

LAURA: *No, not very long.*

LAURA smiles again, quite casually, but her eyes remain miserable.

LAURA: *I hardly know him at all, really. . . .*

DOLLY off: *Well, my dear, I've always had a passion for doctors. I can well understand how it is that women get neurotic. Of course some of them go too far. I'll never forget that time Mary Norton had jaundice. The way she behaved with that doctor of hers was absolutely scandalous. Her husband was furious and said he would. . . .*

DOLLY's words fade away. LAURA's mouth remains closed, but we hear her thoughts.

LAURA'S VOICE: *I wish I could trust you. I wish you were a wise, kind friend, instead of just a gossiping acquaintance that I've known for years casually and never particularly cared for. . . . I wish. . . . I wish. . . .*

Close shot of DOLLY over LAURA's shoulder.

DOLLY: *Fancy him going all the way to South Africa. Is he married?*

LAURA: *Yes.*

DOLLY: *Any children?*

Close shot of LAURA.

LAURA: *Yes — two boys. He's very proud of them.*

DOLLY off: *Is he taking them with him, his wife and children?*

LAURA: *Yes — yes, he is.*

Close shot of DOLLY.

DOLLY: *I suppose it's sensible in a way — rushing off to start life anew in the wide open spaces, and all that sort of thing, but I must say wild horses wouldn't drag me away from England. . . .*

Resume on LAURA.

DOLLY off: *. . . and home and all the things I'm used to — I mean, one has one's roots after all, hasn't one?*

LAURA: *Yes, one has one's roots.*

Close shot of DOLLY's mouth.

DOLLY: *A girl I knew years ago went out to Africa you know — her husband had something to do with engineering or something, and my dear. . . .*

Close shot of LAURA.

DOLLY off: *She really had the most dreadful time — she got some awful kind of germ through going out on a picnic and she was ill for months and months. . . .*

DOLLY's voice has gradually faded away, and we hear LAURA's thoughts — her lips do not move.

LAURA'S VOICE: *I wish you'd stop talking — I wish you'd stop prying and trying to find out things — I wish you were dead! No — I don't mean that — that was unkind and silly — but I wish you'd stop talking. . . .*

DOLLY's voice fades in again.

DOLLY off: *. . . all her hair came out and she said the social life*

*was quite, quite horrid — provincial, you know, and very nouveau riche. . . .*
LAURA wearily: *Oh, Dolly. . . .*
Close shot of DOLLY over LAURA's shoulder.
DOLLY: *What's the matter, dear — are you feeling ill again?*
LAURA: *No, not really ill, but a bit dizzy — I think I'll close my eyes for a little.*
DOLLY: *Poor darling — what a shame and here am I talking away nineteen to the dozen. I won't say another word and if you drop off I'll wake you just as we get to the level crossing. That'll give you time to pull yourself together and powder your nose before we get out.*
Close shot of LAURA.
LAURA: *Thanks, Dolly.*
She leans her head back and closes her eyes. The background of the railway compartment darkens and becomes a misty movement. The noise of the train fades away and music takes its place.
LAURA'S VOICE: *This can't last — this misery can't last — I must remember that and try to control myself. Nothing lasts really — neither happiness nor despair — not even life lasts very long — there will come a time in the future when I shan't mind about this any more — when I can look back and say quite peacefully and cheerfully 'How silly I was' — No, no, — I don't want that time to come ever — I want to remember every minute — always — always — to the end of my days. . . .*
LAURA's head gives a sudden jerk as the train comes to a standstill.
DOLLY off: *Wake up, Laura! We're here!*
Simultaneously the background of the compartment comes back to normal. Station lights flash past onto LAURA's face.
The music stops, and the screech of brakes takes its place.
A porter's voice is heard calling:
PORTER off: *Ketchworth — Ketchworth — Ketchworth!*
Dissolve to Ketchworth Station. It is night. LAURA and DOLLY walk along the platform. The lights from the stationary train illuminate their faces.
DOLLY: *I could come to the house with you quite easily, you know — it really isn't very much out of my way — all I have to do is to*

127

*cut through Elmore Lane — past the Grammar School and I shall be home in two minutes.*

LAURA: *It's sweet of you, Dolly, but I really feel perfectly all right now. That little nap in the train did wonders.*

DOLLY: *You're quite sure?*

LAURA: *Absolutely positive.*

LAURA and DOLLY pass the barrier, where they give up their tickets. A whistle blows and the train can be heard leaving the station. They stop in the station yard beyond.

LAURA: *Thank you for being so kind.*

DOLLY: *Nonsense, dear. Well — I shall telephone in the morning to see if you've had a relapse.*

LAURA: *I shall disappoint you.* She kisses DOLLY. *Good night.*

DOLLY: *Good night — give my love to Fred and the children.*

Dissolve to the exterior of LAURA's house. LAURA is seen approaching the gate of a solid, comfortable-looking house. As she enters the gate, she feels in her handbag for her latch-key, finds it, opens the front door and goes inside.

Seen from the hallway, LAURA enters the front door, glances around, shuts the door quietly and moves out of shot towards the stairs.

The foreground of the shot is framed by a man's hat and coat on a hat-stand. Beyond is the stairway and an open door leading to the sitting-room. LAURA enters frame and starts to go up the stairs.

FRED off, from the sitting-room: *Is that you, Laura?*

LAURA stopping on the stairs: *Yes, dear.*

FRED off: *Thank goodness you're back, the house has been in an uproar.*

LAURA: *Why — what's the matter?*

FRED off: *Bobbie and Margaret have been fighting again, and they won't go to sleep until you go in and talk to them about it.*

MARGARET off: *Mummy — Mummy! Is that you, Mummy?*

LAURA: *Yes, dear.*

BOBBIE off, from upstairs: *Come upstairs at once, Mummy — I want to talk to you.*

LAURA on the way upstairs again: *All right. I'm coming — but you're both very naughty. You should be fast asleep by now.*

On the upstairs landing, LAURA crosses to the half-open door of the children's night nursery.

Inside the night nursery, the foreground is framed by two small twin beds. The room is in darkness and LAURA is silhouetted in the doorway.

LAURA: *Now what is it, you two?*

BOBBIE: *Well, Mummy, tomorrow's my birthday and I want to go to the circus, and tomorrow's not Margaret's birthday, and she wants to go to the pantomime, and I don't think it's fair.*

MARGARET: *I don't see why we've got to do everything Bobbie wants, just because it's his silly old birthday. Besides, my birthday is in June, and there aren't any pantomimes in June.*

BOBBIE persuasively: *Mummy, why don't you come and sit down on my bed?*

MARGARET: *No, Bobbie, Mummy's going to sit on my bed. She sat with you last night.*

LAURA: *I'm not going to sit with either of you. In fact I'm not going to come into the room. It's far too late to discuss it tonight, and if you don't go to sleep at once I shall tell Daddy not to let you go to either.*

BOBBIE and MARGARET together: *Oh, Mummy!*

Dissolve to the interior of the dining room. Close shot of LAURA and her husband FRED, who is a pleasant-looking man in his forties. They are seated at a round dining-room table and are just finishing their meal. LAURA is officiating at the Cona machine. (*Still*) The dining room is furnished comfortably without being in anyway spectacular.

FRED: *Why not take them to both? One in the afternoon and one in the evening?*

LAURA: *You know that's impossible. We shouldn't get home to bed until all hours — and they'd be tired and fractious.*

FRED: *One on one day, then, and the other on the other.*

LAURA handing him a cup of coffee: *Here you are, dear. You're always accusing me of spoiling the children. Their characters would be ruined in a month if I left them to your over-tender mercies.*

FRED cheerfully: *All right — have it your own way.*

Close shot of LAURA.

LAURA: *Circus or pantomime?*

FRED off: *Neither. We'll thrash them both soundly and lock them in the attic, and go to the cinema ourselves.*

LAURA's eyes suddenly fill with tears.

LAURA: *Oh, Fred!*

Close shot of FRED.

FRED: *What on earth's the matter?*

LAURA frantically dabbing her eyes: *Nothing — really it's nothing.*

FRED rises and crosses over to her. He puts his arms round her.

Close shot of FRED and LAURA.

FRED: *Darling — what's wrong? Please tell me. . . .*

LAURA: *Really and truly it's nothing — I'm just a little run-down. I had a sort of fainting spell in the refreshment room at Milford — wasn't it idiotic? Dolly Messiter was with me and talked and talked and talked until I wanted to strangle her — but still she meant to be kind — isn't it awful about people meaning to be kind? . . .*

FRED gently: *Would you like to go up to bed?*

LAURA: *No, Fred — really. . . .*

FRED: *Come and sit by the fire in the library and relax — you can help me with The Times crossword.*

LAURA forcing a smile: *You have the most peculiar ideas of relaxation.*

FRED: *That's better.*

LAURA rises with his arms still round her.

Dissolve to the interior of the library. FRED and LAURA are sitting on either side of the fire. FRED is in the foreground; on his lap is The Times, opened at the crossword puzzle. (*Still*) He holds a pencil in his hand. LAURA has some sewing to do. The library is cosy and intimate.

Close shots of LAURA and FRED individually, as they speak.

FRED: *But why a fainting spell? I can't understand it.*

LAURA: *Don't be so silly, darling — I've often had fainting spells and you know it. Don't you remember Bobbie's school concert and Eileen's wedding, and that time you insisted on taking me to that Symphony Concert in the Town Hall?*

FRED: *That was a nose bleed.*

LAURA: *I suppose I must just be that type of woman. It's very humiliating.*

FRED: *I still maintain that there'd be no harm in you seeing Doctor Graves.*

LAURA a little tremulously: *It would be a waste of time.*

FRED looks at her.

LAURA: *Do shut up about it, dear — you're making a fuss about nothing. I'd been shopping and I was tired and the refreshment room was very hot and I suddenly felt sick. Nothing more than that — really nothing more than that. Now get on with your old puzzle and leave me in peace.*

FRED: *All right — have it your own way.* After a pause: *You're a poetry addict — help me over this — it's Keats — ' When I behold upon the night starred face, huge cloudy symbols of a high ' — something — in seven letters.*

LAURA with an effort: *Romance, I think — yes, I'm almost sure it is. ' Huge cloudy symbols of a high romance ' — It'll be in the Oxford Book of English Verse.*

FRED: *No that's right, I'm certain — it fits in with ' delirium ' and ' Baluchistan '.*

LAURA: *Will some music throw you off your stride?*

FRED: *No, dear — I'd like it.*

> LAURA crosses the room, turns on the radio and returns to her chair. She has tuned in to the opening movement of the Rachmaninoff Concerto in C minor.
>
> Close shot of LAURA. She takes up her sewing, then puts it down again and looks at her husband.
>
> Close shot of FRED. He is concentrating hard and scratching his head thoughtfully with the pencil.
>
> Close shot of LAURA, as her eyes fill with tears again. Her mouth remains closed but we hear her thoughts. . . .

LAURA'S VOICE: *Fred — Fred — dear Fred. There's so much that I want to say to you. You are the only one in the world with enough wisdom and gentleness to understand — if only it were somebody else's story and not mine. As it is you are the only one in the world that I can never tell — never — never — because even if I waited until we were old, old people, and told you then, you would be bound to look back over the years . . . and be hurt and oh, my dear, I don't want you to be hurt. You see, we are a happily married couple, and must never forget that. This is my home. . . .*

> A shot of FRED over LAURA's shoulder. He is engrossed in his crossword puzzle.

LAURA'S VOICE: *. . . you are my husband — and my children are upstairs in bed. I am a happily married woman — or rather, I was,*

*until a few weeks ago. This is my whole world and it is enough —*
*or rather, it was, until a few weeks ago.*

Close shot of LAURA.

LAURA'S VOICE: *. . . But, oh, Fred, I've been so foolish. I've fallen*
*in love! I'm an ordinary woman — I didn't think such violent things*
*could happen to ordinary people.*

Again a shot of FRED over LAURA's shoulder.

LAURA'S VOICE: *It all started on an ordinary day, in the most ordin-*
*ary place in the world.*

The scene, with the exception of LAURA, slowly starts to dim
out. LAURA remains a solid figure in the foreground. As the room
fades away, the station refreshment room takes its place. LAURA,
as well as being in the foreground of the picture, is also seated
on one of the tables in the refreshment room, thus giving the
impression that she is watching herself. Dissolve.

It is now night time, about 5.30 p.m. The scene takes place in
the refreshment room at the Milford Junction Station. There
are only two or three other people in the room. MYRTLE and
BERYL are behind the counter, against which ALBERT is lolling,
sipping a cup of tea.

LAURA'S VOICE: *. . . the refreshment room at Milford Junction. I*
*was having a cup of tea and reading a book that I'd got that morn-*
*ing from Boots — my train wasn't due for ten minutes. . . . I looked*
*up and saw a man come in from the platform. He had on an ordinary*
*mac with a belt. His hat was turned down, and I didn't even see his*
*face. He got his tea at the counter and turned — then I did see his*
*face. It was rather a nice face. He passed my table on the way to his.*
*The woman at the counter was going on as usual. You know, I told*
*you about her the other day — the one with the refined voice. . . .*

Cut to MYRTLE, BERYL and ALBERT at the counter.

BERYL: *Minnie hasn't touched her milk.*

MYRTLE: *Did you put it down for her?*

BERYL: *Yes, but she never came in for it.*

ALBERT conversationally: *Fond of animals?*

MYRTLE: *In their place.*

ALBERT: *My landlady's got a positive mania for animals — she's*
*got two cats, one Manx and one ordinary; three rabbits in a hutch*
*in the kitchen, they belong to her little boy by rights; and one of*

*them foolish-looking dogs with hair over his eyes.*

MYRTLE: *I don't know to what breed you refer.*

ALBERT: *I don't think it knows itself. . . .*

Cut to LAURA, as she glances at the clock, and collects her parcels in a leisurely manner.

MYRTLE off: *Go and clean off Number Three, Beryl, I can see the crumbs on it from here.*

LAURA walks over to the door leading to Number 2 platform.

ALBERT off: *What about my other cup? I shall have to be moving — the five-forty will be in in a minute.*

MYRTLE off: *Who's on the gate?*

ALBERT off: *Young William.*

Outside, the express roars into Milford Junction Station.

LAURA is standing on the platform with the windows of the refreshment room behind her. The lights from the express flash across her face as it streaks through Number 2 platform. She suddenly puts her hand to her face as a piece of grit gets into her eye. She takes out a handkerchief and rubs her eye for a few moments, then turns and walks back into the refreshment room.

MYRTLE is in the foreground of the shot. LAURA enters through the door, comes over to the counter and stands beside ALBERT, who is drinking his second cup of tea. She rubs her eye. (*Still*)

LAURA: *Please, could you give me a glass of water? I've got something in my eye and I want to bathe it.*

MYRTLE: *Would you like me to have a look?*

LAURA: *Please don't trouble. I think the water will do it.*

MYRTLE handing her a glass of water: *Here.*

MYRTLE and ALBERT watch in silence as LAURA bathes her eye.

ALBERT: *Bit of coal-dust, I expect.*

MYRTLE: *A man I knew lost the sight of one eye through getting a bit of grit in it.*

ALBERT: *Nasty thing — very nasty.*

MYRTLE as LAURA lifts her head: *Better?*

LAURA obviously in pain: *I'm afraid not — oh!*

ALEC comes in.

ALEC: *Can I help?*

LAURA: *Oh, no please — it's only something in my eye.*

MYRTLE: *Try pulling down your eyelid as far as it'll go.*

ALBERT: *And then blow your nose.*

ALEC: *Please let me look. I happen to be a doctor.*

LAURA: *It's very kind of you.*

ALEC: *Turn round to the light, please.*

Close shot of LAURA and ALEC.

ALEC: *Now — look up — now look down — I can see it. Keep still. . . .*

He twists up the corner of his handkerchief and rapidly operates with it.

ALEC: *There. . . .*

LAURA blinking: *Oh, dear — what a relief — it was agonizing.*

ALEC: *It looks like a bit of grit.*

LAURA: *It was when the express went through. Thank you very much indeed.*

ALEC: *Not at all.*

There is the sound of a bell on the platform.

ALBERT off: *There we go — I must run.*

LAURA: *How lucky for me that you happened to be here.*

ALEC: *Anybody could have done it.*

LAURA: *Never mind, you did, and I'm most grateful.*

ALEC: *There's my train — good-bye.*

ALEC leaves the buffet and goes out of the door to Number 3 platform.

Outside, he comes out of the refreshment room and hurries along the platform and down the subway.

LAURA also comes out of the refreshment room door on to Number 4 platform. She idly glances across at the opposite platform and sees ALEC.

He emerges from the subway entrance, walks a few steps. His train pulls into the station and he is hidden from view.

Close-up of LAURA. She watches the train as it draws to a standstill.

LAURA'S VOICE: *. . . That's how it all began — just through me getting a little piece of grit in my eye.*

LAURA looks up as she hears her own train approaching.

A shot of Number 3 and 4 platforms. The engine of ALEC's train is in the background. LAURA's train steams into Number 3 platform, hiding it from view.

From outside the window of LAURA's compartment, we see

142

LAURA sitting down, opening her book and starting to read.

LAURA'S VOICE: *I completely forgot the whole incident — it didn't mean anything to me at all, at least I didn't think it did.*

There is the sound of a guard's whistle and the train starts to move off. Fade out.

As the screen goes black, we hear LAURA's voice.

LAURA'S VOICE: *The next Thursday I went into Milford again as usual. . . .*

Fade in on Milford High Street where LAURA walks along, carrying a shopping basket. She checks the contents of the basket with a shopping list and, having decided on her next port of call, she quickens her step. Dissolve.

We are inside Boots Chemist. LAURA is walking away from the library section and goes over to a counter with soaps, tooth-brushes, etc.

LAURA'S VOICE: *I changed my books at Boots — Miss Lewis had at last managed to get the new Kate O'Brien for me — I believe she'd kept it hidden under the counter for two days! On the way out I bought two new toothbrushes for the children — I like the smell of a chemist's better than any other shop — it's such a mixture of nice things — herbs and scent and soap. . . .*

Close shot of MRS LEFTWICH at the end of the counter.

LAURA'S VOICE: *. . . that awful Mrs Leftwich was at the other end of the counter, wearing one of the silliest hats I've ever seen.*

Cut to LAURA placing the toothbrushes in her shopping bag and leaving the counter.

LAURA'S VOICE: *. . . fortunately she didn't look up, so I got out without her buttonholing me. Just as I stepped out on to the pavement. . . .*

Dissolve to LAURA as she comes out of Boots. ALEC comes by walking rather quickly. He is wearing a turned-down hat. He recognizes her, stops, and raises his hat.

ALEC: *Good morning.*

LAURA jumping slightly: *Oh — good morning.*

ALEC: *How's the eye?* (*Still*)

LAURA: *Perfectly all right. How kind it was of you to take so much trouble.*

ALEC: *It was no trouble at all.*

After a slight pause.

ALEC: *It's clearing up, I think.*

LAURA: *Yes — the sky looks much lighter, doesn't it?*

ALEC: *Well, I must be getting along to the hospital.*

LAURA: *And I must be getting along to the grocer's.*

ALEC with a smile: *What exciting lives we lead, don't we? Good-bye.*

Dissolve to the interior of the subway. It is night time. LAURA is walking along, a little out of breath.

LAURA'S VOICE: *That afternoon I had been to the Palladium as usual, but it was a terribly long film, and when I came out I had had to run nearly all the way to the station.*

LAURA starts to go up the steps leading to Number 3 platform. She comes up the subway on to the platform.

LAURA'S VOICE: *As I came up on to the platform the Churley train was just puffing out.*

Cut to the train leaving Number 4 platform.

Close shot of LAURA, watching the Churley train.

LAURA'S VOICE: *I looked up idly as the windows of the carriages went by, wondering if he was there. . . . I remember this crossing my mind but it was quite unimportant — I was really thinking of other things — the present for your birthday was worrying me rather. It was terribly expensive, but I knew you wanted it, and I'd sort of half taken the plunge and left a deposit on it at Spink and Robson's until the next Thursday. The next Thursday. . . .*

Dissolve to the interior of Spink and Robson. Close-up of a travelling clock with a barometer and dates, all in one. It is standing on a glass show case.

LAURA is looking down at it admiringly.

LAURA'S VOICE: *. . . Well — I squared my conscience by thinking how pleased you would be, and bought it — it was wildly extravagant, I know, but having committed the crime, I suddenly felt reckless and gay. . . . .*

Dissolve to Milford High Street. LAURA walks along the street, carrying a small parcel in her hand. It is a sunny day and she is smiling. A barrel organ is playing.

LAURA'S VOICE: *The sun was out and everybody in the street looked more cheerful than usual — and there was a barrel organ at the* corner by Harris's, and you know how I love barrel organs — it was playing ' Let the Great Big World Keep Turning ', and I gave the man sixpence and went to the Kardomah for lunch.

Dissolve to inside of a Kardomah Café. LAURA is sitting at an alcove table. A waitress is just finishing taking her order.

LAURA'S VOICE: *It was very full, but two people had got up from the table just as I had come in — that was a bit of luck, wasn't it? Or was it? Just after I had given my order, I saw him come in. He looked a little tired, I thought, and there was nowhere for him to sit, so I smiled and said . . .*

LAURA: *Good morning.*

Close-up of ALEC.

ALEC: *Good morning. Are you alone?*

Resume on LAURA and ALEC.

LAURA: *Yes, I am.*

ALEC: *Would you mind very much if I shared your table — it's very full and there doesn't seem to be anywhere else?*

LAURA moving a couple of parcels and her bag: *Of course not.*

ALEC hangs up his hat and mackintosh and sits down next to her.

ALEC: *I'm afraid we haven't been properly introduced — my name's Alec Harvey.*

LAURA shaking hands: *How do you do — mine's Laura Jesson.*

ALEC: *Mrs or Miss?*

LAURA: *Mrs. You're a doctor, aren't you? I remember you said you were that day in the refreshment room.*

ALEC: *Yes — not a very interesting doctor — just an ordinary G.P. My practice is in Churley.*

A waitress comes to the table.

WAITRESS: *Can I take your order?*

ALEC to LAURA: *What did you plump for?*

LAURA: *The soup and the fried sole.*

ALEC to WAITRESS: *The same for me, please.*

WAITRESS: *Anything to drink?*

ALEC: *No, thank you.*

ALEC pauses and looks at LAURA.

ALEC: *That is — would you like anything to drink?*

LAURA: *No, thank you — just plain water.*

ALEC to WAITRESS: *Plain water, please.*

As the WAITRESS goes away, a Ladies Orchestra starts to play very loudly. LAURA jumps.

Cut to a view of the Ladies Orchestra. They are playing with enthusiasm.

Close shot of LAURA and ALEC. They both laugh. ALEC catches LAURA's eye and nods towards the cellist.

Close shot of the cellist. She is a particularly industrious member of the orchestra.

LAURA'S VOICE: *I'd seen that woman playing the cello hundreds of times, but I've never noticed before how funny she looked.*

Close shot of LAURA and ALEC.

LAURA: *It really is dreadful, isn't it — but we shouldn't laugh — they might see us.*

ALEC: *There should be a society for the prevention of cruelty to musical instruments — you don't play the piano, I hope?*

LAURA: *I was forced to as a child.*

ALEC: *You haven't kept it up?*

LAURA smiling: *No — my husband isn't musical at all.*

ALEC: *Bless him!*

LAURA: *For all you know, I might have a tremendous, burning professional talent.*

ALEC shaking his head: *Oh dear, no.*

LAURA: *Why are you so sure?*

ALEC: *You're too sane — and uncomplicated!*

LAURA fishing in her bag for her powder puff: *I suppose it's a good thing to be so uncomplicated — but it does sound a little dull.*

ALEC: *You could never be dull.*

LAURA: *Do you come here every Thursday?*

ALEC: *Yes, to spend a day in the hospital. Stephen Lynn — he's the chief physician here — graduated with me. I take over from him once a week — it gives him a chance to go up to London and me a chance to study the hospital patients.*

LAURA: *I see.*

ALEC: *Do you?*

LAURA: *Do I what?*

ALEC: *Come here every Thursday?*

LAURA: *Yes — I do the week's shopping, change my library book, have a little lunch, and generally go to the pictures. Not a very exciting routine, really, but it makes a change.*

ALEC: *Are you going to the pictures this afternoon?*
LAURA: *Yes.*
ALEC: *How extraordinary — so am I.*
LAURA: *But I thought you had to work all day in the hospital.*
ALEC: *Well, between ourselves, I killed two patients this morning by accident and the Matron's very displeased with me. I simply daren't go back. . . .*
LAURA: *How can you be so silly. . . .*
ALEC: *Seriously — I really did get through most of my work this morning — it won't matter a bit if I play truant. Would you mind very much if I came to the pictures with you?*
LAURA hesitatingly: *Well — I. . . .*
ALEC: *I could sit downstairs and you could sit upstairs.*
LAURA: *Upstairs is too expensive.*

She smiles. The orchestra stops playing.

LAURA'S VOICE: *The orchestra stopped as abruptly as it had started, and we began to laugh again, and I suddenly realized that I was enjoying myself so very much.*

The WAITRESS arrives back with the soup.

LAURA'S VOICE: *I had no premonitions although I suppose I should have had. It all seemed so natural — and so — so innocent.*

Close-up of ALEC over LAURA's shoulder, followed quickly by a close-up of LAURA over ALEC's shoulder.

Dissolve to close shot of the luncheon bill on a plate. ALEC's hand comes into view and picks it up. LAURA's hand tries to take it from him.

LAURA'S VOICE: *We finished lunch, and the idiot of a waitress had put the bill all on one.*

Close shot of LAURA and ALEC.

ALEC: *I really must insist.*
LAURA: *I couldn't possibly.*
ALEC: *Having forced my company on you, it's only fair that I should pay through the nose for it!*
LAURA: *Please don't insist — I would so much rather we halved it, really I would — please.*
ALEC: *I shall give in gracefully.*
LAURA'S VOICE: *We halved it meticulously — we even halved the tip.*

LAURA and ALEC get up from the table and the orchestra plays again. They start laughing as they leave the restaurant.

Dissolve to Milford High Street. The camera tracks with LAURA and ALEC as they are walking along.

LAURA: *We have two choices — 'The Loves of Cardinal Richelieu' at the Palace, and ' Love in a Mist' at the Palladium.*

ALEC: *You're very knowledgeable.*

LAURA: *There must be no argument about buying the tickets — we each pay for ourselves.*

ALEC: *You must think me a very poor doctor if I can't afford a couple of one and ninepennies!*

LAURA: *I insist.*

ALEC: *I had hoped that you were going to treat me!*

LAURA: *Which is it to be — Palace or Palladium?*

ALEC with decision: *Palladium, I was once very sick on a channel steamer called ' Cardinal Richelieu '.*

Dissolve to inside of the cinema where we see the Palladium Proscenium. On the screen a trailer is being shown, advertising a coming attraction. Superimposed over four spectacular shots in ever increasing sizes, are the following words, which zoom up towards the audience:

STUPENDOUS! COLOSSAL!!
GIGANTIC!!! EPOCH-MAKING!!!!

A burst of flame appears, followed by the title of the picture ' Flame of Passion ' coming shortly. The trailer ends abruptly and the first of a series of advertisements is flashed on the screen. It is a drawing of a pram with the words:

BUY YOUR PRAM AT BURTONS
22, MILFORD HIGH STREET.

Close shot of LAURA and ALEC who are seated in the middle of the front row of the circle. A beam of light from the projector forms the background of the scene.

LAURA leaning forward over the edge of the circle: *I feel awfully grand perched up here — it was very extravagant of you.*

ALEC: *It was a famous victory.*

LAURA: *Do you feel guilty at all? I do.*

ALEC: *Guilty?*

LAURA: *You ought to more than me really — you neglected your work this afternoon.*

ALEC: *I worked this morning — a little relaxation never did any harm to anyone. Why should either of us feel guilty?*

LAURA: *I don't know.*

ALEC: *How awfully nice you are.*

There is a deafening peal of organ music.

With ALEC and LAURA in the foreground, a woman organist rises from the depths of the orchestra pit, organ and all, playing away as though her life depended on it.

Close shot of LAURA and ALEC, as they are watching the organist. A surprised look appears on both their faces. They look at each other, then lean forward to get a better view of the organist.

Close shot of the organist, acknowledging the applause from the audience. She is the woman that plays the cello at the Kardomah Café.

Close shot of LAURA and ALEC.

LAURA: *It can't be.*

ALEC: *It is.*

They both roar with laughter.

Dissolve to Milford Junction Station, showing the yard and booking hall. It is night time. The camera tracks with LAURA and ALEC, who are walking across the station yard.

LAURA'S VOICE: *We walked back to the station. Just as we were approaching the barrier he put his hand under my arm. I didn't notice it then, but I remember it now.*

LAURA: *What's she like, your wife?*

ALEC: *Madeleine? Oh — small, dark, rather delicate —*

LAURA: *How funny — I should have thought she would be fair.*

ALEC: *And your husband — what's he like?*

They enter the lighted booking hall.

LAURA: *Medium height, brown hair, kindly, unemotional, and not delicate at all.*

ALEC: *You said that proudly.*

LAURA: *Did I?*

They pass the ticket barrier, where ALBERT is on duty, and out on to Number 1 platform.

LAURA: *We've just got time for a cup of tea before our trains go.*

Dissolve to the refreshment room. From behind the counter,

MYRTLE and BERYL are seen gossiping in the foreground, while ALEC and LAURA enter through the door. LAURA goes over to a table out of shot. ALEC comes forward to the counter.

MYRTLE: *And for the third time in one week he brought that common man and his wife to the house without so much as by your leave.* To ALEC: *Yes?*

ALEC: *Two teas, please.*

MYRTLE: *Cakes or pastry?*

LAURA off: *No, thank you.*

ALEC: *Are those Bath buns fresh?*

MYRTLE: *Certainly they are — made this morning.*

ALEC: *Two, please.*

MYRTLE puts two Bath buns on a plate. Meanwhile BERYL has drawn two cups of tea.

MYRTLE: *That'll be sevenpence.*

ALEC: *All right.*

He pays her.

MYRTLE: *Take the tea to the table, Beryl.*

ALEC: *I'll carry the buns.*

LAURA has now seated herself at a table. BERYL brings the tea while ALEC follows with the buns.

ALEC: *You must eat one of these — fresh this morning.*

LAURA: *Very fattening.*

ALEC: *I don't hold with such foolishness.*

BERYL goes out of view towards the counter.

BERYL off: *What happened then, Mrs Bagot?*

LAURA gives ALEC a nudge to draw his attention to MYRTLE and BERYL.

Close shot of MYRTLE and BERYL behind the counter.

MYRTLE slightly relaxed in manner: *Well — it's all very faine, I said, expecting me to do this, that and the other, but what do I get out of it? You can't expect me to be a cook-housekeeper and char rolled into one during the day, and a loving wife in the evening, just because you feel like it. Oh, dear, no. There are just as good fish in the sea, I said, as ever came out of it, and I packed my boxes then and there and left him.*

BERYL: *Didn't you never go back?*

MYRTLE: *Never, I went to my sister's place at Folkestone for a bit, and then I went in with a friend of mine and we opened a tea-shop in Hythe.*

BERYL: *And what happened to him?*

MYRTLE: *Dead as a doornail inside three years.*

BERYL: *Well, I never.*

Close shot of LAURA and ALEC.

LAURA: *Is tea bad for one? Worse than coffee, I mean?*

ALEC: *If this is a professional interview my fee is a guinea.*

LAURA: *Why did you become a doctor?*

ALEC: *That's a long story. Perhaps because I'm a bit of an idealist.*

LAURA: *I suppose all doctors ought to have ideals, really — otherwise I should think their work would be unbearable.*

ALEC: *Surely you're not encouraging me to talk shop?*

LAURA: *Why shouldn't you talk shop? It's what interests you most, isn't it?*

ALEC: *Yes — it is. I'm terribly ambitious really — not ambitious for myself so much as for my special pigeon.*

LAURA: *What is your special pigeon?*

ALEC: *Preventative medicine.*

LAURA: *Oh, I see.*

ALEC laughing: *I'm afraid you don't.*

LAURA: *I was trying to be intelligent.*

ALEC: *Most good doctors, especially when they're young, have private dreams — that's the best part of them; sometimes, though, those get over-professionalized and strangulated and — am I boring you?*

LAURA: *No — I don't quite understand — but you're not boring me.*

ALEC: *What I mean is this — all good doctors must be primarily enthusiastic. They must have, like writers and painters and priests, a sense of vocation — a deep-rooted, unsentimental desire to do good.*

LAURA: *Yes — I see that.*

ALEC: *Well, obviously one way of preventing disease is worth fifty ways of curing it — that's where my ideal comes in — preventative medicine isn't anything to do with medicine at all, really — it's concerned with conditions, living conditions and common sense and hygiene. For instance, my speciality is pneumoconiosis.*

LAURA: *Oh, dear!*

ALEC: *Don't be alarmed, it's simpler than it sounds — it's nothing but a slow process of fibrosis of the lung due to the inhalation of particles of dust. In the hospital here there are splendid opportunities for observing cures and making notes, because of the coalmines.*

LAURA: *You suddenly look much younger.*

ALEC brought up short: *Do I?*

LAURA: *Almost like a little boy.*

ALEC: *What made you say that?*

LAURA staring at him: *I don't know — yes, I do.*

ALEC gently: *Tell me.*

LAURA with panic in her voice: *Oh, no — I couldn't really. You were saying about the coal-mines.*

ALEC looking into her eyes: *Yes — the inhalation of coal-dust — that's one specific form of the disease — it's called anthracosis.*

LAURA hypnotized: *What are the others?*

ALEC: *Chalicosis — that comes from metal-dust — steel-works, you know. . . .*

LAURA: *Yes, of course. Steel-works.*

ALEC: *And silicosis — stone-dust — that's gold-mines.*

LAURA almost in a whisper: *I see.*

There is the sound of a bell.

LAURA: *That's your train.*

ALEC looking down: *Yes.*

LAURA: *You mustn't miss it.*

ALEC: *No.*

LAURA again with panic in her voice: *What's the matter?*

ALEC with an effort: *Nothing — nothing at all.*

LAURA socially: *It's been so very nice — I've enjoyed my afternoon enormously.*

ALEC: *I'm so glad — so have I. I apologize for boring you with those long medical words.*

LAURA: *I feel dull and stupid, not to be able to understand more.*

ALEC: *Shall I see you again?*

There is the sound of a train approaching.

LAURA: *It's the other platform, isn't it? You'll have to run. Don't worry about me — mine's due in a few minutes.*

ALEC: *Shall I see you again?*

LAURA: *Of course — perhaps you could come over to Ketchworth one Sunday. It's rather far, I know, but we should be delighted to see you.*

ALEC intensely: *Please — please. . . .*

The train is heard drawing to a standstill. . . .

LAURA: *What is it?*

ALEC: *Next Thursday — the same time.*

LAURA: *No — I can't possibly — I. . . .*

ALEC: *Please — I ask you most humbly. . . .*

LAURA: *You'll miss your train!*

ALEC: *All right.*

He gets up.

LAURA: *Run. . . .*

ALEC taking her hand: *Good-bye.*

LAURA breathlessly: *I'll be there.*

ALEC: *Thank you, my dear.*

He leaves LAURA, and the camera tracks into a big close shot to hold her, smiling with joy.

LAURA collects her shopping basket and goes towards the door to Number 3 platform.

She comes out of the refreshment room on to the platform. She looks up past camera at ALEC's train, which can be heard pulling out of the station.

A shot of ALEC, from LAURA's view-point. He is leaning out of a carriage window, and waves to her as the train starts to pull out of the station.

Close-up of LAURA. She waves back, and her eyes follow the departing train.

LAURA'S VOICE: *I stood there and watched his train draw out of the station. I stared after it until its little red tail light had vanished into the darkness. I imagined him arriving at Churley and giving up his ticket and walking through the streets, and letting himself into his house with his latchkey. Madeleine, his wife, would probably be in the hall to meet him — or perhaps upstairs in her room — not feeling very well — small, dark and rather delicate — I wondered if he'd say ' I met such a nice woman in the Kardomah — we had lunch and went to the pictures ' — then suddenly I knew that he wouldn't — I knew beyond a shadow of doubt that he wouldn't say a word, and at that moment the first awful feeling of danger swept over me.*

A cloud of steam from an incoming engine blows across the screen, almost obscuring LAURA. The grinding of brakes and hiss of steam as her train draws to a standstill, interrupts her thoughts. She walks out of view towards the train.

Through the clearing steam we see her enter a third-class compartment, crowded with people.

She sits down between two other passengers, and glances around the carriage.

LAURA'S VOICE: *I looked hurriedly around the carriage to see if anyone was looking at me.*

The camera pans along the passengers seated on the opposite side of the carriage.

LAURA'S VOICE: *. . . as though they could read my secret thoughts. Nobody was looking at me except a clergyman in the opposite corner.*

The clergyman catches her eye and turns his head away.

Close-up of LAURA as she opens her library book.

LAURA'S VOICE: *I felt myself blushing and opened my library book and pretended to read.*

The train gives a jerk as it starts to move off.

Dissolve to Ketchworth Station, where LAURA walks along the platform towards the barrier. There are several other passengers around her.

LAURA'S VOICE: *By the time we got to Ketchworth, I had made up my mind definitely that I wouldn't see Alec any more.*

A WOMAN'S VOICE: *Good evening, Mrs Jesson.*

LAURA does not hear.

LAURA'S VOICE: *It was silly and undignified flirting like that with a complete stranger.*

She walks on a pace or two, then turns.

LAURA: *Oh — oh — good evening.*


Dissolve to LAURA's house. She walks up the path to the front door.

LAURA'S VOICE: *I walked up to the house quite briskly and cheerfully. I had been behaving like an idiot admittedly, but after all no harm had been done.*

LAURA opens the front door.

She enters the hall, and looks up towards the stairs.

LAURA'S VOICE: *You met me in the hall. Your face was strained and worried and my heart sank.*

LAURA: *Fred, what's the matter?*

Cut to FRED, who walks down the stairs into the hall.

FRED: *It's all right, old girl, but you've got to keep calm and not be upset.*

LAURA: *What is it? What's wrong?*

FRED: *It's Bobbie — he was knocked down by a car on the way home from school. . . .*

LAURA gives a little cry.

FRED: *It's not serious — he was just grazed by the mudguard but it knocked him against the kerb and he's got slight concussion — the doctor's upstairs with him now. . . .*

LAURA flings down her parcels and book and goes upstairs at a run, tearing off her coat as she goes. FRED follows.

Through the open door of the night nursery we see LAURA arrive on the landing and hurry towards the room. She stops in the doorway as she sees the doctor standing beside BOBBIE's bed. BOBBIE is lying with his eyes shut, and his head and right arm bandaged. The doctor puts his fingers to his lips.

DOCTOR: *It's all right, Mrs Jesson — nothing to worry about — he'll be as right as rain in a few hours.*

LAURA goes across the room and kneels at the side of BOBBIE's bed. The DOCTOR now becomes an unimportant part of the scene; his legs only being visible.

LAURA whispering: *You're sure — you're sure it's not serious?*

DOCTOR smiling: *Quite sure — but it was certainly a very lucky escape.*

The DOCTOR moves off out of view.

DOCTOR off: *I've given him a little sedative, and I should advise keeping him at home for a couple of days. It must have been a bit of a shock and his right arm is rather badly bruised.*

The DOCTOR's voice gradually fades away.

LAURA'S VOICE: *I felt so dreadful, Fred — looking at him lying there with that bandage round his head. I tried not to show it, but I was quite hysterical inside as though the whole thing were my fault — a sort of punishment — an awful, sinister warning.*

Dissolve to LAURA and BOBBIE. She is seated on his bed, as the maid comes into view and hands BOBBIE a plate of bread and milk.

LAURA'S VOICE: *An hour or two later, of course, everything became quite normal again. He began to enjoy the whole thing thoroughly, and revelled in the fact that he was the centre of attraction. Do you remember how we spent the whole evening planning his future?*

Dissolve to FRED and LAURA in the library. They are seated on either side of the fire. FRED is on the sofa with a crossword puzzle and LAURA is smoking a cigarette.

LAURA: *But he's much too young to decide really.*

FRED: *It's a good life — and if the boy has a feeling for it. . . .*

LAURA: *How can we possibly really know that he has a feeling for it? He'll probably want to be an engine driver next week.*

FRED: *It was last week that he wanted to be an engine driver.*

LAURA: *But it seems so final somehow, entering a child of that age for the Navy.*

FRED: *It's a healthy life.*

LAURA with slight exasperation: *I know it's a good life, dear, and I know that he'll be able to see the world, and have a wife in every port and keep on calling everybody ' sir ' — but what about us?*

FRED: *How do you mean? ' What about us? '*

LAURA: *We shall hardly ever see him. . . .*

FRED: *Nonsense.*

LAURA: *It isn't nonsense. He'll be sent away to sea as a smooth-faced boy, and the next thing we know he'll be walking in with a long beard and a parrot.*

FRED: *I think you take rather a Victorian view of the Navy, my dear.*

LAURA: *He's our only son and I should like to be there while he's growing up.*

FRED: *All right, old girl. We'll put him into an office and you can see him off on the eight-fifty every morning.*

LAURA crushing her cigarette out: *You really are very annoying — you know perfectly well that I should hate that.*

LAURA rises and goes round to the sofa table, behind FRED. On the table is a work basket, out of which she starts to take some wool, etc.

FRED: *All right — all right, have it your own way.*

After a pause we resume on close-ups of FRED and LAURA, individually.

LAURA suddenly: *Fred. . . .*

FRED busily counting spaces: *Yes —*

LAURA: *I had lunch with a strange man to-day and he took me to the movies.*

FRED: *Good for you.*

LAURA: *He's awfully nice — he's a doctor. . . .*

FRED rather abstractedly filling in a word: *A — very — noble — profession. . . .*

LAURA helplessly: *Oh dear!*

FRED: *It was Richard the Third who said ' My kingdom for a horse ', wasn't it?*

LAURA: *Yes, dear.*

FRED: *Well, all I can say is that I wish he hadn't — it ruins everything.*

LAURA: *I thought perhaps we might ask him over to dine one evening. . . .*

FRED: *By all means.* He looks up. *Who?*

LAURA: *Doctor Harvey. The one I was telling you about.*

FRED: *Must it be dinner?*

LAURA: *You're never at home for lunch.*

FRED: *Exactly.*

LAURA leaves the table and goes over to sit beside FRED.

LAURA starting to laugh, almost hysterically: *Oh, Fred!*

Close shot of FRED and LAURA.

FRED looking up: *What on earth's the matter?*

LAURA laughing more: *It's nothing — it's only that. . . .*

She breaks off and goes on laughing helplessly until she has to wipe her eyes.

LAURA: *Oh, Fred. . . .*

FRED: *I really don't see what's so terribly funny.*

LAURA: *I do — it's all right, darling, I'm not laughing at you — I'm laughing at me, I'm the one that's funny — I'm an absolute idiot — worrying myself about things that don't really exist — making mountains out of molehills. . . .*

FRED: *I told you when you came in that it wasn't anything serious — there was no need for you to get into such a state. . . .*

LAURA: *No — I see that now — I really do. . . .*

She goes on laughing.

Dissolve to interior of the Kardomah Café. LAURA is sitting at the same table; she is alone. The Ladies Orchestra is playing away as usual.

LAURA'S VOICE: *I went to the Kardomah and managed to get the*

*same table. I waited a bit but he didn't come. . . . The ladies'*
*orchestra was playing away as usual — I looked at the cellist — she*
*had seemed to be so funny last week, but to-day didn't seem funny*
*any more — she looked pathetic, poor thing.*

Dissolve to LAURA, who is walking past the hospital.

LAURA'S VOICE: *After lunch I happened to pass by the hospital —*
*I remember looking up at the windows and wondering if he were*
*there, and whether something awful had happened to prevent him*
*turning up.*

Dissolve to the refreshment room. It is night time. LAURA is
leaving the counter, carrying a cup of tea, which MYRTLE has
just poured out for her. She walks over to a table and sits down.

LAURA'S VOICE: *I got to the station earlier than usual. I hadn't*
*enjoyed the pictures much — it was one of those noisy musical*
*things and I'm so sick of them — I had come out before it was over.*

MYRTLE comes over to the stove in the centre of the room.
She bends down to put more coal into it. ALBERT GODBY enters
and perceiving her slightly vulnerable position he tiptoes
towards her.

LAURA is watching ALBERT. After a moment there is a loud
smack, off. LAURA smiles.

MYRTLE springs to an upright position.

MYRTLE: *Albert Godby, how dare you?*

ALBERT: *I couldn't resist it.*

MYRTLE: *I'll trouble you to keep your hands to yourself.*

MYRTLE walks out of view towards the counter.

ALBERT: *You're blushing — you look wonderful when you're angry*
*— like an avenging angel.*

ALBERT follows her.

At the counter we see individual close-ups of MYRTLE and
ALBERT.

MYRTLE: *I'll give you avenging angel — coming in here taking*
*liberties. . . .*

ALBERT: *I didn't think after what you said last Monday you'd*
*object to a friendly little slap.*

MYRTLE: *Never you mind about last Monday — I'm on duty now.*
*A nice thing if Mr Saunders had happened to be looking through*
*the window.*

ALBERT: *If Mr Saunders is in the 'abit of looking through windows,*

*it's time he saw something worth looking at.*
MYRTLE: *You ought to be ashamed of yourself!*
ALBERT: *It's just high spirits — don't be mad at me.*
MYRTLE: *High spirits indeed! Here, take your tea and be quiet.*
ALBERT: *It's all your fault, anyway.*
MYRTLE: *I don't know what you're referring to, I'm sure.*
ALBERT: *I was thinking of to-night.*
MYRTLE: *If you don't learn to behave yourself there won't be a to-night — or any other night, either. . . .*
ALBERT: *Give us a kiss.*
MYRTLE: *I'll do no such thing. The lady might see us.*
ALBERT: *Just a quick one — across the counter.*
   He grabs her arm across the counter.
MYRTLE: *Albert, stop it!*
ALBERT: *Come on — there's a love.*
MYRTLE: *Let go of me this minute.*
ALBERT: *Come on, just one. . . .*
   They scuffle for a moment, upsetting a neat pile of cakes on to the floor.
MYRTLE: *Now look at me Banburys — all over the floor.*
   ALBERT bends down to pick them up.
   Cut to STANLEY as he enters the door.
STANLEY: *Just in time or born in the vestry.*
   LAURA glances up at the clock, takes up her shopping basket, and during the following dialogue, the camera pans with her to the door which leads to Number 3 platform.
MYRTLE off: *You shut your mouth and help Mr Godby pick up them cakes. Come along, what are you standing there gaping at?*
   LAURA comes out of the refreshment room door on to Number 3 platform.
LAURA'S VOICE: *As I left the refreshment room I saw a train coming in — his train. He wasn't on the platform, and I suddenly felt panic-stricken at the thought of not seeing him again.*
   Dissolve to the subway entrance to Number 2 and 3 platforms.
   ALEC dashes up the steps on to the platform, and runs towards LAURA.
ALEC breathlessly: *Oh, my dear, I'm so sorry — so terribly sorry.*
LAURA: *Quick — your train — you'll miss it.*
   They both rush along the platform towards the subway.

159

ALEC as they go: *I'd no way of letting you know — the house surgeon had to operate suddenly — it wasn't anything really serious, but I had to stand by as it was one of my special patients.*

Inside the subway LAURA and ALEC are running down the steps.

ALEC: *. . . You do understand, don't you?*

LAURA now rather breathless: *Of course — it doesn't matter a bit.*

They turn the corner at the foot of the steps, and the camera tracks with them as they run along the subway towards Number 4 platform.

ALEC: *I thought of sending a note to the Kardomah, but I thought they would probably never find you, or keep on shouting your name out and embarrass you, and I. . . .*

They start running up the steps leading to Number 4 platform.

LAURA: *Please don't say any more — I really do understand. . . .*

A whistle blows as LAURA and ALEC hurry on to the platform.

LAURA: *Quickly — oh, quickly. The whistle's gone.*

They hurry to the waiting train. ALEC opens the door of a third-class compartment and turns to LAURA.

ALEC: *I'm so relieved that I had a chance to explain — I didn't think I would ever see you again.*

LAURA: *How absurd of you.*

The train starts to move off.

LAURA: *Quickly — quickly. . . .*

ALEC jumps into the train, and leans out of the window. LAURA walks along a few paces with the train.

ALEC: *Next Thursday.*

LAURA: *Yes. Next Thursday.*

The train gradually gains on LAURA, and ALEC goes out of view. LAURA watches ALEC's departing train, waves after it and stands quite still until the sound of it has died away in the distance. A strident voice from the loudspeaker breaks in:

LOUDSPEAKER: *The train for Ketchworth is standing at Number 3 platform.*

LAURA suddenly realizes that she is about to miss her own train, and she makes a dash for the subway steps.

Dissolve to a close shot of LAURA and ALEC sitting in the front row of the circle at the Palladium Cinema. They are both laughing and are obviously very happy. The lights go up.

ALEC: *The stars can change in their courses, the universe go up in flames and the world crash around us, but there'll always be Donald Duck.*

LAURA: *I do love him so, his dreadful energy, his blind frustrated rages. . . .*

The lights begin to dim.

ALEC: *It's the big picture now — here we go — no more laughter — prepare for tears.*

Dissolve to the main title of the big picture, flashed on to the screen. It is the film advertised in the trailer of two weeks ago, ' Flame of Passion '.

LAURA'S VOICE: *It was a terribly bad picture.*

Dissolve to LAURA and ALEC walking up the last few steps of the circle towards the exit. The back of an usherette forms the foreground of the shot.

LAURA'S VOICE: *We crept out before the end, rather furtively, as though we were committing a crime. The usherette at the door looked at us with stony contempt.*

Dissolve to a medium shot of LAURA and ALEC coming out of the cinema. ALEC takes LAURA'S arm, as they walk along the street.

LAURA'S VOICE: *It really was a lovely afternoon, and it was a relief to be in the fresh air. Do you know, I believe we should all behave quite differently if we lived in a warm, sunny climate all the time. We shouldn't be so withdrawn and shy and difficult.*

Dissolve to a picturesque shot of ALEC and LAURA as they walk along by the side of a lake.

LAURA'S VOICE: *Oh, Fred, it really was a lovely afternoon. There were some little boys sailing their boats — one of them looked awfully like Bobbie — that should have given me a pang of conscience I know, but it didn't! . . .*

After a few moments ALEC stops walking and turns to LAURA.

LAURA'S VOICE: *Alec suddenly said that he was sick of staring at the water and that he wanted to be on it.*

The foreground of the scene is now composed of one or two rowing boats, which have been covered up for the winter. On the landing stage in the background, a boatman is pushing ALEC and LAURA away from the shore.

LAURA'S VOICE: *All the boats were covered up but we managed to persuade the old man to let us have one.*

Close shot of the boatman.

LAURA'S VOICE: *He thought we were raving mad. Perhaps he was right.*

The boat is in the water, with the boatman in the foreground.

LAURA'S VOICE: *. . . Alec rowed off at a great rate, and I trailed my hand in the water — it was very cold but a lovely feeling.*

ALEC and LAURA are in the boat. LAURA is in the foreground of the shot. ALEC catches a crab and an oar slips out of its rowlock.

LAURA: *You don't row very well, do you?*

ALEC putting the oar back in the rowlock: *I'm going to be perfectly honest with you. I don't row at all, and unless you want to go round in ever narrowing circles, you had better start steering.* (Still)

LAURA laughs and picks up the steering ropes. They start off again.

The boat is following a somewhat erratic course.

LAURA'S VOICE: *We had such fun, Fred. I felt gay and happy and sort of released — that's what's so shameful about it all — that's what would hurt you so much if you knew — that I could feel as intensely as that — away from you — with a stranger.*

The camera is tracking with the boat. LAURA is in the foreground of the shot. They are approaching a very low bridge.

LAURA: *Oh, look out . . . we shan't get through.*

ALEC glancing behind: *Pull on your left.*

As the bridge looms nearer and nearer, ALEC rises to his feet. LAURA pulls the wrong rope and looks up inquiringly at ALEC. There is a crash and a shudder as the boat hits the bridge.

LAURA'S VOICE: *I never could tell left from right.*

The boat rocks violently and there is a loud splash. LAURA looks towards the water and begins to laugh.

ALEC is standing in the lake. The water only comes up to his knees. He is very wet.

Close-up of LAURA, who is roaring with laughter.

Dissolve to the interior of the boathouse. ALEC's trousers are hanging over a line in front of an open ' Ideal ' boiler. ALEC himself is seated on an upturned dinghy. He is wearing an overcoat, which is obviously not his own, and is smoking a cigarette. He looks at LAURA.

She is kneeling by the boiler, laying out ALEC's shoes and socks to dry.

She gets up and goes over to a carpenter's bench, where a kettle is boiling on a gas ring. Beside the ring is a bottle of milk and two cups. In the background of the shot are a collection of punts, boats, oars, etc. LAURA starts to make tea.

LAURA: *The British have always been nice to mad people. That boatman thinks we are quite dotty, but just look how sweet he has been: overcoat, tea, milk — even sugar.*

Close shot of ALEC as he watches her prepare the tea. After a moment we hear the sound of LAURA walking across the boathouse towards ALEC. He follows her with his eyes. Her hand comes into view and gives him a cup of tea.

ALEC: *Thank you.*

LAURA sits down on an old wooden chair, and they both begin to stir their tea.

ALEC quietly: *You know what's happened, don't you?*

LAURA: *Yes — yes, I do.*

ALEC: *I've fallen in love with you.*

LAURA: *Yes — I know.*

ALEC: *Tell me honestly — my dear — please tell me honestly if what I believe is true. . . .*

LAURA in a whisper: *What do you believe? (Still)*

ALEC: *That it's the same with you — that you've fallen in love too.*

LAURA near tears: *It sounds so silly.*

ALEC: *Why?*

LAURA: *I know you so little.*

ALEC: *It is true, though — isn't it?*

LAURA with a sigh: *Yes — it's true.*

ALEC making a slight movement towards her: *Laura. . . .*

LAURA: *No please . . . we must be sensible — please help me to be sensible — we mustn't behave like this — we must forget that we've said what we've said.*

ALEC: *Not yet — not quite yet.*

LAURA panic in her voice: *But we must — don't you see!*

ALEC leaning forward and taking her hand: *Listen — it's too late now to be as sensible as all that — it's too late to forget what we've said — and anyway, whether we'd said it or not couldn't have mattered — we know — we've both of us known for a long time.*

163

LAURA: *How can you say that — I've only known you for four weeks — we only talked for the first time last Thursday week.*

ALEC: *Last Thursday week. Hadn't it been a long time since then — for you? Answer me truly.*

LAURA: *Yes.*

ALEC: *How often did you decide that you were never going to see me again?*

LAURA: *Several times a day.*

ALEC: *So did I.*

LAURA: *Oh, Alec.*

ALEC: *I love you — I love your wide eyes and the way you smile and your shyness, and the way you laugh at my jokes.*

LAURA: *Please don't. . . .*

ALEC: *I love you — I love you — you love me too — it's no use pretending that it hasn't happened because it has.*

LAURA with tremendous effort: *Yes it has. I don't want to pretend anything either to you or to anyone else . . . but from now on I shall have to. That's what's wrong — don't you see? That's what spoils everything. That's why we must stop here and now talking like this. We are neither of us free to love each other, there is too much in the way. There's still time, if we control ourselves and behave like sensible human beings, there's still time to — to. . . .*

She puts her head down and bursts into tears.

ALEC: *There's no time at all.*

ALEC goes over to her, takes her in his arms and kisses her. Cut to close-up of the station bell, ringing loudly at Milford Junction Station. It is night time.

LAURA and ALEC come on to Number 1 platform from the booking hall.

LAURA: *There's your train.*

ALEC: *Yes.*

LAURA: *I'll come with you — over to the other platform.*

They walk along the platform and down the subway steps. In the subway ALEC stops and takes her in his arms. She struggles a little.

LAURA: *No dear — please . . . not here — someone will see.*

ALEC kissing her: *I love you so.*

They are interrupted by the sound of feet coming down the subway steps. A shadow appears on the wall behind them. They hurry off through the subway.

In the foreground of the shot, the dim outline of LAURA can be seen. She is watching herself and ALEC as they walk along the subway towards Number 4 platform. The sound of an express train roaring overhead, becomes the sound of loud music. FRED's voice is heard.

FRED'S VOICE: *Don't you think we might have that down a bit, darling?*

After a slight pause.

FRED'S VOICE: *Hoi — Laura!*

Dissolve to a shot over LAURA's shoulder. The subway has suddenly disappeared, and FRED and the library have taken its place.

LAURA jumping: *Yes, dear?*

FRED: *You were miles away.*

LAURA: *Was I? Yes, I suppose I was.*

FRED rising: *Do you mind if I turn it down a little — it really is deafening. . . .*

He goes towards the radio.

LAURA with an effort: *Of course not.*

She bends down and starts sewing. FRED turns down the radio, and returns to his place.

FRED: *I shan't be long over this, and then we'll go up to bed. You look a bit tired, you know. . . .*

LAURA: *Don't hurry — I'm perfectly happy.*

She continues her sewing for a moment or two, then she looks up again. FRED's head is down, concentrating on the paper.

LAURA passes her hand across her forehead wearily.

LAURA'S VOICE: *How can I possibly say that? ' Don't hurry, I'm perfectly happy.' If only it were true. Not, I suppose, that anybody is perfectly happy really, but just to be ordinarily contented — to be at peace. It's such a little while ago really, but it seems an eternity since that train went out of the station — taking him away into the darkness.*

Dissolve to LAURA walking in the subway. The sound of her train is heard pulling in overhead.

LAURA'S VOICE: *I went over to the other platform and got into my train as usual.*

Close shot of LAURA in the railway compartment. She is seated in a corner.

LAURA'S VOICE: *This time I didn't attempt to read — even to pretend to read — I didn't care whether people were looking at me or not. I had to think. I should have been utterly wretched and ashamed — I know I should but I wasn't — I felt suddenly quite wildly happy — like a romantic schoolgirl, like a romantic fool! You see he had said he loved me, and I had said I loved him, and it was true — it was true! I imagined him holding me in his arms — I imagined being with him in all sorts of glamorous circumstances. It was one of those absurd fantasies — just like one has when one is a girl — being wooed and married by the ideal of one's dreams — generally a rich and handsome Duke.*

As LAURA turns to look out of the window, the camera tracks and pans slowly forward until the darkened countryside fills the screen.

LAURA'S VOICE: *I stared out of the railway carriage window into the dark and watched the dim trees and the telegraph posts slipping by, and through them I saw Alec and me.*

The countryside fades away and ALEC and LAURA are seen, dancing a gay waltz. The noise of the train recedes, and is replaced by music.

LAURA'S VOICE: *Alec and me — perhaps a little younger than we are now, but just as much in love, and with nothing in the way.*

The sound of the train returns for a moment and the dancing figures fade away. The train noise dies away again, and is replaced by the sound of an orchestra tuning up, as the passing countryside changes to a picture of ALEC and LAURA in a theatre box. ALEC gently takes a beautiful evening cloak from her shoulders and hands her a programme and opera glasses.

LAURA'S VOICE: *I saw us in Paris, in a box at the Opera. The orchestra was tuning up. Then we were in Venice — drifting along the Grand Canal in a gondola.*

LAURA and ALEC are reclining in a gondola. There is the sound of lovely tenor voices and mandolins coming over the water. The scene changes to one of ALEC and LAURA in a car. They are driving through beautiful countryside, and the wind blowing LAURA's hair accentuates the feeling of speed.

LAURA'S VOICE: *I saw us travelling far away together; all the places I have always longed to go.*

We now see the rushing wake of a ship; then a ship's rail.

LAURA'S VOICE: *I saw us leaning on the rail of a ship looking at the sea and the stars — standing on some tropical beach in the moonlight with the palm trees sighing above us. Then the palm trees changed into those pollarded willows by the canal just before the level crossing. . . .*

The camera pulls back from the window of the railway compartment and pans to include LAURA.

LAURA'S VOICE: *. . . and all the silly dreams disappeared, and I got out at Ketchworth and gave up my ticket. . . .*

Dissolve to the booking hall and station yard of Ketchworth Station. LAURA gives up her ticket and walks away across the station yard.

LAURA'S VOICE: *. . . and walked home as usual — quite soberly and without any wings at all.*

Dissolve to the interior of LAURA's bedroom. It is night time. LAURA is seated at her dressing table. The camera shoots on to the mirror of the dressing table.

LAURA'S VOICE: *When I had changed for dinner and was doing my face a bit — do you remember? I don't suppose you do, but I do — you see you don't know that that was the first time in our life together that I had ever lied to you — it started then, the shame of the whole thing, the guiltiness, the fear. . . .*

The reflection of FRED can be seen coming into the bedroom. He comes forward and kisses LAURA lightly.

FRED: *Good evening, Mrs Jesson.*

LAURA: *Hullo, dear.*

FRED: *Had a good day?*

LAURA: *Yes, lovely.*

FRED: *What did you do?*

LAURA: *Well — I shopped — and had lunch — and went to the pictures.*

FRED moving away: *All by yourself?*

LAURA in sudden panic: *Yes — no — that is, not exactly.*

FRED cheerfully: *How do you mean, not exactly?*

LAURA with a rush: *Well I went to the pictures by myself, but I had lunch with Mary Norton at the Kardomah — she couldn't come to the pictures because she had to go and see her in-laws — you know, they live just outside Milford — so I walked with her to the bus and then went off on my own.*

FRED: *I haven't seen Mary Norton for ages. How was she looking?*

LAURA: *She was looking very well really — a little fatter, I think. . . .*

FRED: *Hurry up with all this beautifying — I want my dinner.*

LAURA gaily: *Go on down — I shan't be five minutes. . . .*

> FRED goes out. LAURA sits staring at herself in the glass. She puts her hand to her throat as if she were suffocating.
> Dissolve to a close shot of LAURA at the telephone.

LAURA on the telephone: *Is Mrs Norton there, please? Yes, I'll hold on. Hallo, is that you Mary — no — I know — I haven't seen you for ages. Listen, my dear, will you be a saint and back me up in the most appalling domestic lie?* She laughs forcedly. *Yes— my life depends on it. Yesterday I went into Milford as usual to do my shopping with the special intention of buying a far too expensive present for Fred's birthday.*

> MARY NORTON is at the other end of the telephone, as she stands in the hallway of her house. She is plump and rather blousy.

LAURA off: *Well, Spink and Robson's hadn't got what I wanted which was one of those travelling clocks with the barometer, and everything in one, but they rang up their branch in Broadham, and said that there was one there — so I hopped on to the one-thirty train and went to get it.*

> Resume on LAURA, back in her bedroom.

LAURA: *Now then, this is where the black lie comes in — Fred asked me last night if I had had a good day in Milford, and I said yes, and you and I had lunched together at the Kardomah, and that you had gone off to see your in-laws, and I had gone to the pictures, so if by any chance you should run into him — don't let me down. All right?* She laughs again. *Yes, dear, I promise I'll do the same for you. Yes, that would be lovely. No I can't on Thursday, that's my Milford day. What about Friday? Very well — perfect — Good-bye.*

> She hangs up the telephone and the social smile on her face fades.
> Dissolve to FRED and LAURA's bedroom. The lights are out and she is awake, while FRED is asleep.

LAURA'S VOICE: *That week was misery. I went through it in a sort of trance — how odd of you not to have noticed that you were living with a stranger in the house.*

Dissolve to the exterior of the hospital. It is day time. LAURA is walking up and down outside. (*Still*)

LAURA'S VOICE: *Thursday came at last — I had arranged to meet Alec outside the hospital at twelve-thirty.*

ALEC comes out of the main doors of the hospital and down the steps in the background. He sees LAURA and comes up to her.

ALEC almost breathlessly: *Hullo....*

LAURA with a strained smile: *Hullo....*

ALEC: *I thought you wouldn't come — I've been thinking all the week that you wouldn't come.*

LAURA: *I didn't mean to really — but here I am....*

He takes her arm, they turn and walk away together along the road. The camera follows them, shooting on to their backs from a low angle. The background of the scene is composed of roof-tops and trees.

Dissolve to the Royal Hotel restaurant where LAURA and ALEC are seated at a corner table. A wine waiter is standing beside ALEC, who is examining the wine list. LAURA is looking around the room.

LAURA'S VOICE: *Do you know, I hadn't been inside the Royal since Violet's wedding reception? It all seemed very grand.*

The wine waiter leaves the table.

LAURA'S VOICE: *He actually ordered a bottle of champagne! And when I protested he said that we were only middle-aged once! We were very gay during lunch and talked about quite ordinary things.*

Close shot of ALEC over LAURA'S shoulder.

LAURA'S VOICE: *Oh, Fred, he really was charming — I know you would have liked him if only things had been different.*

Dissolve to the hotel entrance lounge. ALEC and LAURA come into view through the door leading from the restaurant.

LAURA'S VOICE: *As we were going out he said that he had a surprise for me, and that if I would wait in the lounge for five minutes he'd show me what it was.*

ALEC runs down some steps towards the main entrance.

LAURA's VOICE: *He went out and down the steps at a run — more like an excited schoolboy than a respectable doctor.*

LAURA watches ALEC as he leaves the hotel. She turns and the camera focuses on the restaurant doorway out of which are emerging MARY NORTON and MRS ROLANDSON. MARY NORTON's clothes are reasonably good but carelessly worn. MRS ROLANDSON is over smartly dressed; her hat is too young for her, and she gives the impression of being meticulously enamelled. They both recognize LAURA.

LAURA smiles with agonized amiability.

MARY: *Laura, it was you after all! Hermione said it was you but you know how shortsighted I am — I peered and peered and couldn't be sure.*

LAURA, with a bright fixed expression, shakes hands with them both.

LAURA: *I never saw you at all — how dreadful of me — I expect it was the champagne — I'm not used to champagne at lunch — or for dinner either for the matter of that — but Alec insisted. . . .*

MARY: *Alec who, dear?*

LAURA with a gay little laugh: *Alec Harvey of course. Surely you remember the Harveys — I've known them for years.*

MARY: *I don't think I ever. . . .*

LAURA: *He'll be back in a minute — you'll probably recognize him when you peer at him closely. . . .*

MRS ROLANDSON: *He certainly looked very charming and very attentive!*

LAURA: *He's a dear — one of the nicest people in the world and a wonderful doctor.*

ALEC comes bounding back up the steps, and joins the group.

LAURA flashes him one anguished look and then introduces him.

LAURA: *Alec — you remember Mrs Norton, don't you?*

ALEC politely shaking hands: *I . . . er . . . I'm afraid I. . . .*

MARY: *It's no use Laura — we've never met before in our lives — I'm sure we haven't. . . .*

LAURA: *How absurd — I made certain that he and Madeleine were there when you dined with us just before Christmas — Alec — this is Mrs Rolandson.*

MRS ROLANDSON: *How do you do.*

They shake hands. There is a pause.

MRS ROLANDSON: *What horrid weather, isn't it?*
ALEC: *Yes.*
MRS ROLANDSON: *Still, I suppose we can't expect spring at this time of the year, can we?*
ALEC: *No.*
There is another pause.
MARY: *Well, we really must be going — I'm taking Hermione with me to see the in-laws — to give moral support — Good-bye, Doctor Harvey.*
ALEC: *Good-bye.*
They shake hands. (*Still*)
MRS ROLANDSON bowing: *Good-bye. Good-bye, Mrs Jesson.*
LAURA: *Good-bye.*
She smiles pleasantly.
MARY to LAURA: *Good-bye, my dear. I do so envy you and your champagne.*
MARY NORTON and MRS ROLANDSON go out of view towards the steps.
LAURA putting her hands over her face: *That was awful — awful....*
ALEC: *Never mind.*
LAURA: *They had been watching us all through lunch — oh dear....*
ALEC with an attempt at brightness: *Forget it — come out and look at the surprise.*
Dissolve to the exterior of the Royal Hotel. In the foreground of the scene is a small two-seater car, which is parked outside the hotel entrance. ALEC and LAURA come out of the hotel and get into the car.
LAURA'S VOICE: *There at the foot of the steps was a little two-seater car. Alec had borrowed it from Stephen Lynn for the afternoon. We got in in silence and drove away.*
Dissolve to the car driving through the outksirts of Milford.
It pulls up near a small bridge over a stream.
LAURA'S VOICE: *When we were out in the real country — I think it was a few miles beyond Brayfield — we stopped the car just outside a village and got out. There was a little bridge and a stream and the sun was making an effort to come out but really not succeeding very well. We leaned on the parapet of the bridge and looked down into the water. I shivered and Alec put his arm around me.*
LAURA and ALEC are leaning on the bridge, looking down into

the water.

ALEC: *Cold?*

LAURA: *No — not really.*

ALEC: *Happy?*

LAURA: *No — not really.*

ALEC: *I know what you're going to say — that it isn't worth it — that the furtiveness and the necessary lying outweigh the happiness we might have together — wasn't that it?*

LAURA: *Yes. Something like that.*

ALEC: *I want to ask you something — just to reassure myself.*

LAURA *her eyes filling with tears: What is it?*

ALEC: *It is true for you, isn't it? This overwhelming feeling that we have for each other — it is as true for you as it is for me — isn't it?*

LAURA: *Yes — it's true.*

She bursts into tears and ALEC puts his arms closer around her. They stand in silence for a moment and then kiss each other passionately.

Dissolve to another shot of LAURA and ALEC. They are now again leaning on the bridge.

LAURA'S VOICE: *I don't remember how long we stayed on that bridge or what we said. I only remember feeling that I was on the edge of a precipice, terrified yet wanting desperately to throw myself over.*

ALEC and LAURA start to move towards the car.

LAURA'S VOICE: *Finally we got back into the car and arrived at Stephen Lynn's garage just as it was getting dark.*

Dissolve to the inside of a small lock-up garage. The camera is shooting towards the entrance. The car drives into the garage towards the camera and stops. The headlights are turned off and ALEC and LAURA get out. They are silhouetted against the entrance, behind which are the lighted windows of the block of flats.

LAURA'S VOICE: *We put the car away and Alec said he had to leave the keys of the car in Stephen Lynn's flat, and suggested that I came up with him. I refused rather too vehemently. Alec reminded me that Stephen wasn't coming back till late, but I still refused.*

ALEC shuts the garage doors.

Dissolve to the exterior of station approach. LAURA and ALEC are walking along towards the camera. In the background of the scene is a signal box and railway lines. An express can be heard approaching in the distance.

ALEC stopping: *I'm going to miss my train. I'm going back.*

LAURA: *Back where?*

ALEC: *To Stephen's flat.*

LAURA: *Oh, Alec.*

They look at each other as the noise of the express rises to a thundering crescendo out of which emerges the scream of the train whistle.

The express hurtles into the tunnel.

LAURA and ALEC are in each other's arms.

LAURA pushing him away in panic: *I must go now. I really must go home.*

She runs off out of view. ALEC stands watching her.

We see LAURA entering the booking hall, from ALEC's viewpoint.

ALEC turns and walks away.

In the refreshment room LAURA takes a cup of tea over to her usual table.

LAURA'S VOICE: *I got my cup of tea at the counter, and went over to our usual table. Two soldiers came in and started to make a scene at the counter.*

LAURA sits at the table, sipping her tea. Her face looks strained and exhausted.

Cut to MYRTLE, BERYL and the two soldiers, BILL and JOHNNIE, who have just arrived at the counter.

BILL: *Afternoon, lady.*

MYRTLE grandly: *Good afternoon.*

BILL: *A couple of splashes, please.*

MYRTLE: *Very sorry, it's out of hours.*

BILL: *Just sneak us a couple under cover of them poor old sandwiches.*

MYRTLE: *Them sandwiches were fresh this morning, and I shall do no such thing.*

BILL: *Come on, be a sport. You could pop it into a couple of teacups.*

MYRTLE: *You can have as much as you want after six o'clock.*

JOHNNIE: *My throat's like a parrot's cage — listen!*

He makes a crackling noise with his throat.

173

MYRTLE: *I'm sorry — my licence does not permit me to serve alcohol out of hours — that's final! You wouldn't want me to get into trouble, would you?*

BILL: *Give us a chance, lady, that's all — just give us a chance.*

They both roar with laughter.

MYRTLE: *Beryl, ask Mr Godby to come 'ere for a moment, will you?*

BERYL: *Yes, Mrs Bagot.*

She runs out of view towards the platform.

BILL: *Who's 'e when 'e's at home?*

MYRTLE: *You'll soon see — coming in here cheeking me.*

JOHNNIE: *Come off it, mother, be a pal!*

MYRTLE losing her temper: *I'll give you mother, you saucy upstart.*

BILL: *Who are you calling an upstart!*

MYRTLE: *You — and I'll trouble you to get out of here double quick — disturbing the customers and making a nuisance of yourselves.*

JOHNNIE: *'Ere, where's the fire — where's the fire?*

ALBERT enters the refreshment room with BERYL.

ALBERT: *What's going on in 'ere?*

He walks towards the counter.

MYRTLE with dignity: *Mr Godby, these gentlemen are annoying me.*

BILL: *We haven't done anything.*

JOHNNIE: *All we did was ask for a couple of drinks. . . .*

MYRTLE: *They insulted me, Mr Godby.*

JOHNNIE: *We never did nothing of the sort — just 'aving a little joke, that's all.*

ALBERT laconically: *'Op it — both of you.*

BILL: *We've got a right to stay 'ere as long as we like.*

ALBERT: *You 'eard what I said — 'op it!*

JOHNNIE: *What is this, a free country or a bloomin' Sunday school?*

ALBERT firmly: *I checked your passes at the gate — your train's due in a minute — Number 2 platform — 'op it.*

JOHNNIE: *Look 'ere now. . . .*

BILL: *Come on, Johnnie — don't argue with the poor basket.*

ALBERT dangerously: *'Op it!*

BILL and JOHNNIE walk towards the door. JOHNNIE turns.

JOHNNIE: *Toodle-oo, mother, and if them sandwiches were made this morning, you're Shirley Temple. . . .*

They go out.

Resume on ALBERT, MYRTLE and BERYL.

MYRTLE: *Thank you, Albert.*

BERYL: *What a nerve, talking to you like that!*

MYRTLE: *Be quiet, Beryl — pour me out a nip of Three Star — I'm feeling quite upset.*

ALBERT: *I've got to get back to the gate.*

MYRTLE graciously: *I'll be seeing you later, Albert.*

ALBERT with a wink: *Okay!*

> ALBERT goes out of view. BERYL brings MYRTLE a glass of brandy.
>
> Close shot of LAURA. A train bell goes. She fumbles in her bag and finds a cigarette. She lights it. There is the sound of her train approaching.

LOUDSPEAKER ANNOUNCEMENT: *The train now arriving at platform five is the five forty-three for Ketchworth.*

> Train noise is heard.

LAURA'S VOICE: *I really must go home.*

ALEC'S VOICE: *I'm going back to the flat.*

LAURA'S VOICE: *I must go home now, I really must go home.*

ALEC'S VOICE: *I'm going back to the flat.*

LAURA'S VOICE: *I'm going home.*

MYRTLE off: *There's the five forty-three.*

> LAURA sits, puffing her cigarette, listening to her train draw into the station. Suddenly she rises, crushes out her cigarette, grabs her bag, and runs to the door leading to Number 3 platform. She runs across the platform and gets into her train.
>
> Entering a third-class compartment, she sits down next to two women.
>
> She is in a nervous state of indecision. The Guard's whistle blows. After a second or two she suddenly jumps up, and stumbles over the women sitting next to her.

LAURA muttering: *Excuse me, I have forgotten something.*

> She gets out of the train, just as it begins to move off. The camera pans with her as she runs along the platform with the train gathering speed behind her. She runs out of shot towards the barrier, leaving a view of the train as it steams away from the station.

Dissolve to the main entrance hallway and staircase of a block of flats. LAURA comes in from the street. It is raining. She pauses for a moment to examine a board on which are listed the names of the tenants and their flat numbers. She walks up the stairs to the door of Stephen Lynn's flat on the second floor, and rings the bell. ALEC opens the door, and she goes quickly past him into the hall almost without looking at him.

ALEC softly: *Oh, darling, I didn't dare to hope.*

ALEC leads her gently through to the sitting room. It is rather a bleak little room. The furniture looks impersonal. He has lit the fire, but it hasn't had time to get under way and is smoking. They stand quite still for a moment, looking at each other.

LAURA: *It's raining.*

ALEC his eyes never moving from her face: *Is it?*

LAURA: *It started just as I turned out of the High Street.*

ALEC: *You had no umbrella and your coat's wet. . . .*

He gently helps her off with her coat.

ALEC: *You mustn't catch cold — that would never do.*

LAURA looking at herself in the glass over the mantelpiece, and slowly taking off her hat: *I look an absolute fright.*

ALEC taking her hat and her scarf: *Let me put these down.*

LAURA: *Thank you.*

ALEC putting them on a chair near the writing desk with the coat: *I hope the fire will perk up in a few minutes. . . .*

LAURA: *I expect the wood was damp.*

ALEC ruefully: *Yes — I expect it was.*

There is silence.

ALEC: *Do sit down, darling. . . .*

LAURA sits down on the sofa.

LAURA with an attempt at gaiety: *I got right into the train and then got out again — wasn't that idiotic?*

ALEC sitting down next to her and taking her in his arms: *We're both very foolish.*

He kisses her.

LAURA weakly: *Alec — I can't stay you know — really, I can't.*

ALEC: *Just a little while — just a little while. . . .*

There is the sound of the lift gates clanging. They both break apart and look up.

From their view-point we see the flat hallway. There is the sound of a step outside on the landing, and then the sound of a key fitted into the front door.

LAURA and ALEC jump to their feet.

LAURA in a frantic whisper: *Quickly — quickly — I must go. . . .*

ALEC snatches up her hat and coat and pushes them into her hand.

ALEC: *Here — through the kitchen — there's a tradesmen's staircase. . . .*

They rush into the small kitchen where there is a door opening on to the fire escape. ALEC tears it open. LAURA runs through it on to a metal staircase, without even looking back. She disappears down the stairs. ALEC shuts the door quietly after her and leans against it for a moment with his eyes closed.

A MAN'S VOICE from the sitting room: *Is that you, Alec?*

ALEC as casually as he can: *Yes.*

He starts to walk back into the sitting room.

STEPHEN LYNN is standing by the entrance to the hall. He is a thin, rather ascetic-looking man. ALEC walks towards him.

ALEC: *You are back early.*

STEPHEN: *I felt a cold coming on so I denied myself the always questionable pleasure of dining with that arch arguer Roger Hinchley, and decided to come back to bed.* Walking to the chair by the writing desk: *Inflamed membranes are unsympathetic to dialectic —*

ALEC: *What will you do about food?*

STEPHEN smiling: *I can ring down to the restaurant later on if I want anything — we live in a modern age and this is a service flat.*

ALEC with a forced laugh: *Yes — Yes — I know.*

STEPHEN still smiling: *It caters for all tastes.*

He lightly flicks LAURA'S scarf off the chair and hands it to ALEC.

STEPHEN: *You know, Alec, my dear, you have hidden depths that I never even suspected.*

ALEC: *Look here, Stephen, I really. . . .*

STEPHEN holding up his hand: *For heaven's sake, Alec, no explanations or apologies — I am the one who should apologize for having returned so inopportunely — it is quite obvious to me that you were interviewing a patient privately — women are frequently neurotic creatures, and the hospital atmosphere upsets them. From the rather undignified scuffling I heard when I came into the hall, I gather that she beat a hurried retreat down the backstairs. I'm surprised at this farcical streak in your nature, Alec — such carryings on were quite unnecessary — after all, we have known each other for years and I am the most broad-minded of men.*

ALEC *stiffly:* I'm really very sorry, Stephen. I'm sure that the whole situation must seem inexpressibly vulgar to you. Actually it isn't in the least. However, you are perfectly right — explanations are unnecessary — particularly between old friends. I must go now.

STEPHEN *still smiling:* Very well.

ALEC: I'll collect my hat and coat in the hall. Good-bye.

STEPHEN: Perhaps you'd let me have my latch key back? I only have two and I'm so afraid of losing them — you know how absent-minded I am.

ALEC *giving him the key:* You're very angry, aren't you? (*Still*)

STEPHEN: No, Alec — not angry — just disappointed.

ALEC goes out without another word.

In the street outside, the camera is tracking on a close shot of LAURA's legs and feet. She is running fast along the pavement. It is pouring with rain.

Close-up of LAURA, who is still running. The background of the scene is composed of the tops of houses. As she approaches a lamp post, the light increases on her face and dies away quickly as she passes it.

The camera tracks to the pavement from LAURA's angle. Her shadow becomes large and elongated as she moves further away from the lamp post.

Resume on LAURA as she approaches another lamp post. She is out of breath and slows down to a walk.

LAURA'S VOICE: *I ran until I couldn't run any longer — I leant against a lamp post to try to get my breath — I was in one of those side-roads that lead out of the High Street. I know it was stupid to run, but I couldn't help myself.*

Close shot of LAURA as she leans against the lamp post.

LAURA'S VOICE: *I felt so utterly humiliated and defeated and so dreadfully, dreadfully ashamed. After a moment or two I pulled myself together, and walked on in the direction of the station.*

The camera starts to track with her along the street.

LAURA'S VOICE: *It was still raining but not very much. I suddenly realized that I couldn't go home, not until I had got myself under*

*more control, and had a little time to think. Then I thought of you*
*waiting at home for me, and the dinner being spoilt.*

LAURA is now at the telephone in a tobacconist's shop. She looks pale and bedraggled.

LAURA'S VOICE: *So I went into the High Street and found a tobac-conist and telephoned to you — do you remember — ?*

LAURA at the telephone (*Still*): *Fred — is that you?* With a tremendous effort she makes her voice sound ordinary: *Yes, dear — it's me — Laura — Yes — of course everything's perfectly all right, but I shan't be home to dinner — I'm with Miss Lewis, dear — the librarian at Boots I told you about — I can't explain in any detail now because she's just outside the telephone box — but I met her a little while ago in the High Street in the most awful state — her mother has just been taken ill, and I've promised to stay with her until the doctor comes — Yes, dear, I know, but she's always been tremendously kind to me and I'm desperately sorry for her — No — I'll get a sandwich — tell Ethel to leave a little soup for me in a saucepan in the kitchen — Yes, of course — as soon as I can. Good-bye.*

She hangs up the telephone.

LAURA'S VOICE: *It's awfully easy to lie — when you know that you're trusted implicitly — so very easy, and so very degrading.*

She walks slowly out of the telephone box.

The camera is shooting from a high angle on to a road leading off the High Street. It has stopped raining but the pavement is still wet and glistening. LAURA is slowly walking towards the camera.

LAURA'S VOICE: *I started walking without much purpose — I turned out of the High Street almost immediately — I was terrified that I might run into Alec — I was pretty certain that he'd come after me to the station.*

The camera is shooting down on to another street. LAURA is still walking.

LAURA'S VOICE: *I walked for a long while. . . .*

Dissolve to a shot of the war memorial. The foreground of the shot is composed of part of the war memorial statue: a soldier's hand gripping a bayoneted service rifle. Beyond it LAURA is seen as a tiny figure walking towards a seat near the base of the memorial.

LAURA'S VOICE: *Finally, I found myself at the war memorial — you know it's right at the other side of the town. It had stopped raining altogether, and I felt stiflingly hot so I sat down on one of the seats.*
Close shot of LAURA on the seat.
LAURA'S VOICE: *There was nobody about, and I lit a cigarette (Still) — I know how you disapprove of women smoking in the street — I do too, really — but I wanted to calm my nerves and I thought it might help.*
She is now in profile to the camera, and has finished her cigarette.
LAURA'S VOICE: *I sat there for ages — I don't know how long — then I noticed a policeman walking up and down a little way off — he was looking at me rather suspiciously. Presently he came up to me.*
The POLICEMAN walks up into a shot over LAURA's shoulder.
POLICEMAN: *Feeling all right, Miss?*
LAURA faintly: *Yes, thank you.*
POLICEMAN: *Waiting for someone?*
LAURA: *No — I'm not waiting for anyone.*
POLICEMAN: *You don't want to go and catch cold you know — that would never do. It's a damp night to be sitting about on seats, you know.*
LAURA rising: *I'm going now anyhow — I have a train to catch.*
Close shot of LAURA and the POLICEMAN.
POLICEMAN: *You're sure you feel quite all right?*
LAURA: *Yes — quite sure — good night.*
POLICEMAN: *Good night, Miss.*
As LAURA walks off the camera pans and tracks with her, shooting at her back.
LAURA'S VOICE: *I walked away — trying to look casual — knowing that he was watching me. I felt like a criminal. I walked rather quickly back in the direction of the High Street.*

Dissolve to Milford Junction Station. The clock on platforms 2 and 3 forms the foreground of shot. The time is six minutes to ten. LAURA comes up out of the subway in the background and walks along the platform. The station is not very well lit, and there is hardly anyone about.
LAURA'S VOICE: *I got to the station fifteen minutes before the last*

*train to Ketchworth, and then I realized that I had been wandering
about for over three hours, but it didn't seem to be any time at all.*
    LAURA comes into the refreshment room.

    It is nearly closing time, and the room is half-lighted. There is
the melancholy noise of a goods train chugging through the
station. BERYL is draping the things on the counter with muslin
cloths while STANLEY, wearing his ordinary clothes, stands
gossiping with her. LAURA comes in through the door in the
background.

BERYL: *Stan, you are awful!*

STANLEY: *I'll wait for you in the yard.*

BERYL: *Oh, all right.*

    STANLEY goes out.

LAURA: *I'd like a glass of brandy, please.*

BERYL: *We're just closing.*

LAURA: *I see you are, but you're not quite closed yet, are you?*

BERYL sullenly: *Three Star?*

LAURA: *Yes, that'll do.*

BERYL getting it: *Tenpence, please.*

LAURA taking money from her bag: *Here — and — have you a piece
of paper and an envelope?*

BERYL: *I'm afraid you'll have to get that at the bookstall.*

LAURA: *The bookstall's shut — please — it's very important — I
should be so much obliged. . . .*

BERYL: *Oh, all right — wait a minute.*

    BERYL goes out.

    LAURA sips the brandy at the counter. She is obviously trying
to control her nerves. After a moment BERYL can be heard
walking back across the refreshment room. She enters the shot
and puts down some notepaper and an envelope.

LAURA: *Thank you so much.*

BERYL: *We close in a few minutes, you know.*

LAURA: *Yes, I know.*

    BERYL goes out of shot and the camera pans with LAURA as she
takes a few paces along the counter in order to be under the
light. She stares at the paper for a moment, takes another sip
of brandy, and then begins to write.

    BERYL looks at LAURA with exasperation.

    Close shot of LAURA. BERYL can be heard walking away across

the refreshment room and slamming the door at the other end. LAURA falters in her writing, then breaks down and buries her face in her hands. In the background the door to the platform opens and ALEC comes in. He looks hopelessly round for a moment, then, seeing her, walks forward.

ALEC: *Thank God — Oh, darling. . . .*

LAURA: *Please go away — please don't say anything. . . .*

ALEC: *I've been looking for you everywhere — I've watched every train.*

LAURA: *Please go away. . . .*

ALEC: *You're being dreadfully cruel. It was just a beastly accident that he came back early — he doesn't know who you are — he never even saw you.*

LAURA: *I suppose he laughed, didn't he?* Bitterly. *I suppose you spoke of me together as men of the world?*

ALEC: *We didn't speak of you — we spoke of a nameless creature who had no reality at all.*

LAURA: *Why didn't you tell him who I was? Why didn't you tell him we were cheap and low and without courage — why didn't you. . . .*

ALEC: *Stop it, Laura — pull yourself together.*

LAURA: *It's true! Don't you see? It's true. . . .*

ALEC: *We know we really love each other — that's true — that's all that really matters.*

LAURA: *It isn't all that matters — other things matter too, self-respect matters, and decency — I can't go on any longer.*

ALEC: *Could you really say good-bye — not see me any more?*

LAURA: *Yes — if you'd help me.*

ALEC after a pause: *I love you, Laura — I shall love you always until the end of my life — all the shame that the world might force on us couldn't touch the real truth of it. I can't look at you now because I know something — I know that this is the beginning of the end — not the end of my loving you — but the end of our being together. But not quite yet, darling — please not quite yet.*

LAURA in a dead voice: *Very well — not quite yet.*

ALEC: *I know what you feel about this evening — I mean about the beastliness of it. I know about the strain of our different lives; our lives apart from each other. The feeling of guilt, of doing wrong is a little too strong, isn't it? Too persistent? Perhaps too great a price to pay for the few hours of happiness we get out of it. I know all this because it's the same for me too.*

LAURA: *You can look at me now — I'm all right.*

ALEC looking at her: *Let's be careful — let's prepare ourselves — a sudden break now, however brave and admirable, would be too cruel. We can't do such violence to our hearts and minds.*

LAURA: *Very well.*

ALEC: *I'm going away.*

LAURA: *I see.*

ALEC: *But not quite yet.*

LAURA: *Please — not quite yet.*

A train bell goes.

The door leading to the staff-room opens and BERYL comes in.

BERYL: *That's the ten-ten. It's after closing time.*

ALEC: *Oh, it is?*

BERYL: *I shall have to lock up.*

BERYL escorts LAURA and ALEC to the door of Number 3 platform. They go out and the camera remains on BERYL as she slams the door and bolts up.

Outside, LAURA and ALEC walk up and down the platform.

ALEC: *I want you to promise me something.*

LAURA: *What is it?*

ALEC: *Promise me that however unhappy you are, and however much you think things over, that you'll meet me next Thursday.*

LAURA: *Where?*

ALEC: *Outside the hospital — twelve-thirty?*

LAURA: *All right — I promise.*

ALEC: *I've got to talk to you — I've got to explain.*

LAURA: *About going away?*

ALEC: *Yes.*

LAURA: *Where are you going? Where can you go? You can't give up your practice.*

ALEC: *I've had a job offered me. I wasn't going to tell you — I wasn't going to take it — but I know now, that it's the only way out.*

LAURA: *Where?*

ALEC: *A long way away — Johannesburg.*

LAURA stopping still: *Oh, Alec. . . .*

ALEC: *My brother's out there. They're opening a new hospital —*

*they want me in it — it's a fine opportunity really. I'll take Made-
leine and the boys. It's been torturing me — the necessity of making
a decision one way or the other. I haven't told anybody — not even
Madeleine. I couldn't bear the idea of leaving you — but now I see,
it's got to happen soon anyway — it's almost happening already.*
LAURA: *When will you go?*
ALEC: *Almost immediately — in about two weeks' time.*
LAURA: *It's quite near, isn't it?*
ALEC: *Do you want me to stay? Do you want me to turn down the
offer?*
LAURA: *Don't be foolish, Alec.*
ALEC: *I'll do whatever you say.*
LAURA *her eyes filling with tears: That's unkind of you, my darling.*
> Close-up of the station loudspeaker.
LOUDSPEAKER: *The train for Ketchworth, Longdean and Perford is
now entering Number Three platform.*
> A train can be heard entering the station.
> Dissolve to LAURA and ALEC. He opens the door of an empty
> third-class compartment and LAURA gets in. ALEC shuts the
> door after her and LAURA leans out of the open window. (*Still*)
ALEC: *You're not angry with me, are you?*
LAURA: *No, I'm not angry — I don't think I'm anything really —
I feel just tired.*
ALEC: *Forgive me.*
LAURA: *Forgive you for what?*
> Close-up of ALEC over LAURA's shoulder.
ALEC: *For everything — for having met you in the first place —
for taking the piece of grit out of your eye — for loving you — for
bringing you so much misery.*
> Close-up of LAURA over ALEC's shoulder.
LAURA *trying to smile: I'll forgive you — if you'll forgive me.*
> Close-up of ALEC over LAURA's shoulder. There is the sound of
> the guard's whistle and the train starts to move. The camera
> and LAURA track away from ALEC as he stands staring after the
> train which pulls out of the station. Fade out.
LAURA'S VOICE: *All that was a week ago — it is hardly credible that
it should be so short a time.*

> Fade in on hospital. It is day time. LAURA is standing by a lamp

post in the foreground of the shot. After a moment ALEC comes down the hospital steps and joins her.

LAURA'S VOICE: *To-day was our last day together. Our very last together in all our lives. I met him outside the hospital as I had promised at 12.30 — this morning — at 12.30 this morning — that was only this morning.*

Dissolve to ALEC and LAURA sitting in a car.

LAURA'S VOICE: *We drove into the country again, but this time he hired a car. I lit cigarettes for him every now and then as we went along. We didn't talk much — I felt numbed and hardly alive at all. We had lunch in the village pub.*

Dissolve to ALEC and LAURA leaning over the bridge. The car is parked nearby.

LAURA'S VOICE: *Afterwards we went to the same bridge over the stream — the bridge that we had been to before.*

Cut to Milford Junction Station and yard. It is night time. LAURA and ALEC are crossing the station yard towards the booking hall. (*Still*)

LAURA'S VOICE: *Those last few hours together went by so quickly. We walked across the station yard in silence and went into the refreshment room.*

ALEC and LAURA are sitting at the refreshment room table. The voices of ALBERT and MYRTLE fade away to a murmur in the background.

ALEC: *Are you all right, darling?*

LAURA: *Yes, I'm all right.*

ALEC: *I wish I could think of something to say.*

LAURA: *It doesn't matter — not saying anything, I mean.*

ALEC: *I'll miss my train and wait to see you into yours.*

LAURA: *No — no — please don't. I'll come over to your platform with you — I'd rather.*

ALEC: *Very well.*

LAURA: *Do you think we shall ever see each other again?*

ALEC: *I don't know.* His voice breaks. *Not for years anyway.*

LAURA: *The children will all be grown up — I wonder if they'll ever meet and know each other.*

ALEC: *Couldn't I write to you — just once in a while?*

LAURA: *No — please not — we promised we wouldn't.*

ALEC: *Laura, dear, I do love you so very much. I love you with all my heart and soul.*

LAURA *without emotion: I want to die — if only I could die.*

ALEC: *If you died you'd forget me — I want to be remembered.*

LAURA: *Yes, I know — I do too.*

ALEC *glancing at the clock: We've still got a few minutes.*

DOLLY *off: Laura! What a lovely surprise!*

LAURA *dazed: Oh, Dolly!*

> DOLLY *joins* LAURA *and* ALEC.

DOLLY: *My dear, I've been shopping till I'm dropping. My feet are nearly falling off, and my throat's parched, I thought of having tea in Spindle's, but I was terrified of losing the train.*

LAURA'S VOICE: *It was cruel of Fate to be against us right up to the last minute. Dolly Messiter — poor, well-meaning, irritating Dolly Messiter. . . .*

> The camera is slowly tracking in to a close-up of LAURA.

DOLLY: *I'm always missing trains and being late for meals, and Bob gets disagreeable for days at a time.* Her voice is fading away. *He's been getting those dreadful headaches, you know. I've tried to make him see a doctor but he won't.*

> Her voice fades out.

LAURA'S VOICE: *. . . crashing into those last few precious minutes we had together. She chattered and fussed, but I didn't hear what she said. I was dazed and bewildered. Alec behaved so beautifully — with such perfect politeness. Nobody could have guessed what he was really feeling — then the bell went for his train.*

> The platform bell rings.

LAURA: *There's your train.*

ALEC: *Yes, I know.*

DOLLY: *Aren't you coming with us?*

ALEC: *No, I go in the opposite direction. My practice is in Churley.*

DOLLY: *Oh, I see.*

ALEC: *I am a general practitioner at the moment.*

LAURA *dully: Doctor Harvey is going out to Africa next week.*

DOLLY: *Oh, how thrilling.*

> There is the sound of ALEC's train approaching.

ALEC: *I must go.*

LAURA: *Yes, you must.*

ALEC: *Good-bye.*

DOLLY: *Good-bye.*

He shakes hands with DOLLY, and looks swiftly once only at LAURA.

Close-up of LAURA. ALEC's hand comes into the shot and gives her shoulder a little squeeze.

LAURA'S VOICE: *I felt the touch of his hand for a moment and then he walked away.* . . .

ALEC is seen from LAURA's view-point. He crosses the refreshment room and goes out of the door on to the platform.

LAURA'S VOICE: . . . *away — out of my life for ever.*

Close shot of LAURA and DOLLY. LAURA is gazing out of the door through which ALEC has just passed. She seems almost unaware of DOLLY at her side, who proceeds to fumble in her handbag for lipstick and a mirror. DOLLY is chattering, but we do not hear her voice.

LAURA'S VOICE: *Dolly still went on talking, but I wasn't listening to her — I was listening for the sound of his train starting — then it did.* . . .

The sound of ALEC's train is heard as it starts to move out of the station.

Close-up of LAURA.

LAURA'S VOICE: *I said to myself — ' He didn't go — at the last minute his courage failed him — he couldn't have gone — at any moment now he'll come into the refreshment room again pretending that he'd forgotten something.' I prayed for him to do that — just so I could see him once more — for an instant — but the minutes went by.* . . .

There is the sound of the station bell.

Close shot of LAURA and DOLLY.

DOLLY: *Is that the train?*

She addresses MYRTLE.

DOLLY: *Can you tell me, is that the Ketchworth train?*

MYRTLE off: *No, that's the express.*

LAURA: *The boat-train.*

DOLLY: *Oh, yes — that doesn't stop, does it?*

DOLLY gets up and moves out of shot towards the counter.

LAURA jumps to her feet and rushes blindly out of the door leading to Number 2 platform. As the camera pans to the door it goes off level, giving the effect of LAURA running uphill.

She runs out of the refreshment room towards the camera and

the railway lines.

The railway lines are seen from above. An express train hurtles through the scene. The camera is tilted.

Close-up of LAURA from a low angle. She is swaying on the edge of the platform. The lights from the express streak past her face. The noise is deafening. She stands quite still. The lights stop flashing across her face and the sound of the train dies away rapidly. Slowly the camera returns to a normal angle.

LAURA'S VOICE: *I meant to do it, Fred, I really meant to do it — I stood there trembling — right on the edge — but then, just in time I stepped back — I couldn't — I wasn't brave enough — I should like to be able to say that it was the thought of you and the children that prevented me — but it wasn't — I had no thoughts at all — only an overwhelming desire not to be unhappy any more — not to feel anything ever again. I turned and went back into the refreshment room — that's when I nearly fainted. . . .*

Dissolve to the library at LAURA's house. It is night time. Close-up of LAURA, who is sitting with her sewing in her lap. She is staring straight in front of her.

Close-up of FRED, who is looking at her. He continues to look at her in silence for a moment or two.

FRED gently: *Laura!*

She doesn't answer. He gets up.

Close shot of LAURA. FRED kneels beside her and softly touches her hand.

FRED: *Laura. . . .*

LAURA turning her head slowly and looking at him — her voice sounds dead: *Yes, dear?*

FRED: *Whatever your dream was — it wasn't a very happy one, was it?*

LAURA in a whisper: *No.*

FRED: *Is there anything I can do to help?*

LAURA: *Yes, my dear — you always help. . . .*

FRED: *You've been a long way away?*

LAURA nodding, her eyes fill with tears: *Yes, Fred.*

FRED moves a little closer to her and quietly rests his face against her hand.

FRED with a catch in his voice: *Thank you for coming back to me.*

Fade out.

# HENRY V

# THE MAKING OF
# HENRY V

## Laurence Olivier

It is now possible for a new generation of moviegoers, and many of those who enjoyed the earlier version of HENRY V, to set it in a new form. I hope very much that they will enjoy the latest techniques now used in the projection of what was, perhaps, the first serious attempt to make a truly Shakespearian film.

Shakespeare, in a way, "wrote for the films." His splitting up of the action into a multitude of small scenes is almost an anticipation of film technique, and more than one of his plays seems to chafe against the cramping restrictions of the stage.

"Can this cockpit *(a reference to the shape of the Globe Theatre)* hold the vasty fields of France?" asks the Chorus in the Prologue. From the very beginning the play suggests a film. The seed of it is there: "With winged heels, like English Mercuries"; the rapid change of scene: "And thence to France shall we convey you safe, and bring you back."

There were, however, many difficult things to be done. Firstly, there was the question of the script. In its long and chequered career, the play has often been altered alarmingly. In the Restoration period it was mutilated almost out of recognition. Kemble cut the text to tatters, and Fielding wrote scornfully: "Shakespeare is already good enough for people of taste, but he must be altered to the palates of those that have none." Remembering this, we made only a few minute alterations in the text, and the cuts are even less than those invariably made in a stage production.

The settings were a still greater problem. We decided that the treatment would have to be new, yet in keeping with the period. The middle part of the film especially must have the feeling of the fifteenth century, but we could only achieve this if the settings and composition of the shots caught the spirit of contemporary paintings.

Further unknown factors were the conditions of colour and lighting. Artists of Henry V's day drew attention to certain parts of their pictures by using strong colours and shapes. In translating this technique to the screen, a correct balance had to be struck between the colours and forms of the costumes and those of the background.

Our costume designer, Roger Furse, discovered the correct family arms and accoutrements for the knights and soldiers from an old book. He also designed 100 costumes for the thirty principals. The horses had to be correctly caparisoned, and this, too, called for expert knowledge. We made their saddles of wood on the pattern of Henry V's own saddle. By careful choice of fabrics, we kept the costumes as close as possible to fifteenth century originals, which were principally made of woollen cloth and heavy silk. Our colours had to correspond with the vegetable dyes of the Middles Ages, with due allowance for variations in colour photography.

We had to discover the rules as we went along. But rules alone could never have made Henry V live unless we had been lucky enough to assemble such a magnificent cast.

*O for a muse of Fire, that would ascend*
*The brightest heaven of invention:*
*A kingdom for a stage, princes to act,*
*And monarchs to behold the swelling scene!*

# EDITOR'S NOTE

Although Laurence Olivier was faithful to Shakespeare's text on the whole, he cut whole subplots, such as the treason of Lord Scrope and the Earl of Cambridge and Sir Thomas Grey. He also abridged long-winded scenes, such as the Archbishop of Canterbury's exposition of King Henry V's right to the French throne. Occasionally, lines were transposed in their order in the scene, and also given to other players for the sake of 'character' – some of Canterbury's warlike lines, for instance, were given to the Duke of Exeter.

Generally, however, the screenplay is a model of how to adapt a classic stage play to the needs of the cinema. It was adapted by Olivier himself with Alan Dent.

*THE CAST LIST AND THE CREDITS will be found at the end of the screenplay.*

## *Acknowledgements*

Lorrimer Publishing wishes to thank Cyril Howard of the Rank Organisation Plc for his kindness in making available the shooting script of *Henry V*, and the British Film Institute for its provision of the script and the photographic stills for this book, which was edited by Andrew Sinclair.

# HENRY V

*We see an aerial view of London, based on Visscher's engraving of 1600. Track back to show the City in long shot, then track in on the Bear Playhouse and then on to the Globe Playhouse, where a flag is being hoisted.*
*The flag on the Globe Playhouse unfurls and flutters.*
*At the foot of the flagpole inside the Globe, a man on a small platform tightens the rope and makes it secure. He picks up a trumpet and blows two fanfares. Track down to show the theatre orchestra beginning to play in the gallery beneath. Pan left to show people filling the top gallery, then pan round and down to the second gallery. A girl drops a handkerchief out of shot.*
*In the third gallery down, a man catches the handkerchief. Pan left to the ground floor entrance where more people are coming in. An Orange Girl steps down into the theatre.*
*The Orange Girl walks into the theatre offering her wares. Pan with her and track slowly back to reveal an auditorium with the stage in the background. A Prompter gives a signal to the orchestra to play a fanfare.*
*A low angle shot in the orchestra gallery shows a man blowing his trumpet.*
*A Boy comes through the curtains on to the stage and holds a board up to the audience.*
*He swings the board to show the writing on it:*

The Chronicle History of
HENRY THE FIFTH
with his battle fought at Agin Court.

*Seen from the top gallery with the audience in the foreground, the Boy on the stage swings the board and exits through the curtains. Chorus enters and bows while the audience applauds.*

CHORUS: O for a muse of fire . . .

*Cut to him as the voices die. He walks around the stage as he speaks. Pan with him.*

CHORUS: . . . . That would ascend
The brightest heaven of invention:
A kingdom for a stage, princes to act,
And monarchs to behold the swelling scene.
Then should the warlike Harry, like himself,
Assume the port of Mars, and at his heels,
Leashed in like hounds, should famine, sword, and fire,
Crouch for employment. But pardon, gentles all,
The flat unraisèd spirits that hath dared
On this unworthy scaffold to bring forth
So great an object. Can this cockpit hold
The vasty fields of France? Or may we cram
Within this wooden O the very casques
That did affright the air at Agincourt?

*He walks to speak to us in close-up.*

CHORUS: On your imaginary forces work.

*Track back as music begins to play.*

CHORUS: Suppose within the girdle of these walls
Are now confined two mighty monarchies,
Whose high, uprearèd and abutting fronts
The perilous narrow ocean parts asunder.
Piece out our imperfections with your thoughts;
Think, when we talk of horses, that you see them,
Printing their proud hoofs i' th' receiving earth;
For 'tis your thoughts that now must deck our kings,
Carry them here and there, jumping o'er times,
Turning th' accomplishment of many years
Into an hour-glass . . .

*The music stops.*

CHORUS: . . . . For the which supply
Admit me Chorus to this history,
Who, Prologue-like, your humble patience pray
Gently to hear, kindly to judge, our play.

*He bows and pulls the Stage Curtain aside. The music starts as the Boy with a board steps forward and shows his message to the audience.*
*Close on the Boy with the board which reads:–*

## ANTE CHAMBER IN KING HENRY'S PALACE

*Track up to the stage balcony above him. Through curtains at the back, the* ARCHBISHOP OF CANTERBURY *and the* BISHOP OF ELY *enter and bow. The audience applauds as* CANTERBURY *sits down at a table and studies a paper. He bangs his first. The music stops.*

CANTERBURY: My lord, I'll tell you. That same bill is urged
Which in th' eleventh year of the last king's reign
Was like, and had indeed against us passed,
But that the scrambling and unquiet time
Did push it out of farther question.

ELY: But how, my lord, shall we resist it now?

CANTERBURY: It must be thought on. If it pass against us,
We lose the better half of our possession:
For all the temporal lands which men devout
By testament have given to the Church
Would they strip from us. Thus runs the bill.

ELY: This would drink deep.

*The audience laughs.*

CANTERBURY: 'Twould drink the cup and all.

*The audience laughs again.*

ELY: But what prevention?

CANTERBURY: The King is full of grace and fair regard.

ELY: And a true lover of the holy Church.

CANTERBURY: The courses of his youth promised it not.
Since his addiction was to courses vain,
His companies unlettered, rude and shallow,
His hours filled up with riots, banquets, sports,

And never noted in him any study.

ELY: And so the Prince obscured his contemplation
Under the veil of wildness, which, no doubt,
Grew like the summer grass, fastest by night.

*The audience laughs.*

CANTERBURY: The breath no sooner left his father's body,
But that his wildness, mortified in him,
Seemed to die too. [Sir John Falstaff . . . .

*The audience cheers. We see them in a high angle shot.*

CANTERBURY: (*off*) . . . . and all
His company along with him . . . .

*Return to medium shot of* CANTERBURY *and* ELY.

CANTERBURY: . . . . he banished.

*The audience groans, seen in a high angle shot.*
CANTERBURY *and* ELY *continue talking on stage.*

CANTERBURY: Under pain of death not to come near his
person . . . .

*The audience now boos the actors.*

CANTERBURY: (*off*) . . . . By ten mile].*

CANTERBURY *now stands up at the table.*

CANTERBURY: . . . . Yea, at that very moment,
Consideration like an angel came
And whipped the offending Adam out of him;
Never was such a sudden scholar made;
Never came reformation in a flood,
As in this king.

ELY *gravely agrees.*

ELY: We are blessèd in the change.

*The lines in square brackets are not from Shakespeare's play of Henry V.

200

*The audience jeers as* ELY *walks to join* CANTERBURY.

ELY: But, my good lord,
How now for mitigation of this bill
Urged by the Commons? Doth his majesty
Incline to it, or no?

*They sit down.*

CANTERBURY: He seems indifferent;
Or rather swaying more upon our part.
For I have made an offer to his majesty,
As touching France, to give a greater sum
Than ever at one time the clergy yet
Did to his predecessors part withal.

ELY: How did this offer seem received, my lord?

CANTERBURY: With good acceptance of his majesty,
Save that there was not time enough to hear,
As I perceived his grace would fain have done,
Of his true titles to some certain dukedoms,
And generally to the crown and seat of France,
Derived from Edward, his great grandfather.

ELY: What was th' impediment that broke this off?

CANTERBURY: The French ambassador upon that instant
Craved audience . . . .

*The audience chuckles as* CANTERBURY *looks off
screen.*

CANTERBURY: . . . . and the hour I think is come
To give him hearing. Is it four o'clock?

*In his corner, the Prompter gets up from his chair and
peers through a grille in the door at the side of the stage. A
bell rings three, then four times.*
*Return to* CANTERBURY *and* ELY *on the stage balcony.*

ELY: It is.

CANTERBURY *rises from his chair.*

201

CANTERBURY: Then we go in, to know his embassy:
Which I could with a ready guess declare,
Before the Frenchman speak a word of it.

*He goes out, as the music starts.*

ELY: I'll wait upon you, and I long to hear it.

*The audience titters as* ELY *gathers up the documents and follows* CANTERBURY.
CANTERBURY *and* ELY *come down the stairs from the balcony backstage. Track back to reveal the actors getting ready for their entrances. A* Boy *crosses to a fellow youngster to try on a wig.*
*The two* Boys *try out their headgear. One of them has been shaving prior to playing* MISTRESS QUICKLY.
*Backstage, the English* Herald *and four soldiers take up their positions before their stage entrance. A fanfare sounds. They exit and actors playing the* EARLS OF SALISBURY *and* WESTMORELAND *exit right to a fanfare. They are followed by* EXETER *and* GLOUCESTER. *The actor playing* KING HENRY V *enters left.*
*The music stops. He coughs. The music starts.*
*Pan with him as he goes through a door on to the stage. The audience applauds in the background.*
HENRY V *bows as the music stops.*

KING HENRY: Where is my gracious Lord of Canterbury?

EXETER *enters left.*

EXETER: Not here in presence.

KING HENRY: Send for him, good uncle.

HENRY V *goes off and* EXETER *signals a Herald to fetch the Archbishops. The Herald approaches us.*
*Backstage,* ELY *is robing for his entrance. He drinks beer with a fellow-actor.*

WESTMORELAND: (*off*) Shall we call in th' ambassador, my liege?

*Frontstage, the Herald, seen in close shot, signals to*

HENRY V, *as* ELY *prepares to go onstage.*

KING HENRY: Not yet, my cousin, We would be resolved,
Before we hear him, of some things of weight
That task our thoughts, concerning us and France.

> *Backstage,* CANTERBURY *comes up and ushers* ELY *into position. Pan with him as he goes off right with* ELY *following him.*
> *Frontstage,* CANTERBURY *enters, his hand raised in blessing. Pan with him to show* HENRY V *seated on his throne surrounded by his court. He bows to* CANTERBURY.

CANTERBURY: God and his angels guard your sacred throne,
And make you long become it!

KING HENRY: Sure we thank you.

> ELY *enters in a flurry and* HENRY V *acknowledges him. The audience laughs.*

KING HENRY: My learnèd lord, we pray you to proceed,
And justly and religiously unfold
Why the law Salic that they have in France
Or should or should not bar us in our claim.

> *In medium close shot,* HENRY V *rises from his throne and steps down from it. We track back with him.*

KING HENRY: We charge you in the name of God take heed
How you awake the sleeping sword of war:
For never two such kingdoms did contend
Without much fall of blood, whose guiltless drops
Do make such waste in brief mortality.

CANTERBURY: Then hear me, gracious sovereign, and you peers
That owe your selves, your lives, and services
To this imperial throne. There is no bar
To make against your highness' claim to France.

But this, which they produce from Pharamond.

    CANTERBURY *takes a document from* ELY *and quotes.*
    *(STILL)*

CANTERBURY: *'In terram Salicam mulieres ne succedant'*:
'No woman shall succeed in Salic land':
Which 'Salic land' the French unjustly gloss
To be the realm of France.
Yet their own authors faithfully affirm
That the land Salic lies in Germany,
Between the floods of Saala and of Elbe . . . .

    ELY *hands him another document. Pan with*
    CANTERBURY *as he walks to the left.*

CANTERBURY: Where Charles the Great having subdued
the Saxons,
There left behind and settled certain French
Who, holding in disdain the German women
For some dishonest manners of their life,
Established there this law . . . .

    *As the audience titters,* CANTERBURY *turns and walks*
    *back to centre stage. Pan with him. He continues walking*
    *to the right to stop at the edge of the stage.*

CANTERBURY: . . . . To wit, no female
Should be inheritrix in Salic land:
Which is this day in Germany called Meissen.
Then doth it well appear the Salic Law
Was not devisèd for the realm of France
Nor did the French possess the Salic land,
Until four hundred one-and-twenty years
After defunction of . . . .

    *He looks at his document and signals* ELY *to bring*
    *another.*
    ELY *hands another document to* CANTERBURY. *Pan left*
    *to right with him, as the audience titters.*

CANTERBURY: . . . . King Pharamond,
Idly supposed the founder of this law,

King Pepin, which deposèd Childeric,
Did as heir general, being descended
Of Blithild . . . .

> CANTERBURY *hands the paper back to* ELY. *He slaps*
> ELY'S *hand as another document is proffered. Pan right*
> *to left with* CANTERBURY. *He has to return to* ELY *for the*
> *paper and snatches it from him.* ELY *throws the*
> *remainder of the papers in the air.*
> *The audience titters as* CANTERBURY *finds documents*
> *are falling about his ears.*

CANTERBURY: . . . . Which was daughter to . . . .

> *The audience laughs as* ELY *points to the papers on the*
> *floor. Pan down to the document as* CANTERBURY'S
> *hand comes into the shot.*
> CANTERBURY *picks up a paper.* HENRY V *is beside him*
> *and tries to interrupt.* CANTERBURY *turns left and we pan*
> *with him and back again as he walks to the King.*

CANTERBURY: . . . . King Clothair,
Make claim and title to the crown of France.
Hugh Capet also, who usurped the crown
Of Charles the Duke of Lorraine, sole heir male
Of the true line and stock of . . . .

> CANTERBURY *holds out his hand for another paper.*
> *The audience titters as* ELY *points to the floor. Now the*
> *audience laughs.*
> *See in close-up,* CANTERBURY'S *hand comes into shot,*
> *but his wrist is seized by* HENRY V, *who picks up the next*
> *paper. Pan up to both of them.*

CANTERBURY: . . . . Charles the Great,
Could not keep quiet in his conscience,
Wearing the crown of France, still satisfied
That fair . . . .

> ELY *looks for the relevant paper.*

 . . . . that fair . . . .

*The audience roars with laughter.*

CANTERBURY: (*off*) . . . . that fair . . . .

EXETER, CANTERBURY *and* HENRY V *are kneeling on the floor, while* ELY *is beside them.* CANTERBURY *has found a paper.* ELY *finds him another.* (*STILL*) HENRY V *and* EXETER *rise to their feet.*

CANTERBURY: . . . . Queen Isabel, his grandmother,
Was lineal of the . . . . the Lady Ermengard,
Daughter to Charles the foresaid Duke of Lorraine:
So that, as clear as is the summer's sun . . . .

*The audience laughs.*

. . . . all appear
To hold in right and title of the female:
So do the Kings of France unto this day,
Howbeit, they would hold up this Salic Law
To bar your highness claiming from the female.

HENRY V *and* EXETER *help* CANTERBURY *to his feet. Track in on* HENRY V *as he interrupts* CANTERBURY.

KING HENRY: May I with right and conscience make this claim?

CANTERBURY: The sin upon my head, dread sovereign!

ELY *holds up a Bible for* CANTERBURY.

CANTERBURY: For in the Book of Numbers it is writ,
'When the son dies, let the inheritance
Descend unto the daughter.'

EXETER: (*off*) Gracious Lord, stand for your own.

EXETER *is now seen in close-up.*

EXETER: Look back into your mighty ancestors:
Go, my dread lord, to your great-grandsire's tomb,
From whom you claim; invoke his warlike spirit
And your great-uncle's, Edward . . . .

HENRY V *is in close-up.*

EXETER: (*off*) . . . . the Black Prince.

SALISBURY: (*off*) Your brother kings and monarchs of . . . .

> *Cut to* SALISBURY *and* WESTMORELAND. *Pan with* SALISBURY *as he walks to the left.*

. . . . the earth
Do all expect that you should rouse yourself
As did the former lions of your blood.

> WESTMORELAND *walks up to join him.*

WESTMORELAND: They know your grace hath cause and means and might;
So hath your highness. Never King of England
Had nobles richer and more loyal subjects,
Whose hearts have left their bodies here in England,
And lie pavilioned in the fields of France.

> *A hand taps him on the shoulder. Pan left to reveal* CANTERBURY.

CANTERBURY: O let their bodies follow my dear liege
With blood and sword and fire, to win your right.
In aid whereof . . . .

> ELY *joins* CANTERBURY.

CANTERBURY: . . . . We of the spirituality
Will raise your highness such a mighty sum
As never did the clergy at one time
Bring in to any of your ancestors.

> HENRY V *is in close-up.*

KING HENRY: Call in the messengers sent from the Dauphin.

> *A fanfare sounds as* CANTERBURY *and* ELY *stand aside.* HENRY V *walks to the throne.*

KING HENRY: Now we are well resolved, and, by God's help,

And yours, the noble sinews of our power,
France being ours, we'll bend it to our awe,
Or lay these bones in an unworthy urn,
Tombless, with no remembrance over them.

*The fanfare concludes as the English Herald and the
French Herald enter through a door at the side of the
stage, followed by the French* AMBASSADOR, *the* DUKE
OF BERRI, *and two pages carrying a casket. Track back
to reveal the stage in long shot.*

KING HENRY: : Now are we well prepared to know the
pleasure
Of our fair cousin Dauphin, for we hear
Your greeting is from him, not from the King.

MOUNTJOY, *the French Herald, bows.*

MOUNTJOY: May't please your majesty to give us leave
Freely to render what we have in charge,
Or shall we sparingly show you far off
The Dauphin's meaning and our embassy?

KING HENRY: We are no tyrant, but a Christian king,
Therefore with frank and with uncurbèd plainness
Tell us the Dauphin's mind.

*The French* AMBASSADOR *bows.*

AMBASSADOR: . . . . Thus then in few . . . .

*Seen in medium close shot, the French* AMBASSADOR
*speaks:*

AMBASSADOR: . . . . Your highness lately sending into
France
Did claim some certain dukedoms, in the right
Of your great predecessor, King Edward the Third.
In answer of which claim, the Prince our master
Says that you savour too much of your youth,
He therefore sends you fitter for your study
This tun of treasure . . . .

*The two pages carry the casket round to the front of the
throne.*

208

AMBASSADOR: . . . . and in lieu of this
Desires you let the dukedoms that you claim
Hear no more of you. This the Dauphin speaks.

*HENRY V leans over to EXETER on his left.*

KING HENRY: What treasure, uncle?

*EXETER opens the casket and closes it quickly.*

EXETER: Tennis balls, my liege.

*There is a nervous giggle from the audience.*
*HENRY V is seen in close-up seated on his throne. He*
*shows no anger.*

KING HENRY: We are glad the Dauphin is so pleasant with
us
His present and your pains we thank you for . . . .

*Track back as HENRY V springs to his feet.*

KING HENRY: When we have matched our rackets to these
balls,
We will in France, by God's grace, play a set
Shall strike his father's crown into the hazard.
Tell him, he hath made a match with such a wrangler
That all the courts of France will be disturbed
With chases . . . .

*HENRY V steps down from the throne. Pan with him as he*
*walks to the right of the stage.*

KING HENRY: . . . . And we understand him well
How he comes o'er us with our wilder days,
Not measuring what use we made of them.
But tell the Dauphin we will keep our state,
Be like a king, and show our sail of greatness,
When we do rouse us in our throne of France . . . .

*He turns. Pan with him as he walks back to centre stage.*

KING HENRY: . . . . And tell the pleasant Prince, this
mock of his
Hath turned these balls to gun-stones, and his soul
Shall stand sore-chargèd for the wasteful vengeance

That shall fly from them: for many a thousand
widows . . . .

*Pan with him as he walks to the left.*

KING HENRY: . . . . Shall this his mock mock out of their
dear husbands,
Mock mothers from their sons, mock castles down:
Ay, some are yet ungotten and unborn
That shall have cause to curse the Dauphin's scorn.

*He turns and walks right to stage centre and back to his
throne, turning when he reaches it. Pan with him and
track back to show all the stage.*

KING HENRY: But this lies all within the will of God,
To whom we do appeal, and in whose name
Tell you the Dauphin, we are coming on
To venge us as we may, and to put forth
Our rightful hand in a well-hallowed cause.
So get you hence in peace and tell the Dauphin
His jest will savour but of shallow wit,
When thousands weep more than did laugh at it.
Convey them with safe conduct. Fare you well.

*HENRY V bows to the applause of the audience as the
French AMBASSADOR and the Heralds exit on the right.
He goes to sit down on his throne.*
*HENRY V now sits down on his throne with EXETER
standing on the left.*

EXETER: This was a merry message.

*HENRY V rises and takes off his crown. Pan with him as
he walks to the left and pauses in front of the door leading
from the stage.*

KING HENRY: We hope to make the sender blush at it.
Therefore, let our proportions for these wars
Be soon collected, and all things thought upon
That may with reasonable swiftness add
More feathers to our wings: for, God before,
We'll chide this Dauphin at his father's door.

HENRY V *bows and goes out through the door. The musicians strike up and the audience applauds.*
CHORUS *comes through the other door and draws the curtain across the inner stage. Pan left to right with him. He turns and walks upstage and throws open his arms as he starts speaking. The music and the applause stop.*

CHORUS: Now all the youth of England are on fire,
And silken dalliance in the wardrobe lies;
Now thrive the armourers, and honour's thought
Reigns solely in the breast of every man:
They sell the pasture now to buy the horse,
Following the mirror of all Christian kings
With wingèd heels, as English Mercuries.

CHORUS *throws up his hands and starts to walk away. Pan left with him until he stands in long shot. He throws up his hands again.*

CHORUS: For now sits expectation in the air
And hides a sword, from hilts unto the point
With crowns imperial, crowns and coronets,
Promised to Harry and his followers.
Linger your patience on, for, if we may,
We'll not offend one stomach with our play.

*The audience applauds as* CHORUS *bows and goes out through the door behind him. Two stagehands enter with bundles of rough grass. They look skywards. There is a roll of thunder.*
*Clouds are covering the sun.*
*A high angle shot shows the theatre audience. It starts to rain. Some of the audience go home. A* BOY *with a billboard appears on the balcony in the foreground. There is the sound of rain and of grumbling people.*
*Medium close shot of the* BOY *displaying the billboard to the audience: it reads:–*

### THE BOAR'S HEAD
*He hangs it on a bracket, bows and exits through curtains behind him. Pan with him, then track in to the balcony and curtains.* NYM *pokes his head through the curtains*

*and furtively climbs over the balcony and drops out of shot.*
*Now* NYM *drops into shot.* BARDOLPH *is standing on stage.*

BARDOLPH: Well met, Corporal Nym.

NYM *gets up from the floor of the stage. Pan up to reveal* BARDOLPH *and track back as* BARDOLPH *steps forward.*

NYM: Good morrow, Lieutenant Bardolph.

BARDOLPH: What, are Ensign Pistol and you friends yet?

NYM: For my part, I care not. I say little, but when time shall serve . . . .

NYM *prods* BARDOLPH'S *arm. Pan as* BARDOLPH *walks round* NYM.

BARDOLPH: I will bestow a breakfast to make you friends, and we'll be all three sworn brothers to France. Let it be so, good Corporal Nym.

NYM: Well, I cannot tell.

BARDOLPH: It is certain, Corporal, that he is married to Nell Quickly, and certainly she did you wrong, for you were betrothed to her.

NYM *prods* BARDOLPH's *arm.*

NYM: Things must be as they may. Men may sleep, and they may have their throats about them at that time, and some say knives have edges. Well, I cannot tell.

BARDOLPH *shudders.* NYM *crosses in front of him. The music begins.*

BARDOLPH: Here comes Pistol and his wife. Good corporal, good corporal, be patient here.

BARDOLPH *ushers* NYM *to the side of the stage.*
*The audience in the foreground applauds the actors on stage.* PISTOL *and* MISTRESS QUICKLY *come through the door in the background. Track in to them as* PISTOL

*flourishes his hat.*
*The audience on the edge of the stage applauds ecstatically.*
PISTOL *flourishes his hat. Pan with him up to*
BARDOLPH.

BARDOLPH: How now, mine host Pistol?

*The music stops as* PISTOL *steps back in disgust.*

PISTOL: Base tyke, call'st thou me host?

*The audience laughs.*

PISTOL: Now by this hand I swear I scorn the title . . . .

*He walks over to* MISTRESS QUICKLY.

PISTOL: Nor shall my Nell keep lodgers.

*The audience laughs as* NYM *crosses his legs and rubs his
hands smugly.*

MISTRESS QUICKLY: (*off*) No, by my troth, not long.

MISTRESS QUICKLY *and* PISTOL *are seen in a medium
close shot.*

MISTRESS QUICKLY: For we cannot lodge and board a
dozen or fourteen gentlewomen that live honestly by the
prick of their needles, but it will be thought we keep a
bawdy house, straight.

PISTOL *leads her by the hand over to* NYM. *Pan right with
them, as the audience titters.*

PISTOL: (*slapping Nym on the shoulder*) O hound of Crete,
think'st thou my spouse to get? I have and I will hold my
honey queen and there's enough. Go to.

NYM: I will prick your guts a little, and that's the truth of it.

*The audience laughs.*

PISTOL: Ha!

MISTRESS QUICKLY *runs to the lip of the stage.*

MISTRESS QUICKLY: Well-a-day, Lady, we shall see wilful

murder and adultery committed.

BARDOLPH *comes into shot as the audience laughs.*

BARDOLPH: Good corporal, good lieutenant, offer nothing here.

NYM *draws his sword.*

NYM: Pish!

PISTOL: Pish for thee, Iceland dog! Thou prick-eared cur of Iceland!

*As the audience laughs,* MISTRESS QUICKLY *walks back to* NYM.

MISTRESS QUICKLY: Good corporal Nym, show thy valour, put up thy sword.

*She helps him to sheath his sword.*

NYM: I will cut thy throat one time or other in fair terms.

PISTOL *crows and brandishes his sword. He comes down to the lip of the stage, then back to the group again. Pan with him as the audience laughs.*

PISTOL: Ha! I can take! Now Pistol's cock is up, and flashing fire will follow.

BARDOLPH *draws his sword.*

BARDOLPH: Hear me, hear me what I say. He that strikes the first stroke, I'll.run him up to the hilts, as I'm a s-s-s-soldier.

PISTOL *walks away from the group. Pan with him as he addresses the audience in the theatre.*

PISTOL: An oath of mickle might, and fury shall abate.

*The audience laughs as* PISTOL *turns round.*

BOY: (*off*) Mine host Pistol . . . .

*The* BOY *on the balcony is seen in a low angle shot.*

BOY: . . . . You must come to Sir John Falstaff.

*The music starts as* PISTOL *comes into shot with* MISTRESS QUICKLY *on the right, followed by* BARDOLPH.

BOY: . . . And you, hostess. He's very sick and would to bed. Good Bardolph, put thy face between his sheets and do the office of a warming-pan.

BARDOLPH: Away, you rogue!

BOY: Faith, he's very ill.

*The* BOY *leaves the balcony. Pan down to show the three below.*

MISTRESS QUICKLY: By my troth, the King has killed his heart. Good husband, come home presently.

MISTRESS QUICKLY *goes out. The music stops.* BARDOLPH *takes* PISTOL *by the arm and leads him over to* NYM.

BARDOLPH: Come, shall I make you two friends? We must to France together. Why the devil should we keep knives to cut one another's throats?

PISTOL: Let floods o'erswell, and fiends for food howl on!

*The audience giggles.*

NYM: You'll pay me the eight shillings I won of you at betting?

PISTOL: Base is the slave that pays.

*The audience laughs.*

NYM: Now that will I have. That's the humour of it.

PISTOL: *(drawing his sword)* As manhood shall compound. Push home.

*The audience laughs, and* BARDOLPH *draws his sword. (STILL)*

BARDOLPH: By this sword, he that makes the first thrust, I'll kill him. By this s-s-sword I will.

*The audience giggles.*

PISTOL: Sword is an oath, and oaths must have their course.

*The audience laughs, as* PISTOL *moves over to the front of the stage to address the audience.*
BARDOLPH *and* NYM *confront each other.*

BARDOLPH: Corporal Nym, an thou wilt be friends, be friends. An thou wilt not, why then, be enemies with me too. Prithee, put up.

BARDOLPH *slaps* NYM'S *sword with his own.* PISTOL *comes into shot.*
MISTRESS QUICKLY *now appears on the balcony.*
*The music soon begins.*

MISTRESS QUICKLY: As ever you come of women, come in quickly to Sir John. He's so shaked of a burning quotidian fever, it's lamentable to behold. Sweet men, come to him.

*She beckons to them, then goes through the curtains behind her. Track back to reveal* BARDOLPH, PISTOL *and* NYM *looking up at the balcony.*

NYM: The King hath run bad humours on the knight.

PISTOL *lays his right hand on* NYM'S *shoulder.*

PISTOL: Nym, thou hast spoke the right. His heart is fracted and corroborate.

BARDOLPH: The King is a good King, but it must be as it may. He passes some humours.

PISTOL *takes a step forward.*

PISTOL: Let us condole the knight. For, lambkins, we will live.

*He turns round and places a hand on* BARDOLPH'S *and* NYM'S *shoulders, who also turn round. As the audience*

216

*applauds, they bow and flourish their hats. Track right
back to reveal the theatre. The three actors make their exit
through a door, as attendants sweep away the rushes on
the floor and* CHORUS *pulls across the proscenium arch a
curtain depicting Southampton.*
CHORUS *stands in front of the Southampton curtain. He
steps forward to address the theatre audience. The music
begins.*

CHORUS: Linger your patience on and we'll digest
Th' abuse of distance. Force a play.
The King is set from London, and the scene
Is now transported, gentles, to Southampton.
There is the playhouse now, there must you sit,
And thence to France . . . .

> CHORUS *walks back and indicates the curtain. He goes
> out of shot. Track up to the theatre curtain, and dissolve
> to:*
> *A model shot of the City of Southampton in 1415 A.D.,
> exactly as depicted on the curtain. Track on, then pan to
> reveal the stern of a ship, and Southampton quay. The*
> ARCHBISHOP OF CANTERBURY *is giving benediction to
> the kneeling* KING HENRY *and his knights.* HENRY V
> *rises.*

CHORUS: *(off)* . . . shall we convey you safe,
And bring you back charming the narrow seas
To give you gentle pass. And here till then,
Unto Southampton do we shift our scene.

> HENRY V *steps down to the deck of the ship. Track with
> him as he walks to the mast. The music stops.* (STILL)

KING HENRY: Now sits the wind fair.

> *He turns and walks back to a group of noblemen,
> including* EXETER, WESTMORELAND, GLOUCESTER,
> *and* SALISBURY.

KING HENRY: Uncle of Exeter,

Set free the man committed yesterday,
That railed against our person. We consider
It was the heat of wine that set him on,
And, on his wiser thought, we pardon him.

EXETER: That's mercy, but too much security.

WESTMORELAND: Let him be punished, sovereign, lest example
Breed, by his sufferance, more of such a kind.

KING HENRY: O let us yet be merciful . . . .

*He turns to* CANTERBURY *just behind him.*

KING HENRY: . . . . We doubt not now
But every rub is smoothèd on our way.

*HENRY V mounts the gangplank.*

KING HENRY: Then forth, dear countrymen.

*As the soldiers cheer, HENRY V steps ashore, followed by*
CANTERBURY *and the nobles. He walks along the quay
to a table.*

KING HENRY: Let us deliver
Our puissance into the hand of God,
Putting it straight in expedition.
Cheerly to sea the signs of war advance . . . .

*The soldiers cheer as* HENRY V *takes a seal and stamps a
paper on the table.*

KING HENRY: No King of England, if not King of France.

*He turns and walks away followed by* CANTERBURY *and
the nobles.*
*Music starts as we dissolve to the sign of THE BOAR'S
HEAD at night.*

CHORUS: *(off)* Still be kind,
And eke out our performance with your mind.

*The illusion that we have returned to the Globe Theatre is
dissolved with a dissolve to the real upper window of an*

*inn, as it is opened by* MISTRESS QUICKLY. *Track up to,
and through the window. An old man is lying in bed in the
room.* MISTRESS QUICKLY *is by the bed. She goes out
through a door on the right.* SIR JOHN FALSTAFF, *the old
man, struggles and sits up in bed. He is in delirium.*

FALSTAFF: God save thy Grace – King Hal – my royal Hal,
God save thee my sweet boy:
My King, my Jove, I speak to thee my heart.

*Track slowly in on* FALSTAFF, *till he is in close-up during*
HENRY V'S *speech.*

KING HENRY: *(off and distant)*
I know thee not, old man, fall to thy prayers.
How ill white hairs become a fool and jester!
I have long dreamed of such a kind of man,
So surfeit swelled, so old and so profane,
But being awaked I do despise my dream.
Reply not to me with a foolish jest,
Presume not that I am the thing I was;
For God doth know, so shall the world perceive
That I have turned away my former self
So shall I those that kept me company.*

*FALSTAFF sinks back on to the pillow, fumbling
convulsively with the sheets.
Now we see a low angle shot of* FALSTAFF *in profile with*
MISTRESS QUICKLY *at the bedside.* (STILL)
*Dissolve to the street outside* THE BOAR'S HEAD *inn.
The street door opens and* NYM, *the* BOY, BARDOLPH
*and* PISTOL *come out. They are followed out by*
MISTRESS QUICKLY *on the balcony.* (STILL) *She comes
down to join them sitting on straw. She touches* PISTOL'S
*arm. The music stops.*

MISTRESS QUICKLY: Prithee, honey, sweet husband, let
me bring thee to Staines.

*Track in on the group as* PISTOL *rouses himself.*

*These lines are taken from Shakespeare's Henry IV, Part Two.*

219

PISTOL: No, for my manly heart doth yearn. Bardolph, be blithe. Nym, rouse thy vaunting veins! Boy, bristle thy courage up. For Falstaff, he is dead. And we must yearn therefore.

BOY: Well, Sir John is gone, God be with him!

*MISTRESS QUICKLY sits down on a stool.* (STILL)

BARDOLPH: Would I were with him wheresome'er he is, either in heaven or in hell.

*Track very slowly up to* MISTRESS QUICKLY.

MISTRESS QUICKLY: Nay, sure he's not in hell. He's in Arthur's bosom. He made a finer end, and went away an it had been any christom child. He parted e'en just betwixt twelve and one, e'en at the turning o' the tide. For after I saw him fumble with the sheets, and play with flowers, and smile upon his fingers' end, I knew there was no way but one. For his nose was now as sharp as a pen, and he babbled of green fields. 'How now, Sir John?' quoth I: 'What, man? Be o' good cheer!' So he cried out: 'God, God, God!' three or four times. And I, to comfort him, bid him he should not think of God. I hoped there was no need to trouble himself with any such thoughts yet. So he bade me lay more clothes on his feet. I put my hand into the bed and felt them, and they were as cold as any stone. Then I felt to his knees . . .

*She touches* PISTOL'S *knee. Track slowly back to show the group again.*

MISTRESS QUICKLY: . . . And they were as cold as any stone, and so upwards and upwards, and all was cold as any stone.

NYM *wipes his nose.*

NYM: They say he cried out for sack.

MISTRESS QUICKLY: Ay, that he did.

BARDOLPH: And for women.

MISTRESS QUICKLY: Nay, that he did not.

BARDOLPH: Ay, that he did! And he said they were devils incarnate.

BOY: He said once, the devil would have him about women.

MISTRESS QUICKLY: He did in some sort, indeed, handle women; but then he was rheumatic. He spoke of the Whore of Babylon.

BOY: Do you not remember, he saw a flea stick up on Bardolph's nose, and said it was a black soul burning in hell-fire.

BARDOLPH: Well, the fuel is gone that maintained that fire. That's all the riches I got in his service.

*NYM stirs and picks up his helmet.*

NYM: Shall we shog? The King will be gone from Southampton.

*PISTOL rouses himself, then turns to MISTRESS QUICKLY.*

PISTOL: Come, let's away. My love, give me thy lips. Look to my chattels and my moveables. Go, clear thy crystals . . . .

*He turns to NYM, BARDOLPH and the BOY.*

PISTOL: . . . Yoke-fellows in arms,
Let us to France, like horse-leeches, my boys,
To suck, to suck, the very blood to suck!

*He signals to BARDOLPH.*

PISTOL: Touch her soft lips and part.

*The music starts.*

BARDOLPH: Farewell, hostess.

*BARDOLPH kisses MISTRESS QUICKLY and goes out, putting on his helmet. NYM moves to go. PISTOL growls at him.*

PISTOL: Huh!

*NYM turns to say goodbye to* MISTRESS QUICKLY. *He kisses his hand to her.*

NYM: I cannot kiss, that's the humour of it, but adieu.

PISTOL *embraces his wife.*

PISTOL: Let housewifery appear. Keep close, I thee command.

*He goes out. The* BOY *runs forward to* MISTRESS QUICKLY, *and she kisses his head. The* BOY *runs out.* PISTOL *and Company are walking along the street away from the inn.* PISTOL *turns and waves his helmet.*

PISTOL: Farewell, farewell, divine Zenocrate –
Is it not passing brave to be a King
And ride in triumph through Persepolis!

*As he finishes quoting Marlowe's lines,* MISTRESS QUICKLY *comes into the foreground.* PISTOL *turns and continues up the street, and* MISTRESS QUICKLY *looks up to* FALSTAFF'S *window. Pan up with her look to centre on the window. The curtain is drawn across it as the music stops, and we fade out.*
*The voice of* CHORUS *is heard over a black screen.*

CHORUS: Thus with imagined wing our scene flies swift.
As that of thought . . .

*Fade in slowly as the music starts, to show* CHORUS *leaning against a dark misty background.*
*Track slowly back as he speaks.*

CHORUS: . . . Suppose that you have seen
The well-appointed King at Hampton Pier
Embark his royalty, and his brave fleet
Play with your fancies; and in them behold
Upon the hempen tackle ship-boys climbing;
Hear the shrill whistle, which doth order give
To sounds confused; behold the threaden sails,
Born with th' invisible and creeping wind,

Draw the huge vessels through the furrowed sea . . .

*He extends his arms, as the mist obscures him.*

CHORUS: . . . Breasting the lofty surge. O do but think
You stand upon the shore and thence behold . . .

*He swings round, now back to us, and is completely
blotted out by mist. A fleet of ships becomes visible
through the mist.*
*Track forward over the model shot of the fleet.*

CHORUS: . . . A city on th' inconstant billows dancing,
Holding due course to Harfleur. Follow, follow!
And leave your England as dead midnight still,
Guarded with grandsires, babies, and old women,
For who is he, whose chin is but enriched
With one appearing hair, that will not follow
These culled and choice-drawn cavaliers to France?

*Dissolve to a long shot of a model of the Palace of the
King of France.*
*Dissolve to a high angle shot inside the Palace, and slowly
track down to ground level where the French* KING
CHARLES *is seated at the base of a pillar. The room is in
the shape of an apse with gothic windows and stone
staircases.*

CHORUS: . . . The French, advised by good intelligence
Of this most dreadful preparation,
Shake in their fear, and with pale policy,
Seek to divert the English purposes.

KING CHARLES *looks nervously off screen, then turns
back again. The music stops.*

KING CHARLES: Thus comes the English with full power
upon us,
And more than carefully it us concerns
To answer royally in our defences.
Therefore, you Dukes of Berri . . .

*As* KING CHARLES *points left, we cut to the* DUKE OF

BERRI *reading at a lectern. He turns to look right.*

KING CHARLES: *(off)* . . . and of Bourbon . . .

*Pan down to show the* DUKE OF BOURBON.

KING CHARLES: *(off)* . . . Lord Constable . . .

*Pan up and right to show the* CONSTABLE *of France.*

KING CHARLES: *(off)* . . . and Orléans shall make forth
. . .

*Continue panning right to show the* DUKE OF ORLEANS.
*Pan with* KING CHARLES, *seen in close-up, as he points
to the left and rises and walks across the palace room. The*
DAUPHIN *is standing at a window in the background.*

KING CHARLES: . . . And you, Prince Dauphin, with all
swift despatch,
To line and new-repair our towns of war
With men of courage, and with means defendant.

KING CHARLES *has turned round and goes out right.*

DAUPHIN: My most redoubted father,
It is most meet we arm us 'gainst the foe.

*The* DAUPHIN *steps down from the window place.*

DAUPHIN: And let us do it with no show of fear,
No, with no more than if we heard that England
Were busied with a Whitsun morris dance.
For, my good liege; she is so idly kinged
By a vain, giddy, shallow, humorous youth,
That fear attends her not.

CONSTABLE: *(off)* O peace, Prince Dauphin!

*The* DAUPHIN *looks round. The* CONSTABLE *of France
steps down and walks right to the* DAUPHIN. *Pan with
him to leave them standing together. The* CONSTABLE
*smiles at* ORLEANS *as he walks past.*

CONSTABLE: You are too much mistaken in this King.
Question your grace our late ambassadors

224

With what great state he heard their embassy,
How well supplied with agèd counsellors,
How terrible in constant resolution.

DAUPHIN: Well, 'tis not so, my Lord Constable,
But though we think it so, it is no matter.
In cases of defence, 'tis best to weigh
The enemy more mighty than he seems.

   The CONSTABLE *bows slightly.*

KING CHARLES: *(off)* And he is bred out of . . .

   The CONSTABLE *and the* DAUPIN *look right.*
   KING CHARLES *is seated on some stone steps.*

KING CHARLES: . . . that bloody strain
That haunted us in our familiar paths,
When Crécy battle fatally was struck,
And all our Princes captured by the hand
Of that black name, Edward, Black Prince of Wales . . .

   KING CHARLES *shivers and crosses himself.*

KING CHARLES: . . . This is a stem
Of that victorious stock; and let us fear
The native mightiness and fate of him.

   *At the sudden sound of a fanfare of trumpets,* KING
   CHARLES *looks up, startled.*
   *The Dukes of France are seated about in the middle. A*
   MESSENGER *dashes in up the staircase on the left of the
   apse.*

MESSENGER: Ambassadors from Harry, King of England,
Do crave admittance to your majesty.

   KING CHARLES *comes into shot in the foreground, his
   back to us.*

KING CHARLES: We'll give them present audience.
Go and bring them.

   KING CHARLES *points irritably at the* MESSENGER, *then
   turns and scampers to his throne. Track with his*

*movements as the music starts.* KING CHARLES *sits on the throne and an Attendant proffers the casket containing the Crown Jewels.*
KING CHARLES *takes the crown and puts it on his head. The* DAUPHIN *comes in left. The King impatiently continues to put on his regalia.*

DAUPHIN: Good, my sovereign.
Take up the English short, and let them know
Of what a monarchy you are the head.
Self-love, my liege, is not so vile a sin
As self-neglecting.

KING CHARLES *and the* DAUPHIN *look left on the sound of another fanfare. The English and French Heralds come up the staircase followed by* EXETER *and* ERPINGHAM. *Track back as the Heralds take up position on either side of the throne.* EXETER *turns to address the King. The sound of the trumpet ceases.* (STILL)

KING CHARLES: From our brother England?

EXETER: From him, and thus he greets your majesty:
He wills you, in the name of God Almighty,
That you divest yourself and lay apart
The borrowed glories that by gift of heaven,
By law of nature and of nations, 'longs
To him and to his heirs, namely the crown,
Willing you overlook this pedigree . . .

EXETER *indicates a document. Two Messengers unfurl it and hold it up before the throne.*

EXETER: . . . And when you find him evenly derived
From his most famed of famous ancestors,
Edward the Third, he bids you then resign
Your crown and kingdom, indirectly held . . .

KING CHARLES *fingers his crown.*

EXETER: . . . From him, the native and true challenger.

KING CHARLES *of France is seen in close-up.*

KING CHARLES: If not, what follows?

EXETER: Bloody constraint. For if you hide the crown
Even in your hearts, there will he rake for it.
Therefore in fierce tempest is he coming,
In thunder and in earthquake, like a Jove;
That, if requiring fail, he will compel.
This is his claim, his threatening, and my message;
Unless the Dauphin . . .

> *He glances to right and left.*
> KING CHARLES *has the* DAUPHIN *beside him. He edges
> the* DAUPHIN *out of shot on the right.*

EXETER: *(off)* . . . be in presence here,
To whom expressly I bring greeting too.

> KING CHARLES *lays his hand on his breast, then points to
> the left.*

KING CHARLES: For us, we will consider of this further:
Tomorrow shall you bear our full intent
Back to our brother England.

> *The* DAUPHIN *is now seen in medium shot.*

DAUPHIN: For the Dauphin,
I stand here for him. What to him from England?

> EXETER *joins the* DAUPHIN .

EXETER: Scorn and defiance, slight regard, contempt,
And anything that may not misbecome
The mighty sender, doth he prize you at.
Thus says my King; an if your father's highness
Do not, in grant of all demands at large,
Sweeten the bitter mock you sent his Majesty,
He'll make your Paris Louvre shake for it.

> KING CHARLES *now joins them.*

KING CHARLES: Tomorrow shall you know our mind at
full.

EXETER: Dispatch us with all speed, lest that our King

Come here himself to question our delay.

*KING CHARLES faints. As the music begins, we dissolve to:*
*A stormy sea, then dissolve again to:*
*English soldiers are storming Harfleur Beach. (STILL)*
*Then dissolve again to:*
*A few soldiers are hauling a cannon ashore up the beach.*

CHORUS: *(off)*
Work, work your thoughts, and therein see a siege.
Behold the ordnance on their carriages
With fatal mouths gaping on girded Harfleur.

*Track forward as English foot soldiers appear round the cliff in retreat. HENRY V rides round on horseback. (STILL)*
*HENRY V takes off his helmet.*
*The King rides up to his men.*

KING HENRY: Once more unto the breach, dear friends, once more,
Or close the wall up with our English dead.

*The music stops as HENRY V rides into shot from the left, then from the right.*

KING HENRY: In peace there's nothing so becomes a man
As modest stillness, and humility,
But when the blast of war blows in our ears,
Then imitate the action of the tiger.
Stiffen the sinews, conjure up the blood,
Disguise fair nature with hard-favoured rage.
Then lend the eye a terrible aspect.

*Track back slowly until the King is seen in long shot.*
*(STILL)*

KING HENRY: Let it pry through the portage of the head
Like a brass cannon, let the brow o'erwhelm it
As fearfully as doth a gallèd rock
O'erhang and jutty his confounded base,
Swilled with the wild and wasteful ocean.

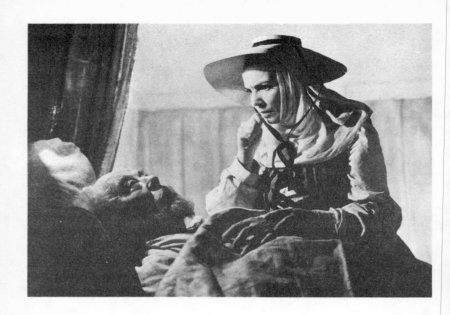

Now set the teeth and stretch the nostril wide,
Hold hard the breath, and bend up every spirit
To his full height. On, on, you noblest English,
Whose blood is fet from fathers of war-proof,
Fathers that like so many Alexanders
Have in these parts from morn till even fought,
And sheathed their swords for lack of argument.
Dishonour not your mothers; now attest
That those whom you called fathers did beget you.
Be copy now to men of grosser blood,
And teach them how to war. And you, good yeomen,
Whose limbs were made in England, show us here
The mettle of your pasture; let us swear
That you are worth your breeding, which I doubt not;
For there is none of you so mean and base
That hath not noble lustre in your eyes.
I see you stand like greyhounds in the slips,
Straining upon the start. The game's afoot.
Follow your spirit, and upon this charge
Cry, 'God for Harry, England and Saint . . .

KING HENRY'S *horse rears and he rides away, followed
by cheering soldiers.*

KING HENRY: . . . George!

*The music strikes up as the soldiers chant:*

SOLDIERS: God for Harry, England and Saint George!

*From a high angle, track down as the soldiers rush up to
the breach.*
BARDOLPH *stands on a rock, waving them on.*

BARDOLPH: On! On! On! On to the breach, to the breach!

BARDOLPH *drops into shot from the rock and takes
refuge beside* PISTOL, NYM *and the* BOY.

NYM : Pray thee, corporal, stay. The knocks are too hot.

*Pan with* PISTOL *as he rises.*

PISTOL: Ah, knocks they come and go;

237

God's vassals drop and die;
And sword and shield
In bloody field
Doth win immortal fame.

*He springs back as a horse leaps from the rock.*
NYM *and the* BOY *shelter by each other.*

NYM: 'Tis honour, and that's the truth of it.

BOY: Would I were in an alehouse in London. I would give all my fame for a pot of ale, and safety.

FLUELLEN: *(off)* God's plud!

*Pan with* FLUELLEN *as he pulls* NYM *and the* BOY *to their feet and kicks them up to the breach.*

FLUELLEN: Up to the breach, you dogs! Avaunt, you cullions!

FLUELLEN *sees* PISTOL *hiding behind the rock.*

FLUELLEN: Ah!

PISTOL: Be merciful, great duke, to men of mould. Abate thy rage, abate thy manly rage.

FLUELLEN: On, on!

*He slashes at* PISTOL *with the flat of his sword.*

PISTOL: Abate thy rage . . .

*Dissolve to a close-up of a flaming linstock touching the powder box of a cannon. Track with its recoil from the explosion.*

CHORUS: *(off)* . . . And the nimble gunner
With linstock now the devilish cannon touches.

*Dissolve to a wall of masonry crashing.*

CHORUS: *(off)* And down goes all before them.

*Dissolve to a bivouac, outside which Captain* GOWER *appears. The music stops.*

238

GOWER: Captain Fluellen!

*Track back to show* FLUELLEN *sitting at a table in the bivouac.*

GOWER: Captain Fluellen, you must come presently to the mines. The Duke of Gloucester would speak with you.

FLUELLEN: To the mines? Tell you the Duke, it is not so good to come to the mines! For look you, the mines is not according to the disciplines of war! The concavities of it is not sufficient. For look you, th' athversary, you may discuss unto the Duke, look you, is digt himself, four yards under the countermines. By Cheshu, I think he will plow up all, if there is not better directions.

GOWER: The Duke of Gloucester, to whom the order of the siege is given, is altogether directed by an Irishman, a very valiant gentleman, i' faith.

FLUELLEN: It is Captain MacMorris, is it not?

GOWER: I think it be.

FLUELLEN: By Cheshu, he is an ass, as in the world. I will verify as much in his beard. He has no more directions in the true disciplines of the wars, look you, of the Roman disciplines, than is a puppy dog.

GOWER *looks right and behind him.*

GOWER: Here he comes, and the Scots captain, Captain Jamy, with him.

FLUELLEN: Ah, Captain Jamy is a marvellous falorous gentleman, that is certain, and of great expedition and knowledge in th' ancient wars.

*Pan slightly right as* CAPTAIN JAMY *and* MACMORRIS *enter.*

JAMY: I say gud day, Captain Fluellen.

FLUELLEN: Gooden to your worship, good Captain James. Captain Jamy is a marvellous falorous gentleman, that is certain.

JAMY *laughs.*

GOWER: How now Captain . . .

MACMORRIS *is seen in close-up.*

GOWER: . . . MacMorris, have you quit the mines? Have the pioneers given o'er?
MACMORRIS: By the Saints, 'tish ill done. The work ish give over, the trumpet sound the retreat. By my hand I swear . . .

*Pan left as he walks to* FLUELLEN.

MACMORRIS: . . . And by my father's soul, tish ill done. The work ish give over. I would have blowed up the town, so God save me, in an hour! O 'tish ill done, by my hand, 'tish ill done!

*Pan right with him as he walks to lean his head against a tree trunk.* (STILL)
JAMY *and* FLUELLEN *are sympathetic.*

FLUELLEN: Captain MacMorris, I beseech you now, will you vouchsafe me, look you, a few disputations with you, partly . . .

*Seen in close-up,* MACMORRIS *leans his head against the tree trunk.*

FLUELLEN: *(off)* . . . to satisfy my opinion, and partly for the satisfaction, look you, of my mind . . . .

JAMY *and* FLUELLEN *watch the sad* MACMORRIS.

FLUELLEN: . . . as touching the direction of the military discipline, that is the point.

JAMY: It shall be very gud, gud faith, gud captains both, and I would fain hear some discourse between you twae!

JAMY *and* FLUELLEN *giggle together.*
*Cut to* GOWER *with* MACMORRIS *standing behind him.*

MACMORRIS: This is no time to discourse, so God save me!

*Pan with him as he walks back to* FLUELLEN.

MACMORRIS: The day is hot, and the weather and the wars and the King and the Dukes. This is no time to discourse. The town is besieched. An the trumpet call us to the breach, and we talk, and by the Holy do nothing, 'tis a shame for us all. So God sa' me . . .

*Pan with him as he walks back to* GOWER.

MACMORRIS: . . . 'Tis a shame to stand still, 'tis a shame by my hand. And there is throats to be cut . . .

*Pan again as he walks back to the table and flops down on it.*

MACMORRIS: . . . And works to be done, and nothing ish done, so help me God!

JAMY *laughs and leans back. Cut to a close-up of him.*

JAMY: By the mess, ere these eyes of mine take themselves to slumber, ay'll de gud service, or ay'll lie i' th' grund for it. Ay, or go to death, and I'll pay't as valorously as I may, that sall I surely do, that is the breff and the long of it.

*Track back to show* JAMY, FLUELLEN *and* MACMORRIS *around the table.*

FLUELLEN: Captain MacMorris, I think, look you, under your correction, there is not many of your nation –

MACMORRIS: Of my nation? What ish my nation? Ish a villain and a bastard and a knave and a rascal? What ish my nation? Who talks of my nation?

FLUELLEN: Look you, if you take the matter otherwise than is meant, Captain MacMorris, peradventure I shall think you do not use me with that affability as in discretion you ought to use me, look you, being as good a man as . . .

FLUELLEN *jumps up into shot in close-up.*

FLUELLEN: . . . yourself, both in the disciplines of war and the derivation of my birth and other particularities.

MACMORRIS'S *head enters the shot.*

MACMORRIS: I do not know you so good a man as myself
. . . so God save me and I will cut off your head.

*Track back as* GOWER *joins them.*

GOWER: Gentlemen both, you will mistake each other.

JAMY: *(laughs)* That's a foul fault.

*He laughs again as a trumpet sounds.*

GOWER: The town sounds a parley.

*The four Captains cheer and grab their helmets.*
*Dissolve to a long shot outside the gates of Harfleur.*
KING HENRY *at the head of his army addresses the*
GOVERNOR *on the city walls. Track in slowly.*

KING HENRY: How yet resolves the Governor of the town?
This is the latest parley we'll admit.

GOVERNOR OF HARFLEUR: Our expectation hath this day
an end.
The Dauphin, of whom succour we entreated,
Returns us word his powers are yet not ready,
To raise so great a siege. Therefore, dread King,
We yield our town and lives to your soft mercy.
Enter our gates, dispose of us and ours.
For we no longer are defensible.

*Seen from a high angle,* KING HENRY *commands at the*
*gates of Harfleur.*

KING HENRY: Open your gates!

GLOUCESTER *stands beside the King.*

KING HENRY: Come, brother Gloucester,
Go you and enter Harfleur. There remain
And fortify it strongly 'gainst the French.
Use mercy to them all. For us, dear brother,
The winter coming on, and sickness growing
Upon our soldiers, we will retire to Calais.

Tonight in Harfleur will we be your guest.
Tomorrow for the march are we addressed.

*To the sound of martial music,* GLOUCESTER *leads the English Army into Harfleur.* HENRY V *watches them. Pan right as he turns and surveys the country ahead. Dissolve to the model shot of the French Palace. Then dissolve again to the door of the Garden Terrace of the Palace. The door opens.* LADY ALICE *followed by* PRINCESS KATHERINE *comes through. A fanfare sounds.* (STILL) PRINCESS KATHERINE *looks over the balcony.*
*From a high angle shot of the Palace Courtyard, we see* MOUNTJOY *escorting* EXETER *and his party. They wait for the gates to be opened.*
MOUNTJOY, EXETER *and his party acknowledge the* PRINCESS *on the balcony.*
KATHERINE *watches the party leave. She turns and walks off shot.*
*She walks down the terrace into the garden, followed by* ALICE.

KATHARINE: Alice, tu as été en Angleterre, et tu bien parles le langage.

ALICE: Un peu, Madame.

KATHARINE: Je te prie, m'enseignez. Il faut que j'apprenne à parler. Comment appelez-vous la main en anglais?

ALICE: La main? Elle est appelée *de hand*.

KATHARINE: *De hand*. Et les doigts?

ALICE: Les doigts? Ma foi, j'oublie les doigts, mais je me souviendrai. Les doigts? Je pense qu'ils sont appelés *de fingres*. Oui, *de fingres*.

KATHARINE: La main, *de hand,* les doigts, *de fingres*. Je pense que je suis le bon écolier; j'ai gagné deux mots d'anglais vitement. Comment appelez-vous les ongles?

ALICE: Les ongles? Nous les appelons *de nails*.

KATHARINE: *De nails*. Écoutez; dites-moi si je parle bien: *de hand, de fingres, de nails*.

ALICE: Ah! C'est bien dit, madame. Il est fort bon anglais.

KATHARINE: Dites-moi l'anglais pour le bras.

ALICE: *De arm*, madame.

KATHARINE: Et le coude?

ALICE: *De elbow*.

KATHARINE: *De elbow*. Je m'en fais la répétition de tous les mots que vous m'avez appris dès à présent.

ALICE: Ça c'est trop difficile, madame, comme je pense.

KATHERINE: Excusez-moi, Alice. Ecoutez: *de hand, de fingres, de nails, de arm, de bilbow*.

ALICE: *De elbow*, sauf votre honneur.

KATHERINE: O Seigneur Dieu, je m'en oublie! *De elbow*. Comment appelez-vous le col?

ALICE: *De nick*.

KATHARINE: *De nick*. Et le menton?

ALICE: *De chin*.

KATHARINE: *De sin*. Le col, *de nick*, le menton, *de sin*.

KATHERINE *has been cutting flowers, and she moves on with* ALICE *following her.*

ALICE: Sauf votre honneur, en vérité, vous prononcez les mots aussi droit que les natifs d'Angleterre.

KATHARINE: Je ne doute point d'apprendre, par la grâce de Dieu, et en peu de temps.

ALICE: N'avez-vous pas déjà oublié ce que je vous ai enseigné?

KATHARINE: Non, je réciterai à vous promptement: *de*

*hand, de fingres, de mails –*

ALICE: *De nails*, madame.

KATHARINE: *De nails, de arm, de bilbow –*

ALICE: Sauf votre honneur, *de elbow*.

KATHARINE: Ainsi dis-je. *De elbow, de nick*, et *de sin*.

KATHARINE *walks right away from* ALICE, *Pan with her.*

KATHARINE: Comment appelez-vous le pied et la robe?

ALICE *speaks after the* PRINCESS.

ALICE: *De foot*, et *de cown*!

ALICE *comes up to the* PRINCESS. *They sit down.* (STILL)

KATHERINE: Oh Seigneur Dieu! Ce sont mots de son mauvais, corruptible, gros, et impudique, et non pour les dames d'honneur d'user. Je ne voudrais pronouncer ces mots devant les seigneurs de France pour tout le monde. Foh! *De foot* et *de cown*! Néanmoins, je réciterai une autre fois ma leçon ensemble: *de hand, de fingres, de nails, de arm, de elbow, de nick, de sin, de foot, de cown.*

ALICE: Oh, Madame, c'est excellent.

KATHARINE: C'est assez pour une fois. Allons-nous à dîner.

*The music starts as they rise and walk to the garden gate and go through on to the terrace. Pan with them as they go. A fanfare sounds, and* KATHARINE *looks over the balcony.*
*Close on* KATHERINE *looking over the balcony.*
*A high angle shot of the courtyard shows us* MOUNTJOY *returning through the gate alone.*
KATHARINE *now looks up to the horizon.*
ESSEX *and his party are riding away in the distance.*
KATHARINE *turns away from the balcony and walks*

*through a door into the Palace. She is followed by* LADY ALICE.

*Inside the French Palace,* KATHARINE *and* ALICE *descend the stairs to the floor of the Banqueting Hall.* (STILL) *At a table at the back,* KING CHARLES, QUEEN ISABEL, *the* DAUPHIN, *the* CONSTABLE, *and the* DUKES OF BOURBON *and* ORLEANS *are seated.*

KING CHARLES: 'Tis certain he hath passed the river Somme.

CONSTABLE: And if he be not fought withal, my lord,
Let us not live in France; let us quit all
And give our vineyards to a barbarous people.

*Track in to feature* BOURBON, KATHARINE *and* ALICE *behind him on the stairs.*

BOURBON: Normans, but bastard Normans. Norman bastards!

ALICE *screams. The music stops.* BOURBON *looks right. He looks left.*

BOURBON: Mort de ma vie!

*He stands up. The music starts.*
KATHARINE *and* ALICE *walk round and take their places at table beside the* QUEEN.
*The* CONSTABLE, ORLEANS *and* BOURBON *sit down.*

BOURBON: If they march along
Unfought withal, then I will sell my dukedom,
To buy a slobbery and dirty farm,
In that nook-shotten isle of Albion.

ORLEANS: Dieu de batailles! Where have they this mettle?
Is not their climate foggy, raw and dull,
On whom as in despite the sun looks pale,
Killing their fruit with frowns?
And shall our quick blood, spirited with wine,
Seem frosty?

BOURBON: By faith and honour,

246

Our madams mock at us and plainly say
Our mettle is bred out, and they will give
Their bodies to the lust of English youth,
To new-store France with bastard warriers.

> QUEEN ISABEL *screams off. The music stops.*
> *Feature the Queen of France,* KATHARINE, *and* ALICE *at*
> *the table. The* QUEEN *pokes* KING CHARLES *on the arm.*
> KING CHARLES *wakes up.*

KING CHARLES: Where is Mountjoy the Herald? Speed
him hence.
Let him greet England with our sharp defiance.

> *We see* KING CHARLES *and his Court seated at table in*
> *long shot. The King of France rises.*

KING CHARLES: . . . Up, princes, and with spirit of
honour edged . . .

> *The three Dukes get up and come down in front of the*
> *table.*

KING CHARLES: . . . Bar Harry England, that sweeps
through our land
With pennons painted in the blood of Harfleur.
Go down upon him, you have power enough,
And in a captive chariot into Rouen
Bring him our prisoner.

CONSTABLE: This becomes the great.
Sorry am I his numbers are so few,
His soldiers sick and famished in their march,
For I am sure, when he shall see our army,
He'll drop his heart into the sink of fear
And for achievement, offer us his ransom.

KING CHARLES: Therefore, Lord Constable, haste on
Mountjoy.

> *The music starts as the three Dukes walk off left. Pan with*
> KING CHARLES *as he turns and walks over to the*
> DAUPHIN.

KING CHARLES: Prince Dauphin, you shall stay with us in Rouen.

DAUPHIN: Not so, I do beseech your majesty.

KING CHARLES: Be patient, for you shall remain with us.

*KING CHARLES turns left.*

KING CHARLES: Now forth, Lord Constable and princes all,
And quickly bring us word of England's fall.

*KING CHARLES turns back to the DAUPHIN and kisses him.*
*Dissolve to the fields of Picardy. MOUNTJOY, preceded by two Heralds and followed by his Standard Bearer, rides up. The Heralds sound a fanfare as MOUNTJOY and the Standard Bearer ride off.*
*KING HENRY V is surrounded by knights. He steps forward as MOUNTJOY and the Standard Bearer ride in. The music stops.*

MOUNTJOY: You know me by my habit.

KING HENRY: Well, then, I know thee. What shall I know of thee?

*We feature MOUNTJOY and the Standard Bearer with KING HENRY on their left in the foreground.*

MOUNTJOY: My master's mind.

KING HENRY: Unfold it.

MOUNTJOY: Thus says my King: 'Say thou to Harry of England: Though we seemed dead, we did but slumber. Tell him we could have rebuked him at Harfleur, but that we thought not good to bruise an injury till it were full ripe. Now we speak upon our cue, and our voice is imperial. England shall repent his folly, see his weakness, and admire our sufferance. Bid him therefore consider of his ransom . . .

*KING HENRY is seen in medium close-up with*

MOUNTJOY *on his right in the foreground..*

MOUNTJOY: . . . Which must proportion the losses we have borne, the subjects we have lost, the disgrace we have digested.

MOUNTJOY *is now in close-up.*

MOUNTJOY: For our losses, his exchequer is too poor; for the effusion of our blood, the muster of his kingdom too faint a number; and for our disgrace, his own person . . .

HENRY V *is now in close-up.*

MOUNTJOY: *(off)* . . . kneeling at our feet, but a weak and worthless satisfaction.

*Resume shot of* MOUNTJOY *and the Standard Bearer with* KING HENRY *on their left.*

MOUNTJOY: To this add defiance, and tell him for conclusion, he hath betrayed his followers, whose condemnation is pronounced. So far my King and master. So much my office.

KING HENRY: What is thy name? I know thy quality.

MOUNTJOY: Mountjoy.

*Resume shot of* KING HENRY *with* MOUNTJOY, *on his right.*

HERALD: *(aside to King Henry)* Mountjoy.

KING HENRY: Thou dost thy office fairly. Turn thee back
And tell thy King I do not seek him now,
But could be willing to march on to Calais
Without impeachment . . .

*Resume shot of* MOUNTJOY *and the Standard Bearer with* KING HENRY *on their left.*

KING HENRY: . . . For, to say the sooth,
My people are with sickness much enfeebled,
My numbers lessened . . .
Go, therefore, tell thy master here I am:

My ransom is this frail and worthless body;
My army, but a weak and sickly guard.

> HENRY V *is seen in close-up.*

KING HENRY: Yet, God before, tell him we will come on,
Though France herself and such another neighbour
Stand in our way . . .
If we may pass, we will; if we be hindered,
We shall your tawny ground with your red blood
Discolour: and so, Mountjoy . . .

> *Resume shot of* MOUNTJOY *and the Standard Bearer
> with* KING HENRY *on their left.*

KING HENRY: . . . Fare you well.
We would not seek a battle as we are,
Nor as we are we say we will not shun it.

> HENRY V *is seen again in close-up.*

KING HENRY: So tell your master.

> MOUNTJOY *flourishes his hat.*

MOUNTJOY: I shall deliver so.

> HENRY V *takes and throws a purse of money.*

KING HENRY: There's for thy labour, Mountjoy.

> MOUNTJOY *catches the purse and rides out followed by
> his Standard Bearer.*

MOUNTJOY: Thanks to your highness.

> *As a fanfare sounds, we feature* HENRY V *and*
> GLOUCESTER. *The King turns to a knight behind him.*

KING HENRY: March to the bridge!

> *A drum roll starts.*

KING HENRY: It now draws towards night.
Beyond the river we'll encamp ourselves,
And on the morrow bid them march away.

KING HENRY, GLOUCESTER *and the army move off.*
*Dissolve to the English army marching wearily away
along the bank of a river in Picardy.*
*As the drum roll stops, fade out to a black screen, over
which the voice of* CHORUS *is heard, accompanied by
music.*

CHORUS: *(off)* Now entertain conjecture of a time
When creeping murmur and the poring dark
Fills the wide vessel of the universe.

*Fade in on a long shot of the French and the English
camps at night.*

CHORUS: *(off)* From camp to camp through the foul womb
of night,
The hum of either army stilly sounds;
That the fixed sentinels almost receive
The secret whispers of each other's watch.
Fire answers fire, and through their paly flames
Each battle sees the other's umbered face.
Steed threatens steed, in high and boastful neighs
Piercing the night's dull ear, and from the tents
The armourers, accomplishing the knights,
With busy hammers closing rivets up,
Give dreadful note of preparation.

*Track in to the French camp.*

CHORUS: Proud of their numbers and secure in soul,
The confident and overlusty French
Do the low-rated English play at dice,
And chide the cripple tardy-gaited night,
Who like a foul and ugly witch doth limp
So tediously away.

*On the sound of a fanfare, dissolve to a shot of the*
CONSTABLE'S *armour inside the tent of the* DUKE OF
ORLEANS. *The music stops.*
*On to the* CONSTABLE *seated at a dining table.*

CONSTABLE: Tut! I have the best armour of the world.

251

*Track back to reveal the* DUKES OF ORLEANS *and* BOURBON.

CONSTABLE: Would it were day!

ORLEANS: You have an excellent armour. But let my horse have his due.

CONSTABLE: It is the best horse of Europe.

BOURBON: Will it never be morning?

*The* DAUPHIN *enters.*

DAUPHIN: My Lord Orléans, my Lord High Constable, you talk of horse and armour?

*The* DUKES *rise.*

ORLEANS: You are as well provided of both as any prince in the world.

*The* DAUPHIN *motions them to sit down and they do so.*

DAUPHIN: What a long night is this! I will not change my horse with any that treads on four hooves. Ça, ha! He bounds from the earth.

*Track in to feature the* DAUPHIN *and the* CONSTABLE.

DAUPHIN: When I bestride him, I soar, I am a hawk; he trots the air, the earth sings when he touches it, he is of the colour of nutmeg. And of the heat of the ginger. He is pure air and fire, and all other jades you may call beasts.

CONSTABLE: It is indeed, my lord, a most absolute and excellent horse.

DAUPHIN: It is the prince of palfreys.

*Pan with the* DAUPHIN *as he walks behind* ORLEANS *and* BOURBON.

DAUPHIN: His neigh is like the bidding of a monarch, and his countenance enforces homage.

BOURBON: No more, cousin.

DAUPHIN: Nay, cousin, the man hath no wit that cannot from the rising of the lark to the lodging of the lamb vary deserved praise on my palfrey.

*Track back to include the whole group as the* DAUPHIN *walks round to the front of the table.* (STILL)

DAUPHIN: I once writ a sonnet in his praise. It began thus, 'Wonder of nature' –

BOURBON: I have heard a sonnet begin so to one's mistress.

DAUPHIN: Then did they imitate that which I composed to my courser, for my horse is my mistress.

CONSTABLE: Methought yesterday your mistress shrewdly shook your back.

ORLEANS: My Lord Constable, the armour that I saw in your tent tonight, are those stars or suns upon it?

CONSTABLE: Stars, my lord.

DAUPHIN: Some of them will fall tomorrow, I hope.

CONSTABLE: That may be.

DAUPHIN: *(looking out of the tent)* Will it never be day?

*Track back as he turns round.*

DAUPHIN: I will trot tomorrow a mile, and my way shall be paved with English faces. Who'll go hazard with me for twenty prisoners?

*There is the sound of a fanfare.*

BOURBON: 'Tis midnight.

DAUPHIN: I'll go arm myself.

*He goes out.*

ORLEANS: Ha! The Dauphin longs for morning.

BOURBON *gets up from the table and walks left to the tent opening.*

BOURBON: He longs to eat the English.

CONSTABLE: I think he will eat all he kills.

ORLEANS: He never did harm, that I heard of.

CONSTABLE: Nor will do none tomorrow. He'll keep that good name still.

ORLEANS: I know him to be valiant.

CONSTABLE: I was told that, by one that knows him better than you.

ORLEANS: What's he?

CONSTABLE: Marry, he told me so himself.

ORLEANS *laughs.*

CONSTABLE: And he said he cared not who knew it.

A MESSENGER *enters and bows down to the* CONSTABLE.

MESSENGER: My Lord High Constable . . .

*The* MESSENGER *and the* CONSTABLE *are seen in close-up.*

MESSENGER: . . . The English lie within fifteen hundred paces of your tents.

CONSTABLE: Who hath measured the ground?

MESSENGER: The Lord Grandpré.

CONSTABLE: A valiant and most expert gentleman.

*The* MESSENGER *withdraws, leaving the* CONSTABLE *and the Dukes.*

CONSTABLE: *(getting up)* Would it were day!

*He turns left to the tent opening. A fanfare sounds as he walks out of the tent.*

CONSTABLE: Alas, poor Harry of England. He longs not for the dawning as we do.

*The* DUKES OF ORLÉANS *and* BOURBON *follow the*

CONSTABLE *outside the tent. It is night. They stand overlooking the English camp in the distance. Another fanfare sounds.*

ORLEANS: What a wretched and peevish fellow is this King of England, to mope with his fat-brained followers so far out of his knowledge.

CONSTABLE: If the English had any apprehension, they'd run away.

ORLEANS: That they lack. For if their heads had any intellectual armour, they could never wear such heavy headpieces.

BOURBON: That island of England breeds very valiant creatures. Their mastiffs are of unmatchable courage.

ORLEANS: Foolish curs, that run winking into the mouth of a Russian bear, and have their heads crushed like rotten apples. You may as well say, 'That's a valiant flea, that dare eat his breakfast on the lip of a lion.'

CONSTABLE: Just, just. And the men are like the mastiffs, give them great meals of beef, and iron and steel, they'll eat like wolves and fight like devils.

ORLEANS: Ah, but those English are shrewdly out of beef.

BOURBON: Then shall we find tomorrow, they have only stomachs to eat, and none to fight.

*Another fanfare sounds.*

CONSTABLE: Now it is time to arm. Come, shall we about it?

*They turn and go back into the tent.*

ORLEANS: It is now two o'clock. But, let me see – by ten we shall have each a hundred Englishmen.

ORLEANS *drops the tent flap.*
*Fade out, then fade in to a long shot of the French camp at night. Then pan slowly left in the direction of the English*

*camp. Music begins.*

CHORUS: *(off)* The country cocks do crow, the clocks do toll
And the third hour of drowsy morning name.
The poor condemnèd English,
Like sacrifices, by their watchful fires
Sit patiently and inly ruminate
The morning's danger; and their gesture sad,
Investing lank lean cheeks and war-worn coats,
Presenteth them unto the gazing moon
So many horrid ghosts.

*We hold the English camp in centre frame and track in.*

CHORUS: *(off)* O now, who will behold
The royal captain of this ruined band
Walking from watch to watch, from tent to tent,
Let him cry, 'Praise and glory on his head!'

*Dissolve to the English camp where we track in slowly to hold an English Soldier warming himself by a brazier.*

CHORUS: *(off)* For forth he goes and visits all his host,
Bids them good morrow with a modest smile
And calls them brothers, friends and countrymen.
A largess universal, like the sun,
His liberal eye doth give to everyone,
Thawing cold fear, that mean and gentle all
Behold, as may unworthiness define,
A little touch of Harry in the night.

*A shadow falls across the Soldier.* KING HENRY, GLOUCESTER, SALISBURY *and their Guard walk away. The music stops.*

KING HENRY: Gloucester!

HENRY V *speaks to his nobles.*

KING HENRY: . . . 'Tis true that we are in great danger,
The greater therefore should our courage be.

ERPINGHAM *comes up from behind.* (STILL)

KING HENRY: Good morrow, old Sir Thomas Erpingham.
A good soft pillow for that good white head
Were better than a churlish turf of France.

ERPINGHAM: Not so, my liege. This lodging suits me better,
Since I may say, 'Now lie I like a king.'

*They all laugh.*

KING HENRY: Lend me thy cloak, Sir Thomas.
I and my bosom must debate awhile,
And then I would no other company.

HENRY V *takes* ERPINGHAM'S *cloak and puts it on.*

ERPINGHAM: The Lord in heaven bless thee, noble Harry!

*The nobles move away.*

KING HENRY: God-a-mercy, old heart!

*He turns and walks away. Track forward to hold a tent flap from which* PISTOL *emerges.*

PISTOL: Qui va là?

HENRY V *swings round.*

KING HENRY: A friend.

PISTOL *draws his sword.*

PISTOL: Discuss unto me: art thou officer, or art thou base, common and popular?

KING HENRY: *(off)* I am a gentleman of a company.

PISTOL: Trail'st thou the puissant pike?

KING HENRY: *(off)* Even so. What are you?

PISTOL: As good a gentleman as the Emperor.

KING HENRY: *(off)* Then you are better than the King.

PISTOL: The King's a bawcock and a heart of gold,
A lad of life, an imp of fame,

Of parents good, of fist most valiant.
I kiss his dirty shoe, and from heart-string
I love the lovely bully.

    PISTOL *comes closer and peers at us*.

PISTOL: What is thy name?

KING HENRY: *(off)* Henry Le Roy.

PISTOL: Le Roy? A Cornish name: are thou of Cornish crew?

KING HENRY: *(off)* No, I'm a Welshman.

PISTOL: Know'st thou Fluellen?

KING HENRY: *(off)* Yes.

PISTOL: Art thou his friend?

KING HENRY: *(off)* I am his kinsman too.

PISTOL: Well, tell him, I'll knock his leek about his head
Upon Saint Davy's day.

KING HENRY: *(off)* Do not wear your dagger in your cap that day,
Lest he knock that about yours.

PISTOL: A fico for thee, then!

    PISTOL *runs back*.

KING HENRY: *(off)* I thank you: God be with you!

PISTOL: My name is Pistol called.

KING HENRY: *(off)* It sorts well with your fierceness.

    PISTOL *goes out*.
    HENRY V *laughs and walks away. Track with him. He suddenly stops.*
    *A man is scrabbling in the undergrowth. It is* FLUELLEN, *who stands up and jumps down to a trench.*

GOWER: *(off)* Captain Fluellen!

    *Pan to show* GOWER *approaching*.

GOWER: Captain Fluellen!

FLUELLEN *jumps up beside him.*

FLUELLEN: Sh! Sh! In the name of Beezlebub, speak lower. If you would take the pains but to examine the wars of Pompey the Great, you shall find, I warrant you, there is no tiddle-taddle nor pibble-pabble in Pompey's camp. I warrant you, you shall find the ceremonies of the wars, and the cares of it, and the forms of it, to be otherwise.

GOWER: Why, the enemy is loud. You can hear him all night.

FLUELLEN: If the enemy is an ass and a fool and a prating coxcomb, is it meet, think you, that we should also, look you, be an ass and a fool and a prating coxcomb? In your own conscience, now?

GOWER: I will speak lower.

FLUELLEN: I pray you and do beseech you that you will.

*They move off.*

KING HENRY: *(off)* Though it appear a little out of fashion There is much care and valour in this Welshman.

*Track back and hold three soldiers,* COURT, BATES *and* WILLIAMS, *seated round a camp fire.*

COURT: Brother John Bates, is not that the morning which breaks yonder?

BATES: I think it be. But we have no great cause to desire the approach of day.

WILLIAMS: We see yonder the beginning of the day, but I think we shall never see the end of it.

*He looks up.*

WILLIAMS: Who goes there?

*The cloaked* KING HENRY *appears.*

KING HENRY: A friend.

WILLIAMS *comes into shot.*

WILLIAMS: Under what captain serve you?

KING HENRY: Under Sir Thomas Erpingham.

WILLIAMS *and* HENRY V *join* COURT *and* BATES *at the camp fire and sit down with them.*

WILLIAMS: A good old commander and a most kind gentleman. I pray you, what thinks he of our estate?

KING HENRY: Even as men wrecked upon a sand that look to be washed off the next tide.

BATES: He hath not told his thought to the King?

KING HENRY: No, nor it is not meet he should. For I think the King is but a man, as I am. The violet smells to him as it doth to me. His ceremonies laid by, in his nakedness he appears but a man. Therefore, when he sees reason of fears, as we do, his fears, without doubt, be of the same relish as ours are. Yet no man should find in him any appearance of fear, lest he, by showing it, should dishearten his army.

WILLIAMS: He may show what outward courage he will, but I believe, as cold a night as 'tis, he could wish himself in Thames up to the neck. So I would he were, and I by him, at all adventures, so we were quit here.

HENRY V *is now seen in close-up.*

KING HENRY: By my troth, I will speak my conscience of the King. I think he would not wish himself anywhere but where he is.

BATES *is seen in close-up.*

BATES: Then I would he were here alone. So should he be sure to be ransomed, and a many poor men's lives saved.

*Resume close-up of* HENRY V.

KING HENRY: Methinks, I could not die anywhere so contented, as in the King's company, his cause being just and his quarrel honourable.

BATES *and* WILLIAMS *are now seen together.*

WILLIAMS: That's more than we know.

BATES: Ay, or more than we should seek after.
For we know enough, if we know we are the King's subjects. If his cause be wrong, our obedience to the King wipes the crime of it out of us.

COURT: *(off)* But if the cause be not good . . .

COURT *is now seen in close-up.*

COURT: . . . the King himself hath a heavy reckoning to make, when all those legs and arms and heads chopped off in a battle shall join together at the latter day, and cry all, 'We died at such a place' – some swearing, some crying for a surgeon, some upon their wives left poor behind them, some upon the debts they owe, some upon their children rawly left. I'm afraid there are few die well that die in a battle, for how can they charitably dispose of anything, when blood is their argument? Now if these men do not die well, it will be a black matter for the King that led them to it.

WILLIAMS: *(off)* Ay!

*All four are seen round the fire.* COURT *begins to fall asleep.*

BATES: Ay!

KING HENRY: So, if a son that is by his father sent about merchandise do sinfully miscarry upon the sea, the imputation of his wickedness, by your rule, should be imposed upon his father that sent him. But this is not so. The King is not bound to answer for the particular endings of his soldiers, nor the father of his son, for they purpose not their deaths when they propose their services. Every subject's duty is the King's, but every subject's soul is his own.

WILLIAMS: Ay, 'tis certain, every man that dies ill, the ill on his own head. The King's not to answer for it.

BATES: I do not desire he should answer for me, and yet I determine to fight lustily for him.

KING HENRY: I myself heard the King say he would not be ransomed.

WILLIAMS: He said so, to make us fight cheerfully, but when our throats are cut, he may be ransomed, and we ne'er the wiser.

KING HENRY: If ever I live to see it, I'll never trust his word after.

*WILLIAMS laughs in close-up, turning to the others.*

WILLIAMS: That's a perilous shot out of a pop-gun, that a poor and a private displeasure can do against a monarch!

*Pan with him as he moves close to* HENRY V.

WILLIAMS: You may as well go about to turn the sun to ice with fanning in his face with a peacock's feather. You'll never trust his word after! Come, 'tis a foolish saying.

KING HENRY: Your reproof is something too round. I should be angry with you, if the time were convenient.

*There is the sound of a fanfare.*

WILLIAMS: Let it be a quarrel between us then, if you live.

BATES: Be . . .

*BATES is seen in close-up.*

BATES: . . . Friends, you English fools . . .

*He grabs WILLIAMS by the arm and they walk away. Track back to leave HENRY V sitting alone with the sleeping COURT.*

BATES: . . . Be friends, we have French quarrels enough if you could tell how to reckon.

HENRY V *speaks a soliloquy in close-up*.

KING HENRY: *(off)* Upon the King!
Let us our lives, our souls, our debts, our careful wives,
Our children, and our sins, lay on the King!
We must bear all. What infinite heartsease
Must kings forego that private men enjoy!
And what have kings that privates have not too,
Save ceremony.
And what art thou, thou idol ceremony,
That sufferest more
Of mortal griefs than do thy worshippers?

> *Track in slowly into a large close-up of* HENRY V.

KING HENRY: What drink'st thou oft, instead of homage
sweet,
But poisoned flattery? O, be sick, great greatness,
And bid thy ceremony give thee cure.
Canst thou, when thou command'st the beggar's knee,
Command the health of it? No, thou proud dream,
That play'st so subtly with a king's repose;
I am a king that find thee, and I know
'Tis not the orb and sceptre, crown imperial,
The throne he sits on, nor the tide of pomp
That beats upon the high shore of this world;
Not all these, laid in bed majestical,
Can sleep so soundly as the wretched slave . . .

> HENRY V *looks down. Track back to show* COURT
> *asleep at his feet.*

KING HENRY: . . . Who with a body filled and vacant
mind,
Gets him to rest, crammed with distressful bread;
Never sees horrid night . . .

> *We still slowly track back as* HENRY V *looks at the sunrise
> in the night sky.*

KING HENRY: . . . The child of hell;
But like a lackey from the rise to set

Sweats in the eye of Phoebus; and all night
Sleeps in Elysium; next day, after dawn,
Doth rise and help Hyperion to his horse,
And follows so the ever-running year
With profitable labour to his grave.
And, but for ceremony, such a wretch,
Winding up days with toil, and nights with sleep,
Had the forehand and vantage of a king.

> HENRY V *sits back against a tree.* (STILL).
> *Seen in close-up,* HENRY V *hears a voice.*

ERPINGHAM: *(off)* My lord!

> *The King looks up.*
> ERPINGHAM *is now in close shot.*

ERPINGHAM: . . . Your nobles, jealous of your absence,
Seek through your camp to find you.

> HENRY V *stands up and comes into shot.*

KING HENRY: Good old knight.

> HENRY V *turns and walks up to the camp, followed by*
> ERPINGHAM. *Track with them, as we hear prayers being*
> *chanted from a tent.*
> HENRY V *pulls back the tent flap and sees a service in*
> *progress. The chanting has stopped and prayers are being*
> *read. Track with the king as he walks on. An 'AMEN' is*
> *chanted and more prayers are spoken from a second tent.*
> *The King stops and turns to* ERPINGHAM.

KING HENRY: Collect them all together at my tent. I'll be
before thee.

> ERPINGHAM *goes out left. Pan with the King walking on*
> *alone. There is the sound of a fanfare as* HENRY V *turns*
> *round and kneels down.*

KING HENRY: O God of battles, steel my soldiers' hearts,
Possess them not with fear, Take from them now
The sense of reckoning lest the opposèd numbers
Pluck their hearts from them.

GLOUCESTER: *(off)* My lord!

GLOUCESTER *comes down the hillside to* HENRY V.

GLOUCESTER: My lord, the army stays upon your presence.

*There is the sound of a fanfare.*

KING HENRY: I know thy errand, I will go with thee.

*Again the trumpets sound.*

KING HENRY: The day, my friends, and all things stay for me.

*As the fanfare sounds for a fourth time,* KING HENRY *takes* GLOUCESTER'S *shoulder and they walk away up the hill.*
*Fade out, then fade in to a fleur-de-lis on a tent flap being swept aside to show the* DAUPHIN *and the French Dukes arming themselves. The music starts.* (STILL)

BOURBON: The sun doth gild our armour! Up, my lords!

DAUPHIN: Monte cheval! My horse! Varlet! Lacquais! Ha!

ORLEANS: O brave spirit!

DAUPHIN: Via les eaux et la terre!

ORLEANS: Rien puis? L'air et le feu!

DAUPHIN: Ciel, cousin Orléans!

*The* CONSTABLE *enters.*

CONSTABLE: Hark, how our steeds for present service neigh.

DAUPHIN: Mount them and make incision in their hides,
That their hot blood may spin in English eyes
And quench them with superior courage. Ha!

*A* MESSENGER *comes in.*

MESSENGER: The English are embattled, you French peers.

*He goes out.*

CONSTABLE: A very little little let us do,
And all is done. Then let the trumpets sound
The tucket sonance and the note to mount.

*Pan with him as he walks down and goes out.*

CONSTABLE: Come, come away!
The sun is high, and we outwear the day.

*In the French camp, the* CONSTABLE *enters and is
escorted to his horse. Pan to show* BOURBON *and*
ORLEANS *following, and finally the* DAUPHIN *is escorted
to his horse.*
*Dissolve to the Cross of St. George, then pan with it to
reveal the Standard Bearer and a group of English
knights.* GLOUCESTER *enters. It is the English camp.*

GLOUCESTER: Where is the King?

SALISBURY: The King himself is rode to view their battle.

WESTMORELAND: Of fighting men they have full three
score hundred.

EXETER: There's five to one, besides they are all flesh.

GLOUCESTER: God's arm strike with us, 'tis a fearful odds.

SALISBURY *shakes hands with his fellow noble knights.*

SALISBURY: Well, God with you, princes all. I'll to my
charge.
If we no more meet till we meet in heaven,
Then joyfully, my noble Westmoreland,
My dear Lord Gloucester, my good Lord Exeter,
And my kind kinsman, warriors all adieu!

WESTMORELAND: Farewell, good Salisbury.

GLOUCESTER: And good luck go with thee!

EXETER: Farewell, kind lord.

SALISBURY *goes out.*

266

WESTMORELAND: O that we now had here
But one ten thousand of those men in England
That do not work today.

KING HENRY: *(off)* What's he that wishes so?

*The music stops as* KING HENRY *enters.*

KING HENRY: My cousin Westmoreland? No, my fair
cousin.

*Pan with him as he walks to the group of noble knights.*

KING HENRY: If we are marked to die, we are enough
To do our country loss; and if to live,
The fewer men, the greater share of honour.
God's will, I pray thee wish not one man more.
Rather proclaim it, Westmoreland, through my host . . .

*Pan with the King as he walks away.*

KING HENRY: . . . That he which hath no stomach to this
fight,
Let him depart. His passport shall be drawn
And crowns for convoy put into his purse.

*He turns round to face us, then walks closer.*

KING HENRY: We would not die in that man's company
That fears his fellowship to die with us.
This day is called the Feast of Crispian:
He that outlives this day, and comes safe home,
Will stand a-tiptoe when this day is named
And rouse him at the name of Crispian.

*He walks still closer to us.*

KING HENRY: He that shall see this day and live t'old age,
Will yearly on the vigil feast his neighbours
And say, 'Tomorrow is Saint Crispian.'
Then will he strip his sleeve and show his scars
And say, 'These wounds I had on Crispian's day.'

*Track with him as he turns and walks left.*

KING HENRY: Old men forget; yet all shall be forgot,
But he'll remember, with advantages,
What feats he did that day. Then shall our names
Familiar in his mouth as household words –
Harry the King, Bedford and Exeter . . .

*He climbs on to a cart. Track slowly back to a long shot to show his army clustered around him.* (STILL)

KING HENRY: Warwick and Talbot, Salisbury and Gloucester –
Be in their flowing cups freshly remembered.
This story shall the good man teach his son,
And Crispin Crispian shall ne'er go by
From this day to the ending of the world
But we in it shall be remembered,
We few, we happy few, we band of brothers.
For he today that sheds his blood with me,
Shall be my brother, be he ne'er so base.
And gentlemen in England, now a-bed,
Shall think themselves accursed they were not here,
And hold their manhoods cheap whiles any speaks
That fought with us upon Saint Crispian's day.

*The soldiers cheer.* SALISBURY *pushes through the soldiers at the side of the cart.*

SALISBURY: My sovereign lord, bestow yourself with speed.
The French are bravely in their battles set
And will with all expedience charge on us.

KING HENRY: All things are ready, if our minds be so.

WESTMORELAND *comes round to the cart.*

WESTMORELAND: Perish the man whose mind is backward now!

HENRY V *is seen in close-up.*

KING HENRY: Thou dost not wish more help from England, coz?

WESTMORELAND *is also seen in close-up.*

WESTMORELAND: God's will, my liege, would you and I alone,
Without more help, could fight this . . .

*Resume close-up of* HENRY V.

WESTMORELAND: *(off)* . . . battle out!

KING HENRY: You know your places. God be with you all!

*Pan with* KING HENRY *as he turns and jumps on a horse.
The music starts as he rides round close to and then away
from us.
English soldiers are driving in stakes with wooden
mallets.* (STILL)
*An English soldier helps* KING HENRY *to put on his chain
mail.
The* DAUPHIN *is lowered by pulley on to his horse.*
(STILL)
*The* DAUPHIN *is settled on his horse. Pan with it as it is led
round.
A line of French drummers waits.*
ORLEANS, *the* DAUPHIN *and* BOURBON *are being
handed cups of wine on horseback.
The* CONSTABLE *and another knight toast the* DAUPHIN
*and company.
The* DAUPHIN *and company acknowledge the toast.*
(STILL)
*Englishmen are banging in stakes.
A line of Englishmen is banging in stakes.
Arrows are being distributed to English archers.
Englishmen are sharpening stakes. There is a fanfare.
The man nearest us looks ahead of him.*
MOUNTJOY *and the Standard Bearer, escorted by two
Heralds, ride up. The Heralds stop to blow a fanfare. Pan
with* MOUNTJOY *and the Standard Bearer as they ride on
into the English camp.*
MOUNTJOY *dismounts and is escorted by the English
Herald out of shot.*

KING HENRY *is in full armour on his horse.* MOUNTJOY
*and the English Herald come in and doff their hats to the
King, who smiles at* MOUNTJOY.
MOUNTJOY *stands by the head of the King's horse. The
music stops.*

MOUNTJOY: Once more I come to know of thee, King
Harry,
If for thy ransom thou wilt now compound
Before thy most assurèd overthrow.

*The King's horse shakes its head.*
KING HENRY *speaks down to* MOUNTJOY.

KING HENRY: Who hath sent thee now?

MOUNTJOY: The Constable of France.

*Drums sound in the distance.*

KING HENRY: I pray thee, bear my former answer back.
Bid them achieve me, and then sell my bones.
Good God, why should they mock poor fellows thus?
The man that once did sell the lion's skin
While the beast lived, was killed with hunting him.
And many of our bodies shall no doubt
Find native graves, upon the which, I trust,
Shall witness live in brass of this day's work
And those that leave their valiant bones in France,
Dying like men, though buried in your dunghills,
They shall be famed. For there the sun shall greet them
And draw their honours reeking up to heaven,
Leaving their earthly parts to choke your clime,
The smell whereof shall breed a plague in France.
Let me speak proudly: tell the Constable
We are but warriors for the working day.
Our gayness and our gilt are all besmirched
With rainy marching in the painful field.
And time hath worn us into slovenry:
But, by the mass, our hearts are in the trim . . .

*The English soldiers cheer. Then the music starts.*

KING HENRY: Come thou no more for ransom, gentle herald,
They shall have none, I swear, but these my bones,
Which if they have as I will leave 'em them,
Shall yield them little. Tell the Constable.

*The King rides off.*
*MOUNTJOY flourishes his hat.*

MOUNTJOY: I shall, King Harry. And so fare thee well.

*He prepares to mount his horse.*
*Now MOUNTJOY is on his horse.*

MOUNTJOY: Thou never shalt hear herald any more.

*To a fanfare, he rides off followed by his Standard Bearer.*
*KING HENRY rides in from the left.*

KING HENRY: Now, soldiers, march away.

*The English soldiers cheer him.*

KING HENRY: And how thou pleasest, God, dispose the day.

*Dissolve to an aerial view of the battlefield.*
*A fanfare announces a shot of the French army ready for battle. (STILL)*
*A fanfare announces a reverse shot of the English army, prepared to fight.*
*A line of French drummers beat their drums.*
*French crossbowmen move up. (STILL)*
*French drummers strike their drums.*
*French cavalry men move up to battle position. The CONSTABLE signals with his sword, and they turn left.*
*French standards dip and move out of shot.*
*Pan across the shining mire to show the reflection and then the hoofs of French cavalry.*
*The French cavalry is in battle order at the walk. (STILL)*
*A line of English bowmen draw their bows.*
*KING HENRY bestrides his horse.*

*The French cavalry break into a trot, then a canter, then a gallop, then a full tilt charge.* (STILL)

*A line of English archers with bows drawn.* (STILL)

*A low angle shot of* HENRY V *with his sword poised for a signal to the archers. His glance changes from left to right.*

*The French cavalry charges at the English stakes in the foreground.*

*The line of English bowmen wait with bows drawn.*

HENRY V *slashes down his sword. The music stops.*

*A line of English archers – they fire.*

*Two lines of English archers – they fire.* (STILL)

*The French cavalry charge at stake emplacements in the foreground. Arrows sizzle through the air overhead and strike home. The French horses rear.*

*The music starts as the English archers fire at the French cavalry.* (STILL)

*Four quick shots show the French cavalry in total confusion.*

*Two quick shots show French chargers rearing madly.*

*The English archers keep on firing.*

*Three quick shots of the confusion of the French horsemen.*

*Two quick shots of horses neighing hysterically.*

*English archers run forward and prepare to fire.*

*A French charger rears.*

*Four more quick shots of the French cavalry in confusion.*

*A second wave of French cavalry charges towards us.*

*The first wave of French cavalry begins to retreat.*

*French horsemen retreat to the right.*

*The second wave of French cavalry charge left.*

*The French cavalry in full retreat.*

*The second wave of French cavalry charging.*

*The first wave of French cavalry in retreat clashes with the second wave of advancing French cavalry.*

*Advancing French cavalry trying to make headway.*

*The two waves of cavalry enmeshed.* (STILL)

*English archers firing.*

*French cavalry enmeshed. Pan to a morass behind them.*

*English archers fire and run forward.*
*French infantry men, in support of their cavalry, become entangled in the morass.*
*French cavalry enmeshed.*
*The French infantry is struggling in the morass.*
*The music stops. Dissolve to the French infantry bogged down in the morass.* (STILL)
*The music starts as we dissolve to the third wave of advancing French cavalry appearing over a hilltop. The horsemen charge towards us.* (STILL)
*The French cavalry charging. English archers are firing from the fringe of a wood, but they retreat. There is a dissolve.*
*Seen from above, the French cavalry is charging through the wood. An English infantryman jumps from the branch of a tree onto a French knight.*
*The infantryman drags the knight from his horse and goes to stab him.*
*Another infantryman jumps from the branch of tree.*
*He hits the ground.*
*Another infantryman jumps from the branch of a tree.*
*The infantryman lands on the ground among the French knights.*
*Two more infantrymen jump from the branches.*
*English and French infantry fighting hand to hand.* KING HENRY *with his Standard Bearer leads a flank attack with his knights.* (STILL) *Pan to hold the Standard.*
*Dissolve to the battlefield as* KING HENRY *rides round from the right. Pan with him.*

KING HENRY: Well have we done, thrice-valiant countrymen.
But all's not done. Yet keep the French the field.

*He has ridden up and on his last word slashes with his sword.*
*Dissolve to a close shot of the English Standard, the Cross of St. George. Pan to show* HENRY V *and the Standard Bearer riding through the thick of the infantry fighting.*
*Dissolve to a close shot of the French Standard. Pan to*

*reveal in long shot French knights and* MOUNTJOY
*fleeing to a hilltop.*
*The French knights are distraught on the hilltop.*

DAUPHIN: O everlasting shame! Let's stab ourselves.
Be these the wretches that we played at dice for?

ORLEANS: Is this the King we sent to for his ransom?

*The* CONSTABLE *rides in.*

CONSTABLE: Shame, and eternal shame, nothing but
shame!
Let's die in honour. Once more back again!

*The* DAUPHIN *and* ORLEANS *look at him.*

ORLEANS: We are enough yet living in the field
To smother up the English in our throngs
If any order might be thought upon.

*The* CONSTABLE *rides round to the foreground.*

CONSTABLE: The devil take order now! I'll to the throng.
Let life be short, else shame will be too long.

*He rides out of shot.*
BOURBON *starts to move off after the* CONSTABLE.
*The* CONSTABLE *and the Standard Bearer ride down the
hill and off.* BOURBON *leads a second party of knights,
who pause to wait for the remaining few, but turn and ride
off.*
*The* DAUPHIN *and* MOUNTJOY *stay on the hilltop,
looking off.*
MOUNTJOY *looks right and left.*
*The* DAUPHIN *looks left.*
*Dissolve to the English Camp. French knights ride in.*
(STILL)
*A French knight rides into the English camp. Pan with
him as he cuts down a tent and kills a Boy.*
*Another camp Boy picks up the dead Boy and looks at
him, then drops him quickly.*
*The second Boy is running hard. A French knight crosses
in front of him.*

*There is a small fire on the ground. A French knight rides in and picks up a fire brand with his sword. He flings it into a tent. Another knight rides in. Pan down to the fire, as this knight spears a fire brand with his sword.*

*Start on a close shot of the fire brand aloft on the sword point. Pan to reveal the knight preparing to fling it into a cart. Another French knight crosses the screen as a Boy runs towards us with a casket in his hand.*

*The Boy runs and stops near a bush with a brazier alongside.*

*The knight flings the fire brand into the cart.*

*The Boy thrusts the casket under the bush and runs out.*

*The knight dashes in and overturns the brazier.*

*The bush catches fire. The music stops.*

*We are inside a tent on fire with a dead Boy. Through the tent opening, French knights are seen to ride away.*

*The music starts as we dissolve to a long shot of the English camp on fire.*

*From the hilltop, the* DAUPHIN *looks at the burning camp. He surveys the scene then rides out.* MOUNTJOY *rides in.*

*The marauding French knights ride in and join* MOUNTJOY. *In the distance, the* DAUPHIN *is seen in flight.*

*The music stops as we dissolve to* FLUELLEN *in the English Camp with a dead Boy in his arms.*

FLUELLEN: God's plud! Kill the boys and the luggage!

GOWER *walks in with a Monk. Track back to medium shot.*

FLUELLEN: 'Tis expressly against the law of arms. 'Tis as arrant a piece of knavery, mark you now, as can be offered. In your conscience now, is it not?

GOWER: 'Tis certain there's not a boy left alive. And the cowardly rascals that ran from the battle ha' done this slaughter.

KING HENRY *on foot, followed by a soldier leading his horse, enters with his Standard Bearer on another horse.*

MONK: Here comes His Majesty.

*Track forward as* HENRY V *approaches them.*

KING HENRY: I was not angry since I came to France
Until this instant.

*He mounts his horse and rides out. The music starts as*
HENRY V *rides full tilt back to the battlefield.* (STILL)
*Pan with his ride.*
*The* CONSTABLE *is in the thick of the fighting.* (STILL)
*The* CONSTABLE *lifts his visor and looks off.*
KING HENRY *followed by his Standard Bearer is riding
up to meet the* CONSTABLE.
*The* CONSTABLE *slams down his visor.*
*The* CONSTABLE *rears his horse and rides off.*
KING HENRY *and the* CONSTABLE *clash swords.*
*The* CONSTABLE *prepares to attack again.*
KING HENRY *swings his horse round and the*
CONSTABLE *rides in. They exchange sword blows.*
(STILL)
*The* CONSTABLE *striking with his sword.*
*The sword crashing on* KING HENRY'S *helmet.*
*The* CONSTABLE'S *horse rearing.*
KING HENRY *rides back. Pan with him as the*
CONSTABLE *rides in.*
*The* CONSTABLE *swinging his horse round to attack
again.*
KING HENRY *swinging his horse round.*
*The* CONSTABLE *riding in.*
KING HENRY *and the* CONSTABLE *exchange sword
blows.*
KING HENRY'S *sword knocks the* CONSTABLE'S *sword
out of his hand.*
KING HENRY'S *horse rearing. The* CONSTABLE *rides
out.*
*The* CONSTABLE *drops his shield. He grabs his mace.*
KING HENRY *rides in. The* CONSTABLE *swings his mace.*
*The* CONSTABLE'S *mace striking* KING HENRY'S *hand,
sending the sword flying out of it.*

KING HENRY'S *sword sticking in the ground.*
*Low angle shot of the* CONSTABLE *raising his mace.*
KING HENRY *looking off.*
*The* CONSTABLE *about to strike.*
*Pan left with* KING HENRY *as he strikes the* CONSTABLE'S *chin with his mailed fist.*
*The* CONSTABLE *falls off his horse. Pan down to the ground with him.*
*The* CONSTABLE *lies on the ground.*
*Two soldiers leave the circle of English watchers and take the* CONSTABLE'S *horse.* KING HENRY *rides to the place where the* CONSTABLE *fell. He bends down to pick up the* CONSTABLE'S *sword. Pan with him as he goes.*
*The* CONSTABLE'S *body lies with* KING HENRY'S *sword beside it.*
KING HENRY *rides down the hill as the English soldiers surge round the body of the* CONSTABLE. *The King rides up to the English Herald.*

KING HENRY: Take a trumpet, Herald.
Ride thou unto the horsemen on yon hill;
If they will fight with us, bid them come down,
Or void the field; they do offend our sight.

> KING HENRY *rides out, and the Herald rides away toward the French knights on the hill.*
> KING HENRY *rides in to join* EXETER *and other English knights.*

EXETER: Here comes the Herald of the French, my liege.

> MOUNTJOY *meets the English Herald on the hillside, and they ride down together.*
> *The English knights address their King, as* MOUNTJOY *approaches.*

SALISBURY: His eyes are humbler than they used to be.

KING HENRY: God's will, what mean's this, Herald?
Com'st thou again for ransom?

> MOUNTJOY *enters and bows. The music stops.* (STILL)

MOUNTJOY *speaks in close-up.*

MOUNTJOY: No, great king.
I come to thee for charitable licence,
That we may wander o'er this bloody field
To book our dead and then to bury them.
The day is yours.

HENRY V *speaks in close-up.*

KING HENRY: Praisèd be God. and not our strength, for it.

*Track back as the King takes off his helmet to show Agincourt Castle in the background. The music starts.*

KING HENRY: What is this castle called that stands hard by?

MOUNTJOY: We call it Agincourt.

KING HENRY: Then call we this the field of Agincourt, Fought on the day of Crispin Crispianus.

*MOUNTJOY kneels and kisses KING HENRY'S hand. The Standard Bearer steps forward and raises the Cross of St. George.*
*The Cross of St. George comes into shot with Agincourt Castle in the background.*
*Dissolve to soldiers lying dead on the Field of the Dead.*
*Dissolve to the English knights drinking in the English Camp.* FLUELLEN *ushers the English Herald forward, who walks over to* KING HENRY *who is surrounded by* EXETER *and other friends. Track with the Herald as he hands the king a paper.*

HERALD: Here is the number of the slaughtered French.

KING HENRY: This note doth tell me of ten thousand French
That in the field lie slain,
Where is the number of our English dead?

*The Herald hands him another paper. The music stops.*

KING HENRY: Edward, the Duke of York, the Earl of Suffolk,

Sir Richard Ketly, Davy Gram Esquire;
And all other men but five-and-twenty score.
O God, thy arm was here!

EXETER: 'Tis wonderful!

KING HENRY: Come, we go in procession to the village.

KING HENRY'S *horse is led in.*

KING HENRY: Let there be sung *Non Nobis* and *Te Deum.*

*The chanting begins as the King mounts his horse.*

KING HENRY: And then to Calais and to England then . . .

*Pan with the King as he leads the procession out of the English camp.*

KING HENRY: . . . Where ne'er from France arrived more happier men.

*Dissolve to a long shot of the English army walking in procession towards Agincourt village.*
*Dissolve to the Field of the Dead.*
*Fade out and cease the chanting in the English army in procession.*
*The music starts as we fade in to a long shot of Agincourt village under snow.*
*Dissolve to the gate to the village. Track forward to reveal* PISTOL *flirting with village women inside a house. Pan to show three boys singing carols, then track forward again as a couple emerge from a house and go into the church alongside. A man comes out of the church, and pan with him to reveal* FLUELLEN *and* GOWER *sitting on a wall. We track in on them. The music stops.* GOWER *laughs.*

GOWER: Nay, that's right. But why wear you your leek today? Saint Davy's day is past.

FLUELLEN: There is occasions and causes why and wherefore in all things, Captain Gower. I will tell you ass my friend, Captain Gower. The rascally beggarly lousy knave Pistol, which you and yourself and all the world know to be no petter than a fellow, look you, of no merits, he is come to me, and prings me pread and salt yesterday, look you, and bid me eat my leek.

GOWER *laughs.*

FLUELLEN: It was in a place where I could not breed no contention with him. But I will be bold as to wear it in my cap till I see him once again, and then I will tell him a little piece of my desires.

GOWER: Why, 'tis a gull, a fool, a rogue, that now and then goes to the wars, to grace himself at his return into London, under the form of soldier, and what such of the camp can do among foaming bottles, and ale-washed wits, is wonderful to be thought on.

*He laughs and points.*

GOWER: Here he comes . . .

*Pan with* PISTOL *as he walks on to bring himself in front of* FLUELLEN *and* GOWER.

GOWER: *(off)* . . . swelling like a turkey-cock.

FLUELLEN: *(off)* 'Tis no matter for his swellings, nor his turkey-cocks.

FLUELLEN *and* GOWER *are now in shot.*

FLUELLEN: God pless you, Pistol! You scurvy lousy knave, God pless you.

PISTOL: Ha! art thou bedlam? Hence! I am qualmish at the smell of leek.

FLUELLEN *jumps off the wall and confronts* PISTOL.

FLUELLEN: I peseech you heartily, scurvy lousy knave, to eat, look you, this leek.

FLUELLEN *snatches the leek from his cap and holds it under* PISTOL'S *nose.*

PISTOL: Not for Cadwallader and all his goats.

PISTOL *walks away. Pan with him, as* FLUELLEN *kicks*

PISTOL'S *backside*.

FLUELLEN: There is one goat for you. Will you be so good, as eat it?

PISTOL *draws his sword*.

PISTOL: Base Trojan, thou shalt die.

FLUELLEN *snatches the sword from* PISTOL *and bangs him on the head with it*. PISTOL *falls to his knees*.

FLUELLEN: You say very true, when God's will is. I will desire you to live in the meantime, and eat your victuals. Come, there is sauce for it.

*He hits* PISTOL *in the face with the leek*.

FLUELLEN: If you can mock a leek, you can eat a leek. Bite, I pray you.

PISTOL: Must I bite?

FLUELLEN: Out of doubt and out of question too.

PISTOL: By this leek, I will most horribly revenge.

FLUELLEN *threatens him with the sword*. (STILL)

PISTOL: I eat. I eat. I swear.

PISTOL *peels the leek*.

FLUELLEN: Nay, pray you, throw none away. The skin is good for your broken coxcomb. When you take occasions to see leeks hereafter, I pray you mock at 'em, that is all.

PISTOL: Good.

FLUELLEN: Ay, leeks is good.

GOWER *sits on the wall and chuckles*.

FLUELLEN: *(off)* Hold you!

FLUELLEN *and* PISTOL *together*.

FLUELLEN: Here is a penny to heal your hand.

PISTOL: Me, a penny?

FLUELLEN: Yes, verily, and in truth you shall take it, or I have another leek in my pocket, which you shall eat.

> PISTOL *takes the penny.* FLUELLEN *kisses* PISTOL'S *head and goes off.*

FLUELLEN: God be wi' you and keep you and heal your head.

> PISTOL *gets up and rushes to the gate at the side of the wall. Pan and track with him, as* GOWER *comes on.*

PISTOL: All hell shall stir for this.

GOWER: Go, go, you are a counterfeit, cowardly knave.
You thought because he could not speak
English in the native garb, he therefore could not
Handle an English cudgel. You find it
Otherwise, and henceforth let a Welsh
Correction teach you a good English condition.

> *Pan with* GOWER *as he walks away from* PISTOL. *He turns and throws a coin away.*
> PISTOL *takes the coin that has fallen into his helmet. He turns and walks straight towards us.*

PISTOL: Doth Fortune play the strumpet with me now?
News have I that my Nell lies dead
I' th' hospital of a malady of France.
And there my rendezvous is quite cut off.
Old do I wax, and from my weary limbs
Honour is cudgelled. Well, bawd I'll turn,
And something lean to cutpurse of quick hand.
To England will I steal, and there I'll steal:
And patches will I get unto these scars,
And swear I got them in these present wars.

> *The music starts as* PISTOL *scurries off and disappears in a barn. Track with him and past the barn.* PISTOL *emerges from the other side of barn with a pig under his arm and a cockerel in his hand. He runs up the hill away*

*from us and disappears.*
*Dissolve to a long shot of the French Palace.*
*Then dissolve again to the great hall of the Palace.*
*A high angle shot shows a choir in the foreground. We*
*track forward and down as the* DUKE OF BURGUNDY
*and attendants take their places, followed by the French*
*King and* KING HENRY V *and their courtiers. The music*
*ceases.*

KING HENRY: Peace to this meeting, wherefore we are met.
Unto our brother France and to our sister,
Health and fair time of day. Joy and good wishes
To our most fair and princely cousin Katharine:
And as a branch and member of this royalty,
We do salute you, Duke of Burgundy:
And Princes French, and peers, health to you all!

> KING CHARLES *and* QUEEN ISABEL *of France are*
> *surrounded by their courtiers.*

KING CHARLES: Right joyous are we to behold your face,
Most worthy brother England, fairly met.
So are you, Princes English, every one.

QUEEN ISABEL: So happy be the issue, brother England,
Of this good day, and of this gracious meeting . . .

> KING HENRY *is surrounded by his court.*

QUEEN ISABEL: *(off)* . . . As we are now glad to behold
your eyes . . .

> *Resume shot of* QUEEN ISABEL *and* KING CHARLES.

QUEEN ISABEL: . . . Your eyes which hitherto have borne
in them
Against the French that met them in their bent,
The fatal balls of murdering basilisks.
The venom of such looks we fairly hope
Have lost their quality, and that this day
Shall change all griefs and quarrels into love.

HENRY V *replies in kind.*

KING HENRY: To cry amen to that, thus we appear.

*He turns to his right.*
KING HENRY *remains in the foreground with* KING
CHARLES, *while the* DUKE OF BURGUNDY *speaks to
them.*

BURGUNDY: My duty to you both, on equal love,
Great Kings of France and England.
Since then my office hath so far prevailed
That face to face and royal eye to eye
You have assembled, let it not disgrace me
If I demand before this royal view,
Why that the naked, poor and mangled peace,
Dear nurse of arts, plenties, and joyful births,
Should not in this best garden of the world,
Our fertile France, put up her lovely visage?

*Close shot of* BURGUNDY. *The music begins.*

BURGUNDY: Alas, she hath from France too long been
chased . . .

*Track with* BURGUNDY *as he steps up to a window.*

BURGUNDY: . . . And all her husbandry doth lie in heaps,
Corrupting in its own fertility.
Her vine, the merry cheerer of the heart . . .

*Pan slowly beyond the window out over the fertile
countryside.*

BURGUNDY: *(off)* . . . Unprunèd, dies; her hedges even-
pleached
Put forth disordered twigs; her fallow leas,
The darnel, hemlock, and rank fumitory
Doth root upon, while that the coulter rusts
That should deracinate such savagery.
The even mead, that erst brought sweetly forth
The freckled cowslip, burnet and green clover,
Wanting the scythe, all uncorrected rank,

Conceives by idleness, and nothing teems
But hateful docks, rough thistles, kecksies, burrs,
Losing both beauty and utility.
Even so our houses and ourselves and children . . .

*The slow pan holds on two children, then slowly pans up to the French castle.*

BURGUNDY: *(off)* Have lost, or do not learn for want of time,
The sciences that should become our country,
But grow like savages, as soldiers will
That nothing do but meditate on blood,
To swearing and stern looks, diffused attire . . .

*Now we dissolve to a shot from outside the window with* BURGUNDY *standing there.*

BURGUNDY: . . . And everything that seems unnatural . . .

*The music stops as* BURGUNDY *turns and steps down from the window.* HENRY V *and his court can be seen in the background. Track forward on them.*

BURGUNDY: Which to reduce into our former favour
You are assembled.

KING HENRY: Then, Duke of Burgundy, you must gain that peace
With full accord to all our just demands.

*Resume the shot of* KING CHARLES *and* QUEEN ISABEL.

KING CHARLES: I have but with a cursory eye
O'erglanced the articles. Pleaseth your grace
To appoint some of your council presently
To sit with us. We will suddenly
Pass our accept and peremptory answer.

KING HENRY *remains gracious.*

KING HENRY: Brother we shall. Will you, fair sister,
Go with the princes, or stay here with us?

QUEEN ISABEL *still stands at the side of* KING CHARLES. PRINCESS KATHARINE *is in the background on the left.* (STILL)

QUEEN ISABEL: Our gracious brother, I will go with them.
Haply a woman's voice may do some good
When articles too nicely urged be stood on.

KING HENRY: *(off)* Yet leave our cousin Katharine here with us.

QUEEN ISABEL: She hath good leave.

*The music starts as* QUEEN ISABEL *leads* PRINCESS KATHARINE *forward. Track back as the French Court take their leave of* HENRY V, *allowing him to be with* KATHARINE *alone. He walks over to her. Pan to show* LADY ALICE *also with them.*

KING HENRY: Fair Katharine and most fair,
Will you vouchsafe to teach a soldier terms
Such as will enter at a lady's ear
And plead his love-suit to her gentle heart?

KATHARINE: Your majesty shall mock at me,
I cannot speak your England.

KING HENRY: O fair Katharine, if you will love me soundly with your French heart, I will be glad to hear you confess it brokenly with your English tongue.

*HENRY V is seen in close-up.*

KING HENRY: Do you like me, Kate?

*PRINCESS KATHARINE is also in close-up with* ALICE *behind her.*

KATHARINE: *Pardonnez-moi*, I cannot tell vat is 'like me'.

*KING HENRY chuckles. He takes KATHARINE by the hand. She comes into shot followed by ALICE as we pan with them and track back. They are now at a window.*

KING HENRY: An angel is like you, Kate, and you are like an angel.

*The music stops.*

KATHARINE: *Que dit-il? Que je suis sembable à les anges?*

ALICE: *Oui, vraiment, sauf votre grâce, ainsi dit-il.*

KATHARINE: *O bon Dieu! Les langues des hommes sont pleines de tromperies.*

KING HENRY: What says she, fair one? That the tongues of men are full of deceits?

ALICE: Oui . . .

*ALICE is now seen in close-up.*

ALICE: . . . dat de tongues of de mans is be full of deceits.

*KING HENRY and PRINCESS KATHARINE are at the window. Pan with him walking to KATHARINE'S right.*

KING HENRY: I' faith, Kate, I am glad thou canst speak no better English, for if thou couldst, thou wouldst find me such a plain King that thou wouldst think I had sold my farm to buy my crown. I know no ways to mince it in love, but directly to say, 'I love you'. Give me your answer, i' faith do, and so clasp hands and a bargain. How say you, lady?

*ALICE nods encouragingly to KATHARINE.*
*KATHARINE replies to KING HENRY.*

KATHARINE: *Sauf votre honneur*, me understand vell.

KING HENRY: Marry, if you put me to verses, or to dance for your sake, Kate, why you undo me. If I might buffet for my love, or bound my horse for her favours, I could lay on like a butcher, and sit like a jackanapes, never off.

*He has stepped down from the window. Track back as he turns his back on us, still talking to KATHARINE.*

KING HENRY: But before God, Kate, I cannot look greenly, nor grasp out my eloquence . . .

*He walks out of shot. Track slowly in towards KATHARINE.*

KING HENRY: *(off)* . . . Nor have I no cunning in protestation. If thou canst love a fellow of this temper, Kate, that never looks in his glass for the love of anything he sees there, whose face is not worth sunburning . . .

*He comes into shot in the foreground.*

KING HENRY: . . . Take me.

*He steps up to the window beside* KATHARINE.

KING HENRY: If not, to say to thee that I shall die, is true – but for thy love, by the Lord, no!

KATHARINE *stands up as he sits beside her.*
ALICE *stands up in alarm.*
KATHARINE *confronts* HENRY V.

KING HENRY: Yet I love thee too.

*He stands up and* KATHARINE *sits down.*

KING HENRY: And while thou livest, dear Kate, take a fellow of plain constancy. For these fellows of infinite tongue, that can rhyme themselves into ladies' favours, they do always reason themselves out again. A speaker is but a prater, a rhyme is but a ballad, a straight back will stoop, a black beard will turn white, a fair face will wither, a full eye will wax hollow, but a good heart, Kate, is the sun and the moon. If thou would have such a one, take me, and take me, take a soldier. Take a soldier, take a King. And what sayest thou then to my love? Speak, my fair, and fairly, I pray thee.

*Pan with* KATHARINE *as she rises and walks alone to a window.*
KATHARINE *stands at the window.*

KATHARINE: Is it possible dat I sould love de enemy of France?

KING HENRY *steps up to the window beside her.*

KING HENRY: No, Kate. But in loving me, you should love the friend of France, for I love France so well that I will not part with a village of it. And Kate, when France is mine, and I am yours, then yours is France, and you are mine.

KATHARTINE: I cannot tell vat is dat.

KING HENRY: No, Kate? I will tell thee in French, which I am sure will hang upon my tongue like a new-married wife about her husband's neck, hardly to be shook off. *Je quand suis le possesseur de France, et quand vous avez le possession de moi, donc vôtre est France et vous être mienne.*

*They both laugh.*

KING HENRY: I shall never move thee in French, unless it be to laugh at me.

KATHARINE: *Sauf votre honneur, le français que vous parlez, il est meilleur que l'anglais lequel je parle.*

KING HENRY: No faith, is't not, Kate. Thy speaking of my tongue, and I thine, must needs be granted to be much alike. But, Kate, dost thou understand thus much English? Canst thou love me?

KATHARINE: I cannot tell.

*KATHARINE walks away from the window.*
*KING HENRY stays at the window.*

KING HENRY: Can any of your neighbours tell, Kate? I'll ask them.

*Track with him as he steps down from the window and walks past ALICE over to KATHARINE.*

KING HENRY: Come, I know thou lovest me, and at night, when you are come into your chamber, you will question this gentlewoman about me, and I know, Kate, you will to her dispraise those parts in me that you love with your heart. But, good Kate, mock me mercifully, the rather, gentle Princess, because I love thee cruelly. What sayest thou, my fair flower-de-luce? *La plus belle Katharine du monde, mon très chēr et divin déesse?*

KATHARINE: Your majesty 'ave *fausse* French enough to deceive de most *sage demoiselle* dat is *en France*.

*Pan with the King as he laughs and comes round to the right of* KATHARINE.

KING HENRY: Now fie upon my false French! But mine honour, in true English, I love thee, Kate. By which honour, though I dare not swear thou lovest me, yet my blood begins to flatter me that thou dost.

*Track back a little.*

KING HENRY: Put off your maiden blushes, avouch the thoughts of your heart with the looks of an empress, take me by the hand, and say, 'Harry of England, I am thine'. Which word thou shalt no sooner bless mine ear withal, but I will tell thee aloud, 'England is thine, Ireland is thine, France is thine, and Henry Plantagenet is thine'. Therefore, Queen of all, Katharine, break thy mind to me in broken English. Wilt thou have me?

KATHARINE: Dat is as it sall please de *roi mon père*.

KING HENRY: Nay, it will please him well, Kate. It shall please him, Kate.

KATHARINE: Den it sall also content me.

KING HENRY: Upon that I kiss your hand, and I call you my queen.

KING HENRY *kisses her hand. Pan with the shocked* KATHARINE *running to a doorway.* ALICE *joins her.*

KATHARINE: *Laissez, mon seigneur, laissez, laissez! Ma foi, je ne veux point que vous abaissiez votre grandeur en baisant la main de votre indigne serviteur*. . .

HENRY V *is seen in close-up.*

KATHARINE: *(off) Excusez-moi, je vous supplie, mon très-puissant seigneur.*

KING HENRY: Oh, then I will kiss your lips, Kate.

*Pan with* KATHARINE *and* ALICE *as they shriek and run to stand behind a window.* KING HENRY *stands in the foreground.*

KATHARINE: *Les dames et demoiselles pour être baisées devant leur noces, il n'est pas la coutume de France.*

KING HENRY *walks up to them behind the window. Track to hold on* KING HENRY *and* KATHARINE. *He turns. Pan to hold on him and* ALICE.

KING HENRY: Madame, my interpreter, what says she?

ALICE: Dat is not be de fashion *pour les* ladies of France – I cannot tell vat is *baiser en* Anglish.

KING HENRY: To kiss.

KATHARINE *is seen in close-up.*

ALICE: *(off)* Your majesty *entendre* better *que moi.*

KING HENRY: *(off)* It is not the fashion for the maids in France to kiss before they are married, would she say?

ALICE: *(off) Oui, vraiment.*

KING HENRY: *(off)* O Kate . . .

*The music starts as* KING HENRY *leads* KATHARINE *from the window and down to us. Pan and track back, then finally move in to a close shot.*

KING HENRY: Nice customs curtsy to great kings. Dear Kate, you and I cannot be confined within the weak list of a country's fashion. We are the makers of manners, Kate. Therefore, patiently and yielding.

*He kisses her. (STILL FRONTISPIECE)*
*In close-up, we see* KING HENRY'S *hand clasping* KATHARINE'S. *The heraldry of England and France can be seen on the rings of their fingers.*

KING HENRY: *(off)* You have witchcraft in your lips, Kate.

*We begin to track back from them.*

BURGUNDY: *(off)* God save your majesty . . .

*The music stops, and track back to a long shot showing the French Court assembled behind* KING HENRY *and* KATHARINE.

BURGUNDY: . . . My royal cousin, teach you our princess English?

*The Court titters.*

KING HENRY: I would have her learn, my fair cousin, how perfectly I love her, and that is good English.

*The Court applauds.*

KING HENRY: Shall Kate be my wife?

KING CHARLES *steps forward and takes the hands of* KING HENRY *and* KATHARINE.

KING CHARLES: Take her, fair son, that the contending kingdoms
Of France and England, whose very shores look pale
With envy of each other's happiness
May cease their hatred; that never war advance
His bleeding sword 'twixt England and fair France.

THE COURT: Amen!

*The music starts, and track back as* KING HENRY *and* KATHARINE *separate,* HENRY *to the English attendants on the left and* KATHARINE *to the French attendants on the right.*
*Now we see a longer shot of the same scene.* KING HENRY *and* KATHARINE *are crowned. Joining hands, they walk away to two thrones. Track forward following them. They sit side by side with* CANTERBURY *behind them.* (STILL)
HENRY V *turns round on reaching the throne. He is wearing the crude Globe Theatre make-up.*
*Applause is heard as we pan to show a* BOY *made-up as* KATHARINE.
*Track back from* KING HENRY *and the* BOY *playing*

KATHARINE *to reveal the stage of the Globe Theatre.*
CHORUS *enters and pulls the curtain across.*

CHORUS: Thus far, with rough and all-unable pen,
Our bending author hath pursued the story,
In little room confining mighty men,
Mangling by starts the full course of their glory.

   CHORUS *walks towards us and flings out his arms.*

CHORUS: Small time, but in that small most greatly lived
This star of England. Fortune made his sword.
And for his sake . . .

   *Shoot down from the top gallery of the theatre past the
   audience towards the stage.*

CHORUS: In your fair minds let this acceptance . . .

   CHORUS *is seen in a closer shot.*

CHORUS: . . . take.

   *He bows. Elizabethan Gallants come onto the stage and
   crowd round* CHORUS. *Track up to the stage balcony
   where the* BISHOP OF ELY *is conducting Choirboys.
   Track in to* ELY *as he looks up and nods.*
   *In the orchestra gallery, the Leader of the orchestra
   acknowledges the signal and the orchestra plays louder.
   The Leader looks up.*
   *Track up to the platform below the flagpole. A man is
   pulling down the Playhouse flag and rolling it up. He
   leaves through the door at the back.*
   *Now we see London in 1600 in a long shot with the Globe
   Playhouse in the foreground. Track back to a wide shot of
   London. A playbill comes fluttering out of the sky and
   hits the camera lens. It has the cast and credits on it, which
   unroll.*

## THE CAST
### In order of appearance

| | |
|---|---|
| Chorus | Leslie Banks |
| Archbishop of Canterbury | Felix Aylmer |
| Bishop of Ely | Robert Helpmann |
| The English Herald | Vernon Greeves |
| Earl of Westmoreland | Gerald Case |
| Earl of Salisbury | Griffith Jones |
| Sir Thomas Erpingham | Morland Graham |
| Duke of Exeter | Nicholas Hannen |
| Duke of Gloucester | Michael Warre |
| King Henry V of England | Laurence Olivier |
| Mountjoy, The French Herald | Ralph Truman |
| Duke of Berri, French Ambassador | Ernest Thesiger |
| Corporal Nym | Frederick Cooper |
| Lieutenant Bardolph | Roy Emerton |
| Ancient Pistol | Robert Newton |
| Mistress Quickly | Freda Jackson |
| Boy | George Cole |
| Sir John Falstaff | George Robey |
| King Charles VI of France | Harcourt Williams |
| Duke of Bourbon | Russell Thorndike |
| The Constable of France | Leo Genn |
| Duke of Orléans | Francis Lister |
| The Dauphin | Max Adrian |
| The French Messenger | Jonathan Field |
| Fluellen ) | Esmond Knight |
| Gower ) Captains in the | Michael Shepley |
| Jamy ) English Army | John Laurie |
| MacMorris ) | Nial MacGinnis |
| The Governor of Harfleur | Frank Tickle |
| Princess Katharine | Renée Ascherson |
| Alice | Ivy St. Helier |
| Queen Isabel of France | Janet Burnell |
| Court ) | Brian Nissen |
| Bates ) Soldiers in the | Arthur Hambling |
| Williams ) English Army | Jimmy Hanley |
| A Priest | Ernest Hare |
| Duke of Burgundy | Valentine Dyall |

Produced and Directed
by
Laurence Olivier

In close association with –

| | |
|---|---|
| The Editor | Reginald Beck |
| The Art Director | Paul Sheriff |

| | |
|---|---|
| Assisted by | Carmen Dillon |
| The Costume Designer | Roger Furse |
| Assisted by | Margaret Furse |
| The Associate Producer | Dallas Bower |
| The Text Editor | Alan Dent |
| The Director of Photography | Robert Krasker |
| The Operating Cameraman | Jack Hildyard |
| The Sound Recorders | John Dennis |
| | Desmond Dew |
| Make-up | Tony Sforzini |
| Hairdressing | Vivienne Walker |
| Special Effects | Percy Day |
| Assistant Director | Vincent Permane |
| Scenic Artist | E. Lindegaard |
| Continuity | Joan Barry |
| Chief Electrician | W. Wall |
| Master of the Horse | John White |
| Production Unit | Alec Hayes |
| | P. G. Bangs |
| | Laurence Evans |

and

| | |
|---|---|
| The music by | William Walton |
| Conducted by | Muir Mathieson |
| Played by | The London Symphony Orchestra |

*Now dissolve to a long shot of London in 1600. The words: THE END: fade in and out of the sky above the city. The music stops.*